Walter's Perspective

WALTER'S
PERSPECTIVE

Walter Jacobson

A Memoir of Fifty Years in Chicago TV News

Walter Jacobson

With a Foreword by Bill Kurtis

Southern Illinois University Press

Carbondale and Edwardsville

Copyright © 2012 by Walter Jacobson
All rights reserved
Printed in the United States of America

Library of Congress Cataloging-in-Publication Data
Jacobson, Walter, 1937–
Walter's perspective : a memoir of fifty years in
Chicago tv news / Walter Jacobson ; with a foreword
by Bill Kurtis.
    p. cm.
Includes index.
    ISBN 978-0-8093-3112-3 (cloth : alk. paper)
    ISBN 0-8093-3112-8 (cloth : alk. paper)
    ISBN 978-0-8093-3113-0 (ebook)
    ISBN 0-8093-3113-6 (ebook)
1. Jacobson, Walter, 1937– 2. Television journalists—
Illinois—Chicago—Biography. 3. Journalists—
Illinois—Chicago—Biography. I. Title.
PN4874.J295A3 2012
070.92—dc23
[B]   2012001300

Printed on recycled paper. ♻
The paper used in this publication meets the minimum requirements of American National Standard
for Information Sciences—Permanence of Paper for
Printed Library Materials, ANSI Z39.48-1992. ∞

Contents

Foreword

Bill Kurtis

T he month of March is when much of the world celebrates the first signs of spring. But not Chicago. I had to scrape away frost on the window of my Holiday Inn room to catch the rose glow of sunrise creeping over Lake Shore Drive. I hadn't felt below-freezing temperatures in three years, and my blood was thinner now. That's what living in California does—or so it feels. But here I was, staring out at ice floes and pondering what the living hell I had done to deserve this. It was 1973, and I was thirty-three years old.

My three-year stint as a correspondent for CBS News, Los Angeles bureau, was my *perfect* job. It was a coming-of-age in my career. You become a fireman to fight fires. As a policeman you'd rather risk your life than direct traffic for thirty years. As a reporter, you want stories, big stories. From LA, we covered eleven western states, including Hawaii and Alaska, and I'd spent more than two hundred days a year away from home. Earthquakes in Los Angeles and Managua, antiwar riots in San Francisco and Berkeley, chasing Howard Hughes to Las Vegas and Vancouver were just a few reportorial adventures sprinkled among more earthly assignments like covering the Charles Manson murder trial for ten months, Angela Davis for six, Daniel Ellsberg. Well, suffice it to say I loved it.

But CBS *corporate* had something else in mind. A CBS News boy-genius of Special Events, Bob Wussler, had been named the general manager of WBBM-TV in Chicago, a CBS-owned and -operated station. Wussler was in charge when Walter Cronkite teared up as Neil Armstrong walked on the moon. In Chicago, he faced a task almost as hard as getting to the moon. WBBM-TV had been in third place for years. An exodus of anchors like Fahey Flynn and John Drury had wound up at competing stations taking viewers with them. Flynn teamed with Joel Daly at WLS-TV (ABC) to prove there is no age barrier when Chicago loves you. WMAQ-TV (NBC) was still enjoying a dynasty of Floyd Kalber, teamed with commentator Len O'Connor. Wussler and his news director, former newspaperman Van Gordon Sauter, sized up the situation and laid out a plan. First, they needed a new anchor team in a new setting, different from the other stations in the market. Since I had worked at WBBM-TV from 1966 to 1970, I had something of a running start. I'd play the straight role. I should say straight to the *extreme*: I was white and male with the look of a midwestern kid from a small town in Kansas. (I'm from Independence, Kansas—one hundred miles from anywhere.) To borrow a more contemporary television description, I *was Friday Night Lights*.

Filling a coanchor-commentator role would be a quirky Jewish kid I'd heard of but never really met, Walter Jacobson. He'd been a batboy for the Cubs, legman for legendary *Chicago Daily News* columnist Jack Mabley, wire-service reporter and backup, and heir apparent to commentator Len O'Connor at WMAQ-TV.

That first cold morning when I reported for work in studio 1, broadcast history seemed to hang from the walls. The first presidential television debate between Kennedy and Nixon had taken place there in 1960. But we were not to broadcast from the cavernous memorial. I was ushered instead to an equally large studio that had been turned into a working newsroom. It looked like one of Wussler's election specials at CBS News. Nice. News from a working newsroom. I was thinking "breakthrough." And he brought more of his *secret sauce* from the network. We would introduce the first local use of the Minicam, a mobile electronic videotape apparatus that was lightweight enough to be taken anywhere at any time in a hurry, and it sent back to the newsroom pictures and sound that we put on the air as we received them. Our broadcasts were urgent, immediate, uncensored, and unedited. Dazzling.

But there was one small change of plans awaiting me. Knowing that I had committed past the point of no return (to my old career path), the wizards behind this historic venture, Wussler and Sauter, casually suggested, "Wow, you guys look so great at the anchor desk (in the middle of the newsroom) maybe you should coanchor." I thought, "Coanchor? You mean side-by-side together? Not like Kalber and O'Connor, an anchor and a commentator. Not what Wussler and Sauter said to me earlier, Bill as solo anchor, Walter as commentator. I wonder if the flights back to LA are still taking off." The marriage of an odd couple, Walter and me, had been arranged. That's what it was, the marriage of an odd couple, everything but Chapel of the Bells in Vegas, not exactly why I had come back to Chicago. And so it began.

Walter would stay inside to work on a commentary called "Perspective," to be included once a day on the 10:00 P.M. newscast. I would be the outside man looking for stories at home and abroad (yes, the correspondent juices kept flowing even though it was a local newscast). Then we would slide in next to each other for our coanchoring chores. He was quirky all right, and unpredictable. Peck's bad boy. And that's exactly what I needed to provide an edge to my down-the-middle style. I think I gave him the freedom to do those things by providing the big brother protection he needed to get away with it (full disclosure: he's four years older than me). To an observer, having two overachieving egos competing for the number of stories to be read, the best stories, the best questions of live guests, looks like a recipe for disaster. In some cases, it is. But Walter and I learned quickly that our futures depended on each other's success. We never had an argument. How many husbands and wives can say that? There was something else. We loved what we were doing. That's what I remember about those early years with Walter. He is still the best political observer that I know.

One measure of how well it all worked is that now, thirty-eight years and several career detours later, we're back together and hearing people say, "Good to have Butch and Sundance back together." Or, "When I was growing up, you guys were Batman and Robin." Why would they say that? To find out you should keep reading. It's not my story. It's Walter's story of a remarkable chapter in the history of local television news, a memoir of a remarkable Chicago journalist who's been a thorn in the sides of mayors Daley and Washington, Byrne and Emanuel, and of the managers of his newsrooms. He punctures arrogance, spies on abuses of power, and is a prickly inquisitor of Louis Farrakhan and Muhammad Ali; Hillary Clinton, Bill O'Reilly, and Barack Obama; Luciano Pavarotti, Liv Ulmann, and Boy George.

We're lucky, Walter and I. All these years in TV news, we've had the best seats in the house.

Preface

I earned my first newspaper byline after visiting a nudist colony whose naked female proprietor told me that if I wanted the story, I'd have to take off my clothes.

Consider that sentence:

I earned my first newspaper byline after visiting a nudist colony whose naked female proprietor told me that if I wanted the story, I would have to take off my clothes.

One of the things I've learned in my fifty-plus years in the newspaper, radio, and television business—and it is a business—is to grab your readers, listeners, or viewers early. Make 'em want to know more so they'll come along for the ride.

Maybe my opening, or *lede*, as we call it, has piqued your curiosity.

What was my reaction to the proprietor's demand? Did I take off my clothes, because I had no inhibitions about doing so or because I was on assignment and didn't want to fail or because, well . . . why not? Did I insist on leaving my clothes on, to let the proprietor know I cover stories dressed as I want to be? The big question is how was I to interview a woman standing before me completely and unabashedly in the buff, stark naked?

In writing a memoir about my life and career, I'm entering territory that is foreign to me. Admittedly, it's not as foreign as that nudist colony, but I'm accustomed to writing relatively short newspaper stories, three-minute television or radio commentaries, or rewriting copy for a half-hour or sixty-minute news broadcast. These are not only shorter than a book, they are about other people, not me.

Here, I am being asked or asking myself to *be* the story in addition to covering or commenting on it—to bare my soul, if not my body. I'd like to say that at the very least I'll know that my primary source—me—is trustworthy, but it's impossible to remember everything that has happened during my lifetime. Stories inevitably take on lives of their own. Facts and the exact words of conversations are forgotten or embellished. I have tried my best on the pages that follow to be truthful and to admit it when my memory is hazy.

Writing a memoir requires a certain amount of audacity and ego—two traits that I have never been accused of lacking. But it also requires a reason. That's another thing I've learned during my career: There has to be a reason, a point. Otherwise, there's no sense in trying to grab anybody.

My reason? An informed public is essential if government and society are to operate effectively and fairly for all. To me, there is no higher calling than ferreting out stories, delivering the news, and offering perspective on how the little guy is affected by the machinations of powerful politicians and big business. I wanted to do that from the time I was in grade school, and I've been blessed with the opportunity to do so for more than half a century. In what other profession would I have had the opportunity to interview presidents and local pols, heavyweight champions and movie stars, mass murderers and movement leaders, and to offer a million fellow citizens my take on the world five nights a week?

In many ways, my career has paralleled the course that journalism itself has taken during the last fifty years—from the days when cities like Chicago had four daily newspapers staffed by reporters straight from the front page who would do anything for a scoop; to the period when television began to flex its muscles and become the primary source of news; to the golden age of local and national television news; to the arrival of the Internet and cable and the decline of traditional news broadcasts. During this period I have had a love-hate relationship with the news business. I've seen it at its best and if not at its worst, close to it.

I have some points to make about another subject, too—politics, which has fascinated me for sixty years, and has been the focus of much of my reporting and commentary. While the ascendance of Chicago's Barack Obama has signaled dramatic and obvious change at the national level, changes at the state and local levels have been more subtle. When I began my career, Illinois governors were indicted with regularity. They still are. As for Chicago, I have two words: Mayor Daley. Richard J. was ruling with an iron fist when I became a reporter. And Richard M., though different than his father in his temperament, his vision, and his politics, wielded similar power for twenty-two years.

So come with me behind the scenes of my world. I have things to say about the Daleys' trade, and about mine, as well as some tips for those of you who'd like to try either one. Where else, for example, are you going to learn where a reporter is supposed to put his notepad (or laptop) upon sitting down for lunch in a nudist colony?

Acknowledgments

There are reporters in Chicago, many of them, who are fighting the good fight—to raise the standards of our television and radio broadcasts. Every day, all day, from first assignment in the morning to a kicker on the ten o'clock news, there are reporters who know stories that need to be told but are not, or that need not be told but are. Journalists committed to the calling of our profession, bucking-up against the nature of our business, which is to appeal to what is perceived as a hunger out there for car crashes and fires, drive-by shootings, el-station murders, and rock stars and movie stars passing through town. A perceived insatiable popular appetite for what doesn't matter. Reporters and writers, producers and editors on the front line of the good fight go home at night or in the middle of the night or the next morning feeling, too much of the time, that there is scant chance the fight can be won. No way will a thirty-minute newscast include four minutes, or three or even two minutes of a story of substantive detail on a state or city budget. But to those who persist in agitating for change, to go back going forward, I dedicate my memoir.

To them, and to those who've inspired my half century on the streets of Chicago and in the studios of television news, I bow in respect; and in gratitude for showing me ways through a lifetime of experiences so rich and far beyond what I imagined when, in seventh grade, I decided to be a reporter and never once changed my mind. Thank you, Edward R. Murrow and Eric Sevareid, whom I never met but dreamed I knew. And Van Gordon Sauter and John Callaway, to whom I listened when told things to do. And to Robert Feder for his principles and outsider inside perspective on television news. If not for Len O'Connor, I could not have come far enough even to try a book that might be of interest to people interested in news.

And if not for Steve Fiffer, there simply wouldn't be this book. An author of many of his own, a writer of enormous sensitivity and skill, he suggested it, loaned me his agent to propose it, then organized and helped me edit it. With the care and warmth of good friendship, he expertly, steadily, and graciously guided me into the publishing world, so that Karl Kageff, editor-in-chief of Southern Illinois University Press, could pilot me through it.

I have four children—Wendy, Peter, Julia, and Genevieve—who live and work in New York and Washington, DC. Thank you, my dear children, for your cross-country interest and support: "Hey, Dad, you okay? How's it going?" And thank you, Susie, my loving, discerning, interesting, and exciting wife, who was twenty-five years in the ad world, and once a national tennis champion, and now a competitive equestrian. My love and gratitude for your patience, and your encouragement and counsel, and for always having my back.

Walter's Perspective

Once a Cubs Fan . . .

(Walter—on-camera)

Election time! Challengers versus incumbents . . . challengers looking for money, incumbents looking at their payrolls to find jobs they can hand out in exchange for support in their campaigns, looking to hire people who will man the precincts . . . and fire those who won't . . .

(Videotape: Coconate)

Like Frank Coconate, for example. Fired from his job after twenty-seven years on the city payroll. Here's his story . . . a Chicago story . . .

Frank Coconate is an independent kind of guy, a whistle-blower-type who discovered waste, he says, and corruption in the city's highly touted $75 million program to prevent flooding in our basements . . .

(Wide shot: blockers stacked behind a city warehouse)

. . . the "rain blocker" program. The blockers didn't work and were an embarrassment to city hall, says Frank. So city employees were instructed to hide the blockers or throw them away. Frank Coconate blew the whistle . . .

(Hidden-camera pix: Coconate and Jackson walking, separately, into restaurant)

. . . then hooked himself up with US congressman Jesse Jackson Jr. in a downtown restaurant to talk quietly about Jesse running for mayor. Well, you can imagine what happened next! Frank received . . .

(Dissolve to: the letter with list of charges)

. . . this letter from his boss listing some charges. And even though Frank emphatically denies those charges, and in twenty-seven years has an extraordinary record of good behavior . . .

(Dissolve to: Coconate)

. . . he's been fired for . . .

(Dissolve to: letter with quote)

. . . quote, "conduct unbecoming a public employee" . . .

(Walter on-camera)

. . . proving once again that in city hall in Chicago conduct unbecoming a public employee is not corruption, but *exposing* it. Or (long pause) . . . supporting the wrong candidate for mayor.

—excerpt from "Walter's Perspective," *Fox News at Nine*, January 19, 1995

I've always had a warm spot in my heart for underdogs like Frank Coconate. Maybe it's because I'm somewhat vertically challenged. Okay, *short*. Maybe it's because as a child I often felt chastened by my dear but domineering mother.

Or because early in my career, I was—due to a mistaken identity, I swear—tagged with the nickname "Skippy," which has stuck to this day. It's an uphill battle to be taken seriously when you wear a moniker like that. In my "honor," Her Honor the playful Chicago mayor Jane Byrne once anointed the symbol of the city's snow-removal program "Skippy the Snowball." I'm still turning around when I hear "Hey, you. Hey, Skippy."

Or how about this—maybe I identify with underdogs because I'm a Chicago Cubs fan (been one since I was eight years old). As most people know, certainly most Chicagoans know, the Cubs have not won a World Series since 1908, haven't even played in a World Series since 1945, when they lost to the Detroit Tigers in seven games. It was during game 4 that year that Billy Sianis, a guy who ran a neighborhood tavern, placed the infamous "curse of the billy goat" on the Cubs. Sianis was angry about being barred from his box seats, along with his pet goat Murphy, who was smelled at a gate by Mr. P. K. Wrigley himself and was declared to be "too stinky" to be allowed in, let alone sit in a box seat.

When the Cubs began the losing ways for which they are now well known, Sianis is reported to have exclaimed, "Who stinks now?"

I remember when I was eight, listening to the '45 Series on the radio with my mother at her ironing board in our apartment in Rogers Park on Chicago's far north side. The Cubs lost, but I was hooked, probably for life. When I was ten or eleven, I began taking the el after school, a fifteen-minute ride to Wrigley Field, where I ducked the ticket-takers to get into the bleachers to catch the last few innings of the games.

When I was fourteen, in the winter before the 1951 season, I wrote a letter to Mr. Wrigley, a chewing-gum magnate who owned the Cubs, asking if I could please be his batboy. Cliff Jaffe, the team's publicity chief, wrote back thanking me for being a Cubs fan, adding: "We're sorry, but the Cubs already have hired a young man, Billy Perkins, to be our batboy."

So I wrote to Mr. Wrigley again the next winter, before the '52 season. This time, I was called in for an interview with Bobby Dorr, the groundskeeper in charge of hiring batboys. My dad drove me to Clark and Addison and waited for me at a back gate, the one on Waveland beyond left field, across the street from the firehouse.

"What happened," he asked when I came out.

"You won't believe it!" I stuttered, heart pounding like a locomotive. "This guy, Mr. Dorr, he asked me about you and mom and school, and how I'd get down here in the spring before school's out. I told him you'd bring me."

"You what?"

"Well, I had to say something. The transportation part seemed important to him. Then he asked me why I love the Cubs. Then he wanted to know how tall I am (five-two) and how much I weigh (120), like he needed to know for a uniform. This can't be happening. It's not gonna happen, I know it."

New Year's passed, and Valentine's Day. I stared at the telephone, crossing my fingers, promising God that for the rest of my life I'd never do anything bad. *Please, please, ring*, I entreated, but it didn't. I figured I'd lost again.

My 0 for 2 batting average seemed confirmed when I tuned in my radio one night in late February to listen, as I did almost every night, to Bert Wilson on the Cubs' News.

". . . Ubson," I heard him say, "has been named the Cubs' new batboy." *Well, lucky Ubson*, I thought, until the phone did ring, and kept on ringing. Friends and cousins calling. Aunts and uncles. It wasn't Ubson. It was Jacobson. I'd missed the first syllable. *Walter Jacobson's been named the new Cubs' batboy.* Ecstasy! If it were true.

My mom called the radio station to make sure. I was at her side, churning in doubt. Yes, she was told, it is true. Next morning, she called Wrigley Field. Confirmed.

We were living in Glencoe by then. Our house was on Green Bay Road, a commuter suburb forty minutes up the north shore from downtown Chicago.

I was a freshman at New Trier High School, which, for better or worse, has given the world such luminaries as Charlton Heston, Ann Margret, Donald Rumsfeld—and now Walter the batboy.

Until 1988 there were no lights at Wrigley Field. The Cubs played all home games in the afternoon. New Trier reluctantly, but understandingly, permitted me to bunch my classes into the morning, and then head off to the ballpark. My dad didn't have to drive me. I took the north shore train to Howard Street, then transferred to the elevated, arriving in time to suit-up, put the bats into racks in the dugout, clean peanut shells and chewed bubble gum off the bench.

During the game, my job was to chase foul balls off the screen behind home plate, mind the resin bag in the on-deck circle, retrieve the leaded bat discarded by the upcoming hitter, make sure the home-plate umpire had a pocketful of unscratched, unsmudged baseballs. And, best of all and most fun, bask in the moments I was kneeling on one knee in the circle alongside some of the biggest boys of summer. When one of them smacked a home run, I jumped to the plate, picked up his Louisville Slugger and, in front of a full house screaming with delight, was the first to shake his hand after he rounded the bases. The next morning I cut out of the newspaper pictures of me and the slugger coming home (I was the one with no number on the back of my wool jersey).

After the game, in the clubhouse, I put dirty socks, jockstraps, and uniforms into the wash, straightened up lockers, swept the floors, and soaped the sinks and urinals. All together, I worked seven, sometimes eight or nine hours a day.

My pay was $2.50, which was fifty cents less than what I spent on the train ride from Glencoe. But so what! I'd have done it for free. I'd have paid the Cubs to let me do it, to be in the same place as Hank Sauer, Hal Jeffcoat, and Frankie Baumholtz in the outfield. Dee Fondy, Eddie Miksis, Handsome Ransom Jackson, and Roy Smalley the infield. Bob Rush on the mound, Harry Chiti behind the plate, and Phil Cavaretta, our manager, who also coached at third.

The dugout buzzed with gutter talk, catcalling, racism, and spittin' tobacco. I was spellbound, and growing up faster than my mother ever could imagine (or desire). But as crude and foul-mouthed as some of the players were, they were Cubs, and I loved them. Did I ever.

My favorite was shortstop Smalley, not a heavy hitter, and soon to be traded to make room for future Hall-of-Famer Ernie Banks. He was the nicest guy you could ever meet. I liked him best because I felt he liked me, and he talked to me, told me stories about making it to the majors, and played catch with me before the games.

I liked him even more because he was having a hard time. When he bungled a grounder at shortstop or threw wildly to first, which he often did, he was booed, mercilessly. Sportswriters parodied that poem by Franklin Pierce Adams about the great Cubs' double plays from Tinker to Evers to Chance—"from Miksis to Smalley to the grandstand." I felt so bad for him.

"Don't worry, Wally," he'd say, his arm around me to keep me from crying. "It's part of the game. I'll make up for it tomorrow." He rarely did.

The Cubs finished even-steven in 1952—seventy-seven wins, seventy-seven losses. Mr. Wrigley's policy was to change batboys every season. But I was so passionate about the job, and good enough at it, that instead of being given my unconditional release, I was assigned to the visiting teams' dugout. Still for $2.50 a day, and visitors' batboy uniforms big enough for two of me. But so what about that, too. During pregame warm up, I caught tosses from Jackie Robinson, Willie Mays, and Stan Musial.

(Before I tell you about the visitors, though, I have a secret to spill about one of my jobs in the Cubs' clubhouse. Those autographed baseballs being sold in the kiosks under the stands for $10 each? Many of them were "autographed" by me. With persistence and practice, I became pretty good at signing the names of all the Cubs. If a fan didn't know precisely how a player signed his name, he or she wouldn't know the difference. I hate to imagine all those people who shelled out their ten bucks in good faith or whose kids or grandkids now cherish the balls—or want to sell them on eBay. All I can say sixty years too late is, I'm sorry.)

The 1953 season was a disaster. Winning only sixty-five games and losing eighty-nine, we finished the season forty games behind the pennant-winning Brooklyn Dodgers. And that was despite my best efforts to help the Cubs by pilfering our opponents' signals. Another secret to spill—after cracking a visitor's code, I'd duck under the stands into the tunnel to the Cubs' dugout.

Who knows? If I hadn't passed my findings on to manager Cavaretta's coaches, the Cubs might have done even worse that season. Not until many years later did I understand that I was a bad boy. A bad batboy.

Looking back, I'm glad to say the scheme was not foolproof. Before a game against the Cincinnati Reds, I was caught listening in on the Reds' manager, the legendary Rogers Hornsby. Caught in the act. Red-handed, you might say, dispatched to the bullpen, and told to stay there. I was warned that if I ever listened again, I'd be fired, which I ought to have been right then and there.

That was minor-league compared to what happened when the Dodgers' pitcher Russ Meyer figured out what I was doing. The "Mad Monk," as Meyer was called due to his temper, actually swung a bat at my head, breaking it in half on a cement post between us. It's a good thing pitchers are not good hitters.

It's also a good thing I didn't get home from work until late, sometimes not until eight o'clock. Life in the Jacobson household often was uncomfortably tense. My father, S. J. (for Samuel John), was an insurance salesman. My mother, Anne, worked on and off as a bookkeeper in his office. Each was the child of Russian immigrants.

I remember my maternal grandparents and my father's mother, who came to Glencoe from Chicago on Sundays for family brunch of brisket, potato pancakes, and politics. (That's where I first heard stories about corruption in city hall). My father's father, Walter, had lost his hand in an accident at the broom factory where he worked, and when the pain became intolerable, he committed suicide.

I was the oldest of four children. My brother Larry was three years younger. The twins, Alan and Janet, a surprise to all, were born when I was ten.

My mother and our religion—a volatile mix if ever there was one—were the source of much of the tension. Growing up Jewish in a largely Christian neighborhood, I felt different and wanted so much to be among the in-crowd that appeared to have stepped out of a Dartmouth College yearbook. Just as much, my mother wanted me to embrace my heritage, which meant attending services at our temple on Friday nights.

One Friday night, feigning illness, I received dispensation to stay home. After the rest of the family left for services, I peddled my bike to meet friends at the Glencoe Theater. When I came out after the movie, obviously not ill, my parents were waiting in their car at the curb.

"Walter," snapped my dad, "come over here—"

My punishment was as ouch a punishment as there could be. That Sunday, two days after the movie, I was to be water boy for a day at Soldier Field for the Chicago Hornets, a professional football team owned by the father of one of my schoolmates. I had been looking forward to it for months. But no temple, no Hornets. My mother wouldn't let me go. Although I had brought the punishment upon myself, I blamed it on her. This precipitated a family brouhaha over Judaism and the Holocaust, one of many while I was in my teens.

My mother believed that what the Nazis did in Germany and Poland in the 1940s was sure to happen again, and that I should be aware. "No way," said I. "The world won't stand for it." She was relentless; I was stubborn. Perhaps had her manner been less aggressive, I'd have yielded. But it wasn't, and I didn't and still don't.

Watching me on television, if you wonder sometimes why I'm like a dog with a bone, think: *his mom*. She was barely five feet and hardly a hundred pounds, with sparkling, beautiful white hair, a warm, loving smile, and a terrorizing tongue: "You listen to me, young man, and pay attention. And mind your manners. Is that clear? Do you understand?"

If on the news on TV, I'm sticking it to authority, that, too, is because of Mom. I equate the power at city hall with the power I felt at home. Guess I just don't like being told what to do. I don't like it when powerless people are forced to knuckle under; I like to expose that kind of thing.

While in high school, I was a reporter on the neighborhood weekly newspaper, the *Glencoe News*. Even then, I knew that's what I was cut out to be. In fact, I'd never wanted to be anything else. I liked the way reporters wrote about skullduggery and defanged big bullies. I wanted to be like the newspapermen I read: city hall investigators like Sandy Smith at the *Chicago Tribune* and Art Petacque at the *Sun-Times*, or foreign correspondents and columnists like Walter Lippman of the *New Republic* and James Reston of the *New York Times*.

I was mesmerized by the sportswriters who covered the Cubs for Chicago's four daily newspapers—especially Jack Mabley at the *Daily News*. Mabley, in his mid-thirties, was urbane and knowledgeable, a terrifically sensitive and creative writer who instinctively knew what people liked to read. He made baseball sing. When I was a batboy, I watched him interview the players, and I read and saved what he wrote. I even spoke to him a few times when he came to Wrigley.

At the end of my two years in the dugouts, instead of asking Mabley a hundred more questions about his work, I asked him if he'd give me a job so I could learn the business. As a summer intern, maybe?

Maybe not. Like the Cubs, Mabley first turned me down. So every year for the next five I tried again. He always took my calls and was nice to me. I never knew why but guessed it was because he liked my persistence.

Maybe he saw some of himself in me. Certainly Jack Mabley was persistent. The best reporters are. But his response to my appeals was always the same.

"No," he said gently. "Not now. Focus on high school and getting into college. Then come back to me." I did what he said, and he finally did give me a job, which is what led me to that nudist colony I mentioned, and then to fifty years in Chicago news looking for trouble.

I'm a Legman

After graduating from high school in 1957, I went to Grinnell, a small liberal arts college in rural Iowa. The campus is an hour from Des Moines, five from Chicago.

Grinnell was, and still is, highly regarded for its academics. But that's not why I chose to go there. As good as the school was in teaching, it was bad in swimming, my sport. Thus: an opportunity for me to move up from second string in high school to first string in college. The promise of being the top guy in the hundred-yard backstroke (in a not-so-hot 1:05) was just too appealing.

We packed up the '55 white Buick. Mom and Dad took turns at the wheel. I was in the back with bags of shoes and clothes that I hoped would register me "cool" on campus. We drove, mostly in silence because of how apprehensive I was, through what seemed like thousands of miles of cornfields.

I'm an urban boy, enraptured by subways, buses, and taxicabs, and the tighter, more jammed my neighborhood the better. Would I be bored in Grinnell, Iowa? And how would I cope with college requirements in math and science and, yuk, poetry? I wasn't much up to "Beowulf" or "Ode on a Grecian Urn."

I ended up doing fine in the pool, in class, and on the *Scarlet and Black*, the weekly newspaper. I covered sports, writing a column that was supposed to be about athletics, but was stretched to everything on which I had an opinion—grades, religion, ethics, professors playing favorites, boys in girls dorms (and vice versa), beer games on Friday night, potatoes for lunch.

I learned early on the unique challenges, disciplines, responsibilities—and pleasures and rewards—of commentary. Reporting is writing about what you see and hear. Commentary is about what you think and feel. Reporting ought to be mixed into commentary; commentary ought not to be mixed into reporting. A reporter must earn a column. A reporter who gets it right may be rewarded with a column one day. Maybe even an editorship.

I thought my reporting and columns for the *Scarlet and Black* were good enough to qualify me for the editorship, but I lost out to a classmate. I was angry—so angry that I decided I should take a break from Grinnell. *Go somewhere else*, I told myself. *Enroll for a semester at a big school, like the University of Illinois or Michigan.*

Or how about the Ivy League? Columbia was home to America's most prestigious graduate school of journalism. I was an undergraduate. But, oh, it would be exciting to be part of the same university.

And, of course, the school was in New York, the city where everything was, where everything happened: the United Nations, Tammany Hall, Wall Street, Broadway and Harlem, the Lower East Side, Fifth Avenue, and Greenwich Village. The Met, the Dodgers, Times Square. Mayor Robert Wagner and Governor Averell Harriman. The *New York Times* and *Herald Tribune,* the *Post,* the *Daily News,* and the *Village Voice.* Norman Mailer, Jimmy Breslin, and Murray Kempton. Huntley and Brinkley . . . and Lynn Strauss, a young woman whom I had fallen for in Chicago. She was a student at Vassar College in Poughkeepsie, a short train ride from Manhattan.

Moved by love for Lynn and the romance of New York, I applied to Columbia. To my surprise and delight, I was accepted.

Soon I'd be off to New York. Where the newspapers and television were jousting for supremacy, and where stories were played big: racial tensions bubbling up from a US Supreme Court decision to integrate public education in Little Rock, Arkansas; a downward spiral from the postwar boom; more unemployment, crime, and class conflict presaging riots and gang warfare. The city's gilded class reaching for Higher Society, scrambling to get tickets for the first transatlantic jet passenger flight to Europe. Frank Lloyd Wright's Guggenheim Museum splashing into the art world. I had to go.

I also had to tell my parents.

"Very funny, Walter," my mother blurted (more like gasped) into the telephone, when I broke the news that I had applied, been accepted, and planned to leave Grinnell for New York in a month. "You are, of course, kidding."

"Mom, I'm not kidding. I . . ."

"Sam" (definitely a gasp), "Sam, pick up the phone!"

Less curious than exasperated, they shouted at me, both of them. "Don't be ridiculous. You're not going to New York. You're not going anywhere, except back here in a few weeks for Hanukkah break." (My mother would not, under any circumstances, say "Christmas" break, or even "Holiday" break.). "Forget it."

Of all places in the world, I was not going to New York. Maybe never would I be going to New York! To Sin City, where there's more crime than in Chicago, to where I'd never once been even overnight? Leave Grinnell, Iowa, to go to New York, New York? By myself? To ride a subway in New York? Out of the question. Out!

The problem for me was that I couldn't go to New York, or anywhere, unless they paid for it. I pleaded that I'd already worked it out with Grinnell so I could take a semester at another school in another city. No Grinnell tuition for the semester, and any credits I earned would transfer back. I winced and went on: "All we have to pay is a little extra for room and board—"

They hung up.

I've never figured out how, but I managed to change their minds. Soon I was on my way to a Manhattan adventure. Home would be a rented room two floors above a Chock Full o' Nuts coffee shop in a beautiful antique building at 116th and Broadway, across the street from Columbia.

My landlady, Florence Stothoff, smaller than me, with curly gray hair, round but severe in her senior years, was mistress of the northwest Manhattan chapter of the Daughters of the American Revolution, not exactly a soul mate, in fact a bit of a biddy, but she was good company, at once intrigued and incensed by the "unacceptable manners and bad behavior of boys, Walter. Staying out after dark, riding around in cars to meet girls. And only the Lord knows what else you're doing. Likely smoking cigarettes."

"Now wait, Missus Flo—" I'd say, sitting next to her in a straight-backed wooden chair in her living room stuffed with William Howard Taft memorabilia—little bronze statues, magazine pictures, and presidential words of wisdom framed and hung on walls papered with flowers.

"No, Mr. Jacobson. You wait!"

My room, like two others she rented to students, was at the end of a long hallway next to an old kitchen without dishwasher or disposal. I didn't dare ask, but I was certain Missus Flo grew up in that apartment, and in 1910 or about then, was corseted there for her sweet-sixteen and coming-out parties.

"Missus Flo," I'd go on, "I'm in my room every night by ten, on the weekends by 11:30, because those are your rules. And I don't have a car, and I positively don't smoke."

"You better not. And no girls or drinking in my house. I'll know if you do."

What good news that was for my mother. She loved to hear it. And though they never met, Mrs. Jacobson loved Missus Flo. Never mind that the DAR in those days was hardly renowned for its fondness for my mother's religion.

Life for me was sublime until the second week after I moved in, when I swelled my chest and swaggered to the campus to register.

"I'm sorry, Walter Jacobson," sniffed the admissions clerk, "you're in the wrong room. This is for Columbia College. You belong two floors up, at the Columbia School of General Studies."

"Is there a difference?"

"Oh, yes, there is." She sniffed again and directed me to a spread of Columbia catalogues on a tabletop, where I discovered that registration for the School of

General Studies was, indeed, where I belonged. I had mistakenly applied to Columbia General Studies, the university's night school for adults.

(Of course there was no such thing in 1958 as the Internet, but if you go to the General Studies Web site today, you'll see that back in 1831 it was "created specifically for students with nontraditional backgrounds." And that "most students at GS, for personal or professional reasons, interrupted their education, never attended college, or can only attend part-time. They bring an average of 8 to 10 years of life experience to the classroom.")

That was not me, not even close. I hadn't interrupted my education, had attended college, planned on going to school full-time, and was bringing nowhere near ten years of life experience to a classroom. I had enrolled in the wrong division of Columbia University. But having boasted to my parents and friends about being accepted by the Ivy League, I wasn't about to turn tail back to Grinnell.

My first class, at 8 P.M., was as advertised. Most of the fifty-some students in a lecture hall were fifty-some years old (I was nineteen), the men in various shades of gray hair and dressed in suits and ties, the women in dresses or skirts and heels. Two of them brought their teenagers to class to hear the lecture, which was on the politics of Franklin Roosevelt's New Deal.

Initially I was numbed by the fear that I had made a terrible mistake, but I soon realized this was the best class I'd ever been in, anywhere. The student next to me, and two in front, had actually lived through the Depression. When they raised their hands and were called on to speak, they delivered riveting personal accounts.

"My dad worked on headlights at Ford in Detroit," said one. "Laid off when he was thirty-eight years old. I had two brothers and a sister . . . I remember the lines for food."

"We were in Detroit, too," said another, smothering tears. "I remember my sister being very sick with whooping cough. We couldn't get her to a hospital, thought she might die."

I was stunned by those stories, and spellbound by the professor, David Miner, who also lectured at Columbia College. Aware that I was much younger than the other students and seemingly out of place, he motioned me forward after one lecture and asked how I happened to be there.

Gulp. "This is hard to explain . . ." and I told my story about Grinnell and New York, even the part about not becoming editor of the *Scarlet and Black*. He seemed as interested in my background as I was in his class.

Professor Miner was so clear, expressive, and sure of what he was saying about American politics that I signed up to hear more. I loved going to General Studies and many years later was elated when Miner called me in the newsroom at Channel 2 in Chicago. He had left Columbia for Northwestern University in Evanston. We talked for an hour about politics and journalism.

I'll always remember that semester in New York, riding the subway wherever it went and walking everywhere else, stopping for a pastrami on rye, dilled pickle, or tomato and a cream soda in a deli hemmed in by a bruising cacophony of cultures slam-banging into one another—out of which relentlessly surged the news, every morning and at noon, and afternoon, night, and all night. In the middle of it, I was living a life that never stopped, or even paused.

You want to be a reporter? Live in New York for a few months, surrender your senses to the drumbeat bad and tingly good of city hall and Gracie Mansion and a Manhattan neighborhood.

I spent a piece of every day, sometimes beginning at three or four in the morning, on the streets. There I could feel the grit and pace of the city and its people. Out of this cauldron came the news.

Talking to people in shops, watching them at subway stops, and listening in class, I began to sense how much power the media has to affect lives. Every word a reporter writes has consequences, so every word must be written with care. Those abstractions—"bias," "fairness," "objectivity," and "slant"—suddenly were real.

By the middle of June 1958, I was on sensory overload. To go home for the summer, then back to Grinnell for my senior year would be good for me. I needed to slow myself down to let New York sink in. I was sure I'd be back one day—to Columbia's School of Journalism. Even my mother believed I would and, thankfully, encouraged me to dream.

On the way, I got the job I tried so hard to get when I was a batboy. The columnist Jack Mabley of the *Daily News* hired me as a summertime assistant, his "legman." He was in the *Daily News* building on the west side of the Chicago River on Madison Street half a block from the Northwestern railroad station.

The *Daily News* was founded in 1875 by Melvin Stone, a newspaper lifer who early in his career ran the Associated Press. When it first hit the streets in 1876, the *News* was literally a penny paper, geared to a less elite, more middle-class audience than the *Tribune*, which already was in its fourth decade.

In fact, the story—perhaps apocryphal—is that we can thank Stone and his paper for popularizing pennies. Neither the paper nor the one-cent piece was a hit in 1876. But according to *The Book of Strange Facts and Useless Information* by Scot Morris, Stone persuaded Chicago shopkeepers that patrons would be more likely to buy items for ninety-nine cents than a dollar. The publisher rightfully figured that the extra penny would then be used to buy his paper. Apparently the scheme was so successful that a penny shortage ensued. No problem. The wily Stone bought barrels of pennies from the US Mint and distributed them to merchants.

When I got to the *Daily News*, when newspapers were still newspapers, it was one of two afternoon dailies in the city. The rival *Chicago's American*, originally a Hearst paper, had been bought by the *Tribune* two years before in 1956. Both were hawked, like in the movies, at railroad stations and the bus and elevated terminals—"Three found murdered in south loop apartment! Get the latest. Get the latest!"

It definitely was the *latest*, with stories that broke after the morning papers had been tossed on stoops and read at breakfast. Just two hours after Mayor Daley was railing about Republicans at a news conference in city hall, or some other politician being indicted in the federal building, the *Daily News* and *American* were on the street luring commuters heading home for dinner.

Hear ye, hear ye, exciting times in Chicago journalism. The competition was ferocious, the headlines monstrous, often so foreboding that you wouldn't dare board a train before standing in line to buy the paper.

The baseball scores at Wrigley Field and Comiskey Park were screaming good news or bad from the top of page 1. The *American*, still echoing William Randolph Hearst, was politically conservative and more flamboyant than the *Daily News*, which was liberal and more substantive. I always bought both papers and, during my career, worked for both.

The *News* won a Pulitzer Prize, journalism's Oscar, in 1957 for, as the judges put it, "determined and courageous public service in exposing a $2,500,000 fraud in the office of the State Auditor that resulted in the indictment and conviction of the Auditor and others."

The job offer from Jack Mabley after Columbia General Studies in the spring of '58 came in the mail in a scribble on his personal notepad: "Walter. You ready? I need an assistant, and can put you to work. Still interested?"

That was a Monday. Wednesday, I was in my place (my place!) in the city room of the *Chicago Daily News*, at a desk up against Mabley's, crowded by a typewriter and telephone. The room was the size of two Blackhawk hockey rinks, the sound a constant click-click of forty typewriters being pounded at once. Working around me, bumping into me in sprints to deadlines, were the columnists and writers whose stories I had been reading, it seemed, since I first opened a newspaper.

The city desk was as I had seen in pictures, a giant horseshoe jammed with rewriters taking dictation from reporters on assignment. There were guys (I can't remember any women) in short-sleeved white shirts and unknotted ties wearing suspenders and green eyeshades. The lighting was fluorescent.

My assignment was to filter Jack's mail (a hundred letters a week, I'd say)—to put aside those that offered ideas or information I thought he could use in a column, the others into a wire basket on the floor behind his chair to await his response and autographed picture—"Thank you for your comments, and for reading the *Daily News*. Sincerely, Jack Mabley." None of that schmaltzy "Best wishes" stuff. Jack was too correct, much too bona fide for that. He had been in the trenches of Chicago newspaper warfare for a long time.

Born in Binghamton, New York, and raised in Chicago, Jack attended the University of Illinois in Urbana-Champaign, where he made quite a name for himself as a reporter for the *Daily Illini*. Most notably, in 1937 he took on an antiprostitution crusade that led to the shutdown of several local bordellos.

After graduating, Jack returned to Chicago to work for the City News Bureau and Associated Press before becoming a reporter for the *Daily News*. He spent four years in the navy during World War II, then back to the *Daily News*, where, in hardly a dozen years, he earned his own column and, shortly thereafter, got himself an assistant—me. In 1961 he took his column to the *American*.

Over the years he solved murders, exposed police corruption, and hobnobbed with just about everybody who was anybody in Chicago and a few somebodies from around the world—as the title of one of his books attests: *Halas, Hef, the Beatles, and Me*. Jack Mabley was so widely read and so popular that he was asked to introduce the Fab Four when they played Chicago in the mid-1960s.

When he went to the *American*, he was being chased and snapped at by a young reporter named Mike Royko, who replaced him at the *Daily News*. I'll have much more to say about Royko later, but for now: Imagine a lion (king Mabley)versus a cheetah (swift and clever Royko); Babe Ruth (powerful Mabley) versus Pete Rose (scrappy Royko); Max Schmeling (smasher Mabley)versus Joe Louis (dancer Royko). A title fight, Mabley versus Royko, sprinkling their columns with personal ideologies, political and social.

In sometimes subtle language, more often unmistakably direct, Mabley called on people to take care of themselves. Royko demanded that government help. When, during a city council showdown over public service, Mayor Daley made his instantly famous remark about minorities, that they ought to "pick *themselves* up by the bootstraps," Mabley understood. Royko went bananas. If the two columnists were writing about Chicago's bid for the 2016 Summer Olympics, Mabley would have been for it. Royko would have been apoplectic.

It's hard to say who was better. Each in his own style was brilliant at his trade. What they had in common was impact. A column by either one about something broken in government or politics or commerce got it fixed, fast. Sometimes overnight. Both had the clout to do good, and they did.

Entertaining? The fun those two would have had with Illinois pols like the disgraced former governor Rod Blagojevich and the fill-in senator Roland Burris. Oh, my.

Mabley's the one I worked for, so I knew him much better than I knew Royko. In oxford button-down, rep tie, and tweedy jacket, at six-two or -three, brown hair kept cut, Mabley was a professor-Marine, thoughtful and decisive, sensitive and exacting.

I didn't always agree with his point of view, but I admired his integrity and fairness, and the generosity that led him to create the Forgotten Children's

Fund for developmentally disabled kids. He was a man of no prejudice and an infinite capacity not only to listen, but to hear.

His standards were high, and he insisted I meet them, which meant, above all else, that I be accurate. In addition to reading his letters and searching for ideas for stories on the telephone, my job was to follow up on his ideas.

"Here's one," he says on a Tuesday morning before lunch. "Maybe for tomorrow. [Governor Otto] Kerner's been crabbing for a week now about the aldermanic perks in Chicago, bodyguards, chauffeurs, expense accounts. What are *his* perks? He's entitled to more than an alderman is, I know, but I'll wager they're excessive. Get the state budget," he commands in fatherly fashion, nodding his head toward the small metal cabinet behind that wastebasket behind his chair. "Add up how much we're paying for the governor's comfort."

Reading a budget, guessing where excesses may be hidden, and finding them is hard to do between lunch time and 3:30, when he begins writing. I start the search—number of personal police bodyguards and drivers, the governor's mansion, the airplane ready to take him anywhere (as Governor Blagojevich would be taking it forty years later, from Springfield to Chicago and back for a hockey game). In a few minutes, I realize I'll never find enough and be able to check it out in time.

"Can't make it, Jack, not for tomorrow. If I work on it tonight and start early tomorrow, maybe for Thursday."

"Okay. Thanks." And he begins to pull out of his hat a substitute column on public school teachers threatening to strike.

I learned a lot that summer about looking for stories. "Ideas come from everywhere," he once said. "There is no formula whatsoever. I write what interests me. That's the one and only standard. I've eaten in the Pump Room maybe twice in twenty years. I haven't attended a single opening night. But I've found a lot of columns pushing a cart in the supermarket, or keeping my ears open as kids stream in and out of our house, and driving around the city, or sitting in the bleachers in Wrigley Field."

Jack explained to me that summer what kind of columns are most popular. As he later put it, "I wrote about our wars and the threat of nuclear bombs and about crooks in government, but invariably a few paragraphs on the best ways to get ketchup out of a narrow-necked bottle generated more response than a column on how the state was losing millions to sales tax gyps." In what was arguably his most famous column, he was the first to write about how toilet usage increased during television commercials and led to water shortages.

The best day for me during my summer with Jack at the *Daily News*—that byline-generating trip to the nudist colony—was occasioned by an invitation to Jack from the proprietors. He smelled a story but didn't want to go. So he sent me, with instructions to bring back notes, not so much about a nudist camp, but what it was like for me to be there. It got me going to where I've been in Chicago news, got me thinking that maybe I was on my way.

I filled a reporter's notebook with notes about the little bag with drawstrings I was given for my pen and paper, standing naked in the cafeteria lunch line, and averting my gaze when caught staring. I wrote it all down, typed it all out when I returned to my desk, and delivered it to Jack, who submitted it as his column the next day, verbatim. Yes, I was on my way. (If I do say so myself, it was a very good column—or at least it got a lot of attention. I'm sorry I can't include it here. I didn't save it, and try as I have, I can't track it down.

Walter Donaldson, a prolific early-twentieth-century American songwriter, is perhaps best known for a tune he penned on his return from World War I. "How Ya Gonna Keep 'Em Down on the Farm," he wondered, "(After They've Seen Paree?)" After my summer with Mabley, the song fit me. I didn't want to go back to Iowa for my senior year at Grinnell, not after seeing Paree, metaphorically, of course.

I didn't know it then, but in two years, I really would see Paris. And Ankara, Damascus, Cairo, Jerusalem, and Amman, where I would feign being a Christian in order to get a visa, and try to become a foreign correspondent.

The City News Bureau, Queen Elizabeth, and Me

Mabley enjoyed mentoring, felt good about teaching me some of the rules of his road, and was pleased with my work. In fact, he said he'd come to depend on my help, and that he'd have a hard time replacing me. He knew how much I didn't want to be replaced, how much I loved being in the city room of the *Daily News*. Why couldn't I stay and continue to help until I was ready to move on?

"Don't even think about it," he said, peering down at me over his patrician nose and reading glasses. "Remember when you finished high school and asked if you could come to work for me? Do you remember that I told you to go to college and come back? That worked out pretty well, didn't it?"

"Yes it did, but—"

"Now I'm telling you to finish college and come back."

"But you'll find someone to take my place."

"I'll be here," he said. And he was. When I finished my senior year, he recommended me for a job at his alma mater, the Chicago City News Bureau, which for more than one hundred years had been hiring aspiring young reporters to cover the courts, governments, and police and fire departments. The information gathered and the stories written by City News were delivered to Chicago newspapers and radio and television stations by way of an elaborate system of pneumatic tubes.

A day in my life at the bureau in the late 1950s:

I'm assigned to cover combat in city hall, where Chicago alderman Leon Despres of the Hyde Park neighborhood, surrounding the University of Chicago, conscience of the city council, is railing at Boss Daley about the political patronage system. I take notes, dash to a telephone in the press room outside the council chambers, or, if the newspaper big shots don't want me in their way, to a public phone. I call "the desk" at City News, and ask for "rewrite."

"I'm ready with the Daley/Despres story," I chirp, self-satisfied at not only gathering information quickly and precisely, but at capturing a mood.

"Okay, okay. GO, will ya. Move it, kid. Dictate, goddamn it. You're fucking late. The papers'll have the thing on fucking page 1 before you get halfway through telling me what the fuck happened. C'mon. Talk, will ya, please. Shit!" (And that was the decent part of what he said.)

"Mayor Richard J. Daley, comma—"

"Everybody knows he's Richard J. We don't need the fucking initial."

". . . sailing along in his third year in office, comma—"

"What?"

". . . has run into a reef."

"Stop already with the sailing and the reef. And you don't have to tell me where the fuck to put the commas, okay?"

"Sorry. I'm trying to add color."

"Cut the color, please. Jus' tell me what the fuck happened," which I do, and he hangs up.

The dictation is yanked from a rewriter's typewriter, rolled and stuffed into a metal can, shoved into one of the pneumatic tubes, and zipped to city desks and radio and TV production meetings throughout the metropolitan area. Not until 1961 were those tubes replaced by teletype.

Founded in the 1890s and funded by Chicago's major newspapers, the City News Bureau did more than supply news. It was like a farm system in Major League Baseball. Most of the bureau reporters were like me—young, ambitious, fresh out of college, and green. The newspapers that many of us would eventually join expected us to learn things at the bureau from the veteran editors who kept us in line. We did.

Many were the times I was told by the editors, a wise and demanding bunch, to return to the scene of a crime or fire in an abandoned warehouse to get more information (as in the old story of the City News reporter who was sent back five miles to find out the color of the eyes of a just-murdered toddler). Other times, I was grilled on the accuracy of my reporting. The mantra of City News was: "If your mother tells you she loves you, make sure you double-check it."

Double-check it! First doubt it, check it, then check it again. I learned to test my accuracy by thinking about what might cause something to be not what it appeared to be. What could make my observation wrong? In collecting evidence of a crime or corruption, or reading transcripts of a police investigation, four eyes are better than two, six better than four. Be careful, because by far the most critical thing in reporting is to confirm what's presumed to be fact. To lodge that mantra forever in my mind, to practice the surest techniques of double-checking, the Chicago City News Bureau was as good a place as any in the country. Because of how fast news moves in Chicago, and how much it's impacted by politics, City News was probably the best place in the country to learn the immutable basics of reporting.

Another day in my life at the bureau:

My assignment is the turf war between gangs in the ghetto on the west side. I'm assigned to do a story about the fighting being more brutal than usual, the summer heat and humidity having driven more bangers than usual out of the projects into the street. It's dusk, and tense. Been that way for several days, since the police began another of their many assaults on drug traffic from the suburbs. Police headquarters at Eleventh and State is preparing for trouble. The press has been tipped.

I'm instructed to hang out on Roosevelt Road, talk to neighbors, count the drug sales that I can see (most of them are out in the open), judge the intensity of police patrols, get a read on their strategy and tactics and on the number of arrests. And as always, find out if Mayor Daley is running the show, on a telephone or walkie-talkie, personally giving orders.

With all that to do, double-checking isn't easy. Well, too bad. Do it anyway. What's crucial is that what I get, I get right. Thank you, City News, for your rigorous on-the-ground, under-pressure training. Journalism 101.

Jack Mabley took 101. He worked at the City News Bureau after college, one among many eventual award-winning reporters and writers to cut their teeth in the clattering little office kitty-corner from city hall at 188 W. Randolph, which, sad to say, is no more. The bureau closed its doors in 2005 for lack of enough money to keep them open. Among its distinguished alums: Seymour Hersh, the internationally heralded investigative reporter who has broken scandals like the My Lai massacre in Vietnam; Mike Royko; David Brooks, columnist for the *New York Times*; novelist Kurt Vonnegut; the painter and sculptor Claes Oldenburg; and the playwright and screenwriter Charles MacArthur, who was once quoted as saying that he modeled several colorful characters in his play *The Front Page* on editors and reporters he had known at City News. (One of his more memorable headlines, above a story about a dentist who had molested a woman: "Dentist Fills Wrong Cavity.")

I had three months at City News as a reporter, half the time working days, the other half overnight. My passion was politics, my assignment was crime. Covering that city hall combat between Daley and Despres was a one-time assignment for me that happened by accident. Our city hall reporter called in sick that morning as I was coming off the night shift, and the city editor needed a substitute. My face was the first one he saw as he hung up the phone.

"You're it, buddy." I took off before he had time to remember I had never covered city hall before.

It was a great day, then back to the streets covering crime and fires. One three-alarm in an abandoned apartment building on the near south side was a tragicomedy for me, an escapade that could have been written into a MacArthur–Ben Hecht play in the '20s or '30s about a young reporter (me) assigned to a fire, and getting himself burned, badly burned, embarrassed, and unforgettably humiliated. Here's how:

The fire is struck, but police and firemen are still inside. I scramble around the exterior of the building in search of a story beyond just the flames and am approached by a strong, dignified serious-looking man twice my age dressed in suit and tie and wearing glasses.

"You a reporter?" he demands to know from me.

"Yeah. City News."

"I'm with the fire marshal," he says. "You want into the building?"

"Sure I do."

"Go ahead, just inside that door. Talk to a few firemen in there, find out what they think the chances are the building's gonna blow . . ."

"Bl—"

"Blow. Collapse. Get back to me, will ya? I need the information."

In I go, propelled by visions of a major scoop. When I come out, soaked to the ankles and covered with soot, brushing off a small notebook full of quotes that I'm certain will land my story on front pages, I aim directly at the marshal's man. He debriefs me, and takes off, away from the fire. What the—?

Another reporter standing nearby senses my confusion. When I tell him what happened, he says derisively, with a laugh, "That guy's as much a marshal's man as you are. That's Jack Lavin of the *Daily News*, sonny boy. He's heading back to his paper with the quotes you gave him. You've been scooped. I mean really scooped."

It was a lesson I wouldn't forget.

Confession: During the years that followed, to be first with a story, I hatched a few tricks of my own. One of the better ones was reading things upside down, like notes and papers on the desks of public officials. I practiced for weeks this peculiar skill and used it on a heavyweight politician in Cook County government.

He's gone, may he rest in peace. I'm not revealing his name because wherever he is (politicians, as General MacArthur said of old soldiers, never die, they just fade away), if he gets wind of this, he'll be ashamed of himself for being outwitted by a rookie reporter. Here's the drill:

First, I pick up a clue that he's preparing an unusually newsworthy announcement. After his lunchtime, I'm waiting for him outside his office in a hallway in the county building. Maybe he's had a martini or a hoagie and is not as sharp as he usually is.

"What's up?" I ask, casually enough to avoid suspicion that I know what's up. "Any news?"

"Yes, Walter, I do have some news, an announcement I'm about to make, but I can't tell you about it, or anyone. Not yet. It's too soon."

"Even if I keep it to myself until you're ready?"

"Even if you keep it to yourself. I'm not ready. Try me next week."

"Okay." But the next day, I ask his secretary if I can see him for a minute about a not-newsworthy matter, thinking if I can get into his office and stand in front of his desk, I might see scribbles about the announcement he's working on. No way he'll suspect I can read upside down, or that if I could, I would. But I can, and I do, and I leave his office with enough information for a front-page story, a day before any other reporter is even close. A trick of the trade.

Here's another one learned during my time at City News—adding chutzpah to a press pass equals a shot at being somewhere I'm not supposed to be, getting a head start on a story.

For example:

It's 1959. Queen Elizabeth is on her way to Chicago, her first visit since her coronation in '52. She's just thirty-three years old, but definitely royally regal. Chicago is enthralled by news of a British monarch coming to town. The hoopla when she arrives on a yacht in front of Buckingham Fountain includes bells and whistles that will not be heard again for nearly a quarter of a century, when Pope John Paul II drops in to pray for us in Soldier Field.

Her Highness is being covered by Chicago's newspaper royalty, but City News is on the story, too. I get a piece of the assignment, to report on her stop at the Museum of Science and Industry, where I discover the upside of being a rookie—nobody in the police or the press corps knows I'm a reporter. Along with a few dozen journalists from around the world, and a few thousand neighbors from around the museum who had read in the papers about the queen's itinerary, or heard of it on the radio, I mill around outside the museum behind a rope at the top of the stairs, awaiting Her Majesty, and plotting to slip under the rope into her entourage of diplomats, city officials, and prominent politicians, including Mayor Daley and the governor of Illinois, William Stratton. I ditch my press credential, into a shallow place in my pocket in case I need it if I get caught doing what I'm about to do.

Amid the cheers and confusion as the queen reaches the last stair before the front door to the museum, and all the attention focused on her and Philip, her prince of a husband, I bend low, duck under the rope, straighten up and saunter in behind Mayor Daley and the governor (they, too, had never seen me before), just half a dozen people away from the royal couple.

The Chicago police must be thinking I'm with Elizabeth. Her police must be thinking I'm with the mayor. Whatever they're thinking, they let me be, and I'm in, and see and hear it all, which isn't much. But hey, no other reporter is so close. Small talk among the entourage, a big scoop for me. What a summer it was, after which I left City News and married Lynn, the gal from Vassar. We moved to New York, and I enrolled at the Graduate School of Journalism, Columbia University.

The curriculum at Columbia was a dream—seminars with reporters, writers, and columnists at the *Washington Post*, the *New York Times*, and the *New York Post* and *Daily News*; major players at the television networks and prominent journalists from Europe, Latin America, and far beyond. I blinked at the star power, and blinked again.

All of Columbia Journalism is in one building, an old graystone that sits, dignified and defiant, just inside the university's wrought-iron entrance on the upper west side in Morningside Heights. No less a figure than Thomas Jefferson, sculpted by William Ordway Partridge in 1914, stands sentinel at the front door. Classes began in 1912, thanks to a $2 million bequest from Joseph Pulitzer, the iconic newspaper publisher.

Initially, the school offered curricula for both undergraduates and graduates. In 1935, the undergraduate program was dropped, and the focus and intensity were sharpened not just on the skills of general reporting, but specifically on how to cover, interpret, edit, and opine on education, the arts, politics, and sports, while always, always, being conscious of the First Amendment, slander, libel and, most importantly, ethics. For me, Columbia was boot camp. It taught me how to meet deadlines and protect sources, and it drilled into me the necessity of being careful, of pressing for a fact until I get it, of never running off without it.

It's the best in the United States, in no small part because it's in New York, the best journalism lab in the country. Nowhere else, except maybe Chicago, is there so much moving, unpredictable grist for a reporter's mill, so much news in so many public and private places. Being in class (1959–60) was being on assignment, covering Mayor Wagner, Governor Rockefeller, the remains of Tammany Hall, and a labor-management storm spreading across Manhattan. Thirty-thousand hospital employees were preparing for a strike. For them to walk off the wards and out of emergency rooms would be calamitous.

For me, an adventure:

Go get the story, my professor commands. Both sides of it. Yes, sir. My first call is to local 1199 of the Drug, Hospital and Health Care Employees Union, whose president, Leon J. Davis, has issued a statement: "It is well that hospital management be fully cognizant of this decision, so that they make no mistake about what their workers are determined to achieve!"

"You plan to shut down eighty-one hospitals?" I ask.

A press officer replies, "Yes we are. You know what this is about, don't you? Dietary employees working split shifts between eight in the morning and seven at night, averaging $35.50 a week, some only $23 a week."

I report that "many employees are housed in projects owned and operated by the hospitals. A 57-year-old woman working in a kitchen at Mount Sinai is fired and ordered out of her apartment because, she says, she refused to eat cold beans that were warmed by being dipped in hot water." I get the other side of the story and turn it in. Job adequately done.

Later, I expanded the story into my master's project, twenty pages on a labor-management crisis in the country's largest, most dynamic, and ever-confrontational urban center. Good training for post-Columbia assignments in Chicago, covering two Mayors Daley, Mayors Jane Byrne and Harold Washington, and the Chicago Federation of Labor. The Columbia faculty pushed us hard. Deadlines were held fast, critiques merciless, and although I didn't know where I'd end up doing what, I believed that after a year at Columbia, I'd be any-street-ready.

As far as I know, none of my "J School" classmates, or any mates before or after, had played Zelig to Elizabeth II, as I did when she came to Chicago, but the alumni roster reads like a Who's Who in American journalism. Prominent graduates are far too many to enumerate, including such giants of the past as *New Yorker* writer A. J. Liebling and Random House co-founder Bennett Cerf.

Here are some other names you might recognize: Molly Ivins, Pat Buchanan, Geraldo Rivera (how's that for a trifecta?), Joseph Lelyveld of the *New York Times* (my classmate), the *Washington Post*'s Howard Kurtz, the *Wall Street Journal*'s Walt Mossberg, *60 Minutes*'s Steve Kroft, NPR's Robert Siegel, and authors Robert Caro, Valerie Wilson Wesley, Ron Suskind, Gail Sheehy, and Erik Larson.

Lynn and I inhaled New York City. We rented a one-bedroom, Pullman-kitchen apartment with three barred windows looking onto a fire escape a block south of Washington Square in Greenwich Village, the center of the universe for the Beat Generation, especially the writers and poets. Jack Kerouac came in off the road, and Allen Ginsberg read "Howl" at the Café Bizarre, a rickety club on Third Street. "Fuck America" (or was it "Amerika"?) was scrawled on the outside of the door. As I recall, the inside was a small, dark, and noisy room about forty feet square. A few dozen folding chairs were spread around a stand-up microphone swirled in a sweet-smelling cloud of marijuana smoke wafting up and around bare pipes that seemed to be holding up the ceiling.

Ginsberg, with a long, curly black beard and in a flannel checkered shirt and Levis, raged at the establishment for a few bucks a night, if that. We of the neighborhood wore Levis. The tourists taxied to the Village to watch us hippies act out the counter culture of the turn of the decade into the '60s. The Big Apple had it all, and then some.

Lynn and I didn't want to leave our pad on Sullivan Street. But we did, for Europe and the Middle East—a honeymoon deferred until we finished school in the spring of 1960, a wedding present from her parents. Before dropping out of New York onto the *Queen Elizabeth* on the Atlantic, I pitched the *Chicago Sun-Times* for a chance to do freelance reporting from some places around the world. Could I be *Walter Jacobson, foreign correspondent*?

I tried my P. K. Wrigley strategy, a letter to the editor of the *Sun-Times*, Larry Fanning, asking for a credential that might allow me access to people making news, and help me cross police or army lines for stories that perhaps the *Sun-Times* would be interested in printing. I'm a Columbia Journalism graduate, I wrote to Fanning. Born and bred in Chicago, blah-blah-blah, twenty-two years old with maybe a perspective he'd enjoy reading.

It worked. Fanning typed on his letterhead a note "To Whom It May Concern" that Walter Jacobson "is authorized to represent the *Chicago Sun-Times*." I couldn't ask for more than that. So Lynn and I sold what we had, including our car, boarded the *Queen* and, as far as I was concerned, sailed off into heaven— three months in France, Germany, Spain, and Italy, then three more in Lebanon, Turkey, Syria, Jordan, Israel, and Egypt.

Jews were not granted visas by most countries in the Middle East, so we signed affidavits attesting to a Christian religion (you can imagine what my mother said about that) and were warned that to admit to being Jewish in nations hostile to, or afraid of, Israel might cause us trouble. We wouldn't have to prove we were Christian. Just say, "Not Jewish."

On our third day in Jordan, in a hot and arid rural somewhere, we were stopped by police and questioned, in English, about religion.

"Oh, I'm Catholic," I stuttered.

"So am I," said Lynn.

"You are welcome in Jordan. Where are you from?"

"Chicago." And, as happens all over the world, the gendarme feigned holding a pistol, and exclaimed something like "Rat-a-tat-tat, Al Capone!" (Michael Jordan, bless his basketball, was to squelch that dialog some twenty-five years later.) "Not to worry," the policeman continued. "Your passports, please," which he examined and returned.

He was one of four officers surrounding us, none of them appearing to be angry or seriously suspicious of anything. They were all smiles as they dug through our duffle bags and camping gear in the trunk, and then motioned us on our way. Pleasant enough, but frightening enough that for the next five days on scrabble dirt roads, one of us looked forward out the windshield and drove while the other glanced backward over shoulders to scout trouble until we passed through the Mandelbaum Gate, the military crossing between Jordan and Israel that was thick with bad feelings and loaded machine guns.

On the Israeli side, I gushed, "Shalom," verily leaping from the car, arms wide open, eyes looking for a hug. "We're Jewish from the United States. It's so wonderful to be here." The Israeli soldiers couldn't have cared less. They weren't nearly as hospitable as the police in Jordan. Later, I learned that many Israelis, especially the Sabras of the military, didn't approve of American Jews visiting Jordan.

I pounded my stories out of a portable typewriter that I toted, because it helped me feel like a pro, and mailed them to the *Sun-Times*. I wrote about the Sabras, civil unrest in Turkey, students in Syria, and American tourists dropping hotdog wrappers and soggy French fries at the base of the Sphinx in Egypt. None of it made the *Sun-Times*. Maybe my writing wasn't good enough, not up to the paper's standards. Or maybe—my fantasy—there was so much else going on that the *Sun-Times* didn't have room for me. John F. Kennedy was running toward the White House, and Mayor Daley was preparing to heist it for him if he had to.

Whatever the reason, I wasn't a budding correspondent. Too bad. It was time to go home to Chicago, and to move on.

We settled into four rooms in an old six-flat on LaSalle Street near the Lincoln Park Zoo and began living the grown-up life—Lynn as a copywriter for the Spiegel mail-order catalogue, I as a reporter for United Press International. I also was a part-time "stringer" for *Time* magazine, doing some telephone reporting for its regular staff.

When working a story about hospitals or, say, public housing or politics in Chicago, *Time* called me with questions that I'd do my best to get answered. Chicago politicians were and still are loathe to talk to inquiring local reporters. But they do respond to, "This is *Time* magazine calling." So the answers I got were pretty good.

My reason for moving back to Chicago was for a job. I figured it would be easier for me to swim in a smaller pond than New York, where I might drown, or at least be forever swimming upstream. Also, when it comes to news about politics and sports, New York's a kiddie pool compared to Chicago.

The hours at UPI were hard, 4 P.M. to midnight or midnight to eight, but I didn't suffer them for long. In less than a year, I was fired. Details on that coming up, but first a note about international wire services.

Many people are familiar with the Associated Press (AP), a news-gathering business that has correspondents around the world and sells stories they cover to newspapers, magazines, and TV and radio stations. It's only the old timers and news junkies who remember UPI, although there was a time when it gave AP a run for its money.

AP evolved out of the Harbor News Association, which was formed by a group of New York newspapers in the 1840s needing to be more cost-efficient in their international reporting. The Mexican-American War was beginning, and the publishers were fearful of how expensive it would be to send correspondents to the border, and keep them there for who-knows-how-long. Why not share the cost of sending one correspondent, and share his stories?

When ships from Europe arrive in New York, why pay a reporter to be one of many in little boats paddling into the harbor to cover the same story, interview the same passengers for the same bits of news. There's not a need to send correspondents to Paris, Moscow, Tokyo, Rio, or Borneo when the wire services have regular staffers already there, and everywhere else? Sign up with a wire service, save big bucks!

In 1882, after AP refused to sell its stories to several of his newspapers, E. W. Scripps launched United Press wire service. As the only major news wire service that was privately owned, UPI never grew to AP's size or was able to command AP's fees. Still, it was a major player in the news game and was at one time or another home to such prominent journalists as Walter Cronkite, David Brinkley, Helen Thomas, and Thomas Friedman.

In its heyday, UPI had about six thousand employees in more than two hundred bureaus in some one hundred countries. Sadly, as daily newspapers, particularly afternoon editions, began failing, UPI lost much of its business and was sold. Then sold and sold again, and again, to seven different owners between 1992 and 2000. When it was bought by Reverend Sun Myung Moon's News World Communications, Helen Thomas, dean of White House reporters, who had been with UPI for fifty-seven years, resigned.

Since 2000, newspapers haven't done much better than that. In 2009, both of Chicago's major dailies, the *Tribune* and the *Sun-Times*, filed for bankruptcy. They soldier on, but beset by increasing costs and declining circulation, they continue cutting their staffs and pages. Bad for the papers. Maybe good for the wire services.

As the newspapers continue to shut down bureaus around the world, they'll have no way of getting stories from where they want them, even places as big and important as Berlin or Madrid or Rome, or Seoul or Beijing. It's not likely, but you never know, maybe a new UPI or some form of news co-op will emerge from the doldrums of the news media. Maybe a better wire service, more carefully budgeted, will increase competition that may sharpen the process of news gathering and enhance the quality of news interpretation and analysis.

How good that would be during this period of not only sinking finances, but sinking news standards. In the past five years, how often have you read all the way through a newspaper, or sat through a half hour of the evening news on television? In the past twenty years?

In 1960, UPI in Chicago, on Madison Street west of Wacker, was a serious if colorless operation of about two dozen journalists looking for a ladder on which to climb to one of Chicago's major dailies or network-owned television stations. The top rung for me was an assignment to cover city hall, where the well-connected, most influential political columnists and commentators (George Tagge and Bob Weidrich at the *Tribune*, John Drieske at the *Sun-Times*, Len O'Connor at the local NBC affiliate) flexed muscle. And where Chicago's incomparable journalism sleuths (Sandy Smith at the *Tribune* and Art Petacque at the *Sun-Times*) scoured government contracts in search of million-dollar deals making Mayor Daley's insiders rich. I yearned to be among them, but I was twenty-three and had a long way to go, and a lot to learn about the meticulous, tedious process of digging for a story while, at the same time, being assigned to cover hard and fast-breaking news, of which, in 1960 and 1961, there was an ample supply: teamsters and milkman strikes; US senator Everett Dirksen, the powerhouse Republican from Illinois, making us guess whether he was pondering a third term; the Blackhawks winning the Stanley Cup; Mayor Daley trying to integrate the public schools, or at least saying he was.

Then there was the story that would lead to my being fired by UPI, causing me to fear that my life as a journalist would end as quickly as it was just beginning.

4

Jacobson versus Royko

I thought I was ready for the big time before I was. After three months of leg-ging it for Jack Mabley, three months at City News, and just five or six at UPI, I was aiming for the *Tribune* or the *Sun-Times*, or either of the two afternoon papers, *Chicago's American* or the *Daily News*. I wanted to stand out, which I guess is a nice way of saying I wanted to make a splash, which I did, all right, a big one. Trouble was, it was the wrong kind, and I almost drowned.

I ventured out on a story to which I was not assigned but hustled on my own and learned a lesson about journalism elitism, about reporters, writers, and television anchors who get to thinking we're better than other people because we believe our work is more important than theirs, and that therefore we deserve special privileges. Well, it's not, and we don't.

Here's what happened, at UPI in 1960:

After reading reports that major department stores in downtown Chicago are more concerned than usual about shoplifting, I "assign" myself to go un-dercover to check it out. When off the clock one morning, I walk from our UPI newsroom five blocks in the rain into Marshall Field's on State Street to take notes on the methods and consequences of shoplifting.

How do lifters work? What percentage of them get away with it? Of those who are caught, are most nabbed in the act, or when leaving the store? What will happen if I try to lift something? How nonchalant need I appear? What's a tipoff to a guard that I'm up to no good?

These are questions that need answers, I say to myself, and I'll be the one to find them. A good idea for a story, good concept. But the execution is just plain stupid, borne of a notion that journalists can do whatever they want to do in search of news.

Inside Field's on the first floor, I mix into a crowd and wander casually from counter to counter seeking my quarry. How about sunglasses, which I can slip easily into the pocket of my coat? What if I try one pair on and look in a mirror while heisting another? Being inexperienced in the manners of thievery—bubble gum, once, out of a jar on a counter in a drugstore when I was six or seven—will I be caught? No, nobody'll notice. Maybe the other shoppers are shoplifting, too.

So I do it, lift a pair of $30 glasses off a revolving showcase, and turn toward an exit. Not three steps from the counter, I'm intercepted by two beefy guys in suits and white shirts and ties. One in front of me, the other behind.

"Excuse me, sir," whispers the front one directly into my face, so if I don't hear him, surely I'll read his lips. He wants not to arouse the curiosity or discomfort of others in the store. "Come with me, please," he says, half flashing what looks like a badge held onto a leather wallet by rubber bands.

"Come with you where? Why?"

No answer. But no compromise, either. I don't have a choice, especially since his partner once behind is now alongside me, prepared to assist should I decline.

No problem, I say to myself. I'm a journalist working on a story, immune to restraints that encumber regular people. I'm special. It's okay for me to walk into a department store and slip a pair of sunglasses into my pocket, because I'm not stealing, I'm reporting. "Where are we going?" I ask rather sternly. "I'm a reporter. United Press . . ."

Still no answer, except "Come with me, please," and he leads me around the down escalator to a dark paneled door that he opens inward to a ten-by-ten-foot room. Nothing in it but a small metal table, two folding chairs, and a telephone. He holds the door for me and the other guy, who closes the door, leans his back up against it, and smiles.

"May I have the sunglasses in your pocket?"

I remove them, place them on the table, and harrumph, "I'd like to speak with your manager, please. I'm a reporter, UPI. Doing a story on—"

"He's on his way." An awkward silence for a minute, until a tall, thin, balding but mustached Marshall Field's executive walks in, is handed the glasses, and glares down at me over a pair of his own.

"I know, dumb thing for me to do, but as I explained to your assistants here, I'm working on a story about shoplift—"

"I understand. May I see some identification, please? Where is it you work?"

"United Press International. I'm a reporter. I don't have my press card with me. Will my driver's license do?" The realization that I may be in trouble suddenly pierces the thickness of my head.

"Yes, that's fine. Is there someone at your office I can call?"

"Sure. Our bureau chief, David Smothers. Here's his direct line," which, during the interrogation, I had scribbled on a page in my reporter's notebook. He punched in the number, identified himself, said, "Marshall Field's," and spoke.

"I have a young man in my office, Mr. Smothers. That's it, isn't it, 'Smothers'? He says his name is Walter Jacobson, that he works for you, and is here doing a story."

As the manager alternately nods and shakes his head, I hear several "um"s and "yes"s, and he hangs up, turns to me, removes his glasses, scowls annoyance, and grumbles a warning: "It's not a good idea to assume you can do as you wish in this department store, or in any store, for that matter. You're free to leave, Mr. Jacobson. Next time, call me. Okay?" He hands me his card.

I leave the store, amble back to the office, approach Smothers, who instructs me to talk to the general manager, who fires me. Sends me packing right then and there with a not-so-gentle reminder that I damn well ought to know that "reporters don't go off doing stories on their own. And they sure as hell don't walk into a store and pocket something off a counter. Who do you think you are?"

Not only am I fired hardly six months into my first full-time job, but I'm humiliated—an arrogant, self-destructive, smart-ass rookie reporter who needs to learn what life's about. I stumble away. "You're finished," I bellow into the rain. "You fathead. There goes your dream. Cooked." Not the best news to be bringing home, where it will be greeted with astonishment and, deservedly, disgust.

Lucky for me, the distress was temporary because I had, several weeks before (presciently? I wonder), started a scrapbook that included copies of UPI in-house memos of commendation for my coverage of government and politics: "Great job on the county payroll flap. You've been consistently out front on it. Congrats, Dave [Smothers]." And "The storms in the suburbs, last week. Thanks, Walter, for your extra hours. Dave." Also lucky for me, I had begun talking about a job with an editor at *Chicago's American*, the feisty afternoon gazette owned by the *Tribune*.

A decade later, after President Richard Nixon's thugs broke into an office of the Democratic Party in the Watergate apartment complex in Washington and triggered the investigation that led Nixon to resign, hordes of America's best and brightest suddenly aspired to careers in investigative journalism. It seemed so glamorous. If your fascination was politics and you had a sense of mission, maybe you, too, could become Bob Woodward and Carl Bernstein, the intrepid Watergate sleuths at the *Washington Post* who went on to become legendary characters, idealized in a smash-hit Hollywood movie starring Robert Redford and Dustin Hoffman.

But before Watergate opened the floodgates, newsrooms were hungry for curious and smart, tireless, persistent, relentless, and nosy, twenty-somethings who didn't understand "No" as an answer to questions and would be happy to work horrendous hours for little pay. Some might be reluctant to vouch for my smarts, but unquestionably I met the other requirements.

With neither a query made nor a word mentioned about my departure from UPI, I was hired by the *American*, assigned to a desk, a telephone, and a typewriter in a city room in the Tribune Tower that was bathed in reflections off the Chicago River and buffeted by the noise of traffic on Michigan Avenue. I was right there above the bridge, less than half a mile, an easy walk in the worst of Chicago's weather, to the city hall and Cook County building, where for as long as I could remember since failing as a pretend *Sun-Times* foreign correspondent in the Middle East, I aimed to be.

One building, two governments. Chicago and Cook County. The city is a piece of the county, about twenty-five miles long on the shore of a beautiful and normally tranquil, though sometimes angry and very nasty, Lake Michigan. It stretches west to a suburban small-town sprawl heading toward Iowa.

Except for an odd four years more than half a century ago, Chicago has been governed—"bullied" may be a more apt description—by Democrats, mostly by the sovereign Mayoral Family Daley. Cook County also is governed by Democrats, including a treasurer and a clerk, and a prosecutor who has the power to incarcerate some of Chicago's most nefarious public officials, but rarely (almost never) uses it, and a county tax assessor who has the power to make people rich, and often (almost always) uses it.

The all-time potentate of assessors was P. J. "Parky" Cullerton, a middle-aged fellow who measured five-foot-five or -six, depending on whether he was standing proud or slinking away from reporters' questions about tax breaks he was granting to his friends. Parky was the ultimate Cook County politician. He was Irish, his eyes always smiling, his nature jolly. But when it came to business, he was ruthless. "Sharky" more than "Parky."

Cullerton held office for twenty-three years, until he died, a comfortably wealthy man. He was a lord of the Democratic Party, committeeman of the Thirty-Eighth Ward on the northwest side, commander of the precinct captains necessary to elect and reelect and reelect him and his party pals. He parceled county and city jobs to his friends and friends of friends according to the number of voters they delivered to the polls on election day and the amount of money they delivered to the Cullerton campaign kitty all other days.

On his family tree were Chicago aldermen Eddie Cullerton (elected in 1871, the year of the Great Chicago Fire), Willie Cullerton and Tom Cullerton; there was ward committeewoman Patty Joe, and there still is John Cullerton, president of the Illinois senate. If there's another family in the western world with that kind of hegemony in representative government, I've not heard of it. The Cullertons reached into everything, anything, having to do with elective politics.

When Parky was county assessor, a ruler of the realm, I was assigned by *Chicago's American* to the county building pressroom, where, one day before Christmas, I was invited upstairs to his office, along with reporters for the *Tribune*, *Sun-Times*, and *Daily News*. From behind a desk much too big for him, the county assessor wished us happy holidays, shook our hands, and gave each of us an envelope containing what we found, upon returning to the pressroom, to be what my colleagues characterized as traditional Cook County holiday cheer—two new $100 bills.

I know not whether Parky Cullerton understood Latin, but he clearly knew the meaning of *quid pro quo*. I can't speak for the others, but on the envelope I received I wrote, "Thank you, but no thank you. Happy Holidays." I signed my name and brought it back upstairs to his polite, but silent and transparently skeptical, secretary.

I tell the story not to proclaim a high standard of ethics, but to reveal the impunity with which elected public officials (Cullerton I know from personal experience, but I suspect many others) attempt to bribe the media as a means of reducing the risks of being caught in quest of outrageously remunerative personal gain. (The number of criminal convictions, all of them federal, attests to that: In much-too-recent history in Cook County, scores of Chicago aldermen, city department heads, and employees—not to mention four Illinois governors—have been sent to prison having been found guilty of extortion, fraud, wire fraud, racketeering, and conspiracy, among an assortment of other felonies. The most recent governor to wear stripes is the famous and infamous Rod "Blago" Blagojevich, convicted on seventeen of twenty counts of misconduct and corruption, including his attempt to sell to the highest bidder the US Senate seat abandoned by Barak Obama when he was elected president.)

When I first checked into my beat covering Cook County, in what the brochures describe as a building "designed to symbolize the strength, dignity and vigor of the functions it contains," the pressroom struck me as an ugly little place set aside, reluctantly, to facilitate reporters' access to the agencies of government. It was more than half a century old and looked, and felt, every day of it. A cement floor of some six hundred square feet was covered by a sheet of muddied linoleum peeling at the corners and cracked most everywhere else. The walls were whitewash turned dirt-gray and smudged by ink-stained fingerprints, pencil scratches, and an array of telephone numbers written in a hurry. Once we secured the numbers in our notepads, we erased them off the wall so as to protect our sources, the lifeblood of journalists competing for an extra dimension to a story known by all—a scoop that excites our editors and distinguishes one of us from the rest.

There were four cheap wooden desks in the pressroom, one for each reporter, painted brown and separated by so little space that we covered our mouths when we talked on the telephone. A large, oblong metal table slopped with old newspapers, county directories, and the Yellow Pages sat in the center of the room underneath fluorescent light fixtures up ten or twelve feet on the ceiling, which also was covered with linoleum. Many of the bulbs were burned out, probably had been for many years. But I loved being there and pretty well mastered the names and inclinations of the most important occupants of county offices.

After being scooped a few times during my first year in that pressroom, I learned how to compete.

Like this:

I'm alone in the room one lunchtime, when Parky opens the door (nobody ever knocks) and walks in carrying a small stack of "Office of the Tax Assessor" press releases.

"Where are the rest of you guys?"

"Out 'n' about." I sense there's big news in the works because of how infrequently The Man himself stops in. "Got something for us?"

"Yeah, I do. A story for you. Taxes goin' up. Pass these around, okay?" He hands me the stack and walks out. I read the one that's on top, instantly recognizing just how big the story is.

"I'll do that," I mumble to Cullerton's back. "Soon as they're here."

I'll do that? No, I won't. What the other guys don't know can't hurt me. I stuff the press releases—all of them—into my pocket, scan the floor to be sure I didn't drop one, and, looking over my shoulder, descend the stairs and walk out of the building as inconspicuously as I think I can, leaving behind nothing for the *Tribune* or *Sun-Times*, or for the *Daily News*, whose beat reporter is the previously mentioned Mike Royko.

I know Royko would do exactly what I'm doing exactly the same way. Nonetheless, when he finds out, he's incensed—which is not a good thing, Mike Royko being incensed. His personal edge is no less jagged than the edge of his column, and he doesn't, or maybe can't, keep it in check. He bounds up the stairs to rail on Assessor Cullerton, who is not to blame, and he sticks me into his craw, and will keep me there for twenty years, occasionally, as you'll see later, spitting me into his columns with anger or sarcasm.

Excepting Studs Terkel, Mike Royko was the best-known and most highly praised Chicago journalist of the last fifty years. He had more than just the talent to write about and advocate for the proletariat. He had the credentials; his father, a Ukrainian immigrant, and his mother, who was Polish American, operated the Blue Sky Lounge on Chicago's northwest side. For a portion of Mike's childhood, the family lived in an apartment over the tavern.

Mike went to college but never finished. His career in journalism began in the air force during the Korean War. The story goes that stationed in the Chicago area, he feared he'd be designated a military policeman or cook. So he told his superior officers a tall tale—that he had worked at the *Daily News*. They made him editor of the base newspaper.

When he died too young at age sixty-four in 1997, the *New York Times* obituary written by Don Terry noted that "for nearly 30 years, every young journalist who ever set foot in a Chicago newsroom wanted to be like Mr. Royko. He had a tough skin and a generous heart, and his column won almost as many awards as a Windy City election has dead voters." Terry also described Mike as having grown "increasingly cantankerous" over the years. I can vouch for that, and that he also had become increasingly nasty.

In the county building pressroom, he more often than not seemed riled and inflamed about something. To his credit and largely to the benefit of Chicago, he channeled a portion of his wrath into fuming columns aimed at deserving politicians. And at times, as I said, at me.

That day I fled the pressroom with Parky Cullerton's press releases, when Royko discovered what I had done too late for his *Daily News* to catch up, his anger propelled him not only to Cullerton's office, but into stairwells and hallways that then echoed his rage.

No matter. I had my story and was hightailing it through the Loop to my editors at the *American*. I wasn't thinking about Royko, only about the deadline for our last edition, and the likelihood we'd be ahead of the *Daily News* by twenty-four hours. I arrived at the city desk short of breath.

"I have a good one." I remember gasping for air. "Cullerton's raising taxes. We have it alone. "

I thrust forward the press releases—all but one of them, which I held onto, awaiting a go-ahead to explain how the taxpayers of Cook County were in for a jolt, a big one. "*Chicago's American* has learned," I typed in a hurry, "that Assessor P. J. Cullerton will soon submit for a vote by the County Board. . . ." A copy boy hovered over my shoulder, waiting to sprint the story, a paragraph at a time, to the city desk a few yards away, where it was edited, dashed into print, and, within an hour, on the street, under a front-page five-column headline and a banner screaming, "EXCLUSIVE!"

What matters to readers is information about taxes. What matters to the newspaper is "*Chicago's American* has learned." During my years in print and on television, I've learned that to managers of the media, the value of a story depends not so much on the substance in it as on the attention it gets, the number of readers who buy, the number of viewers who tune in. And that depends, more often than it ought to, on what a newspaper or television station has that the competition does not.

News managers and marketers, in their ultimate wisdom (as they define it), contend that exclusivity sells. That's why the cable news channels CNN, MSNBC, and Fox incessantly, boorishly promote "Exclusive One-on-One" interviews with any congressman or White House adviser who wants to talk about anything. For how many more minutes can you bear to hear Wolf Blitzer howl, "Only on CNN," or Chris Matthews, "Only on MSNBC?"

I remember watching Barack Obama make the rounds after he became president. Every television star who interviewed him was the "first" or "only" one. If that pitch really sells, then TV news ratings would be soaring. So don't you wonder sometimes where the buyers are? Wouldn't Blitzer and Matthews and Sean Hannity and Rachel Maddow do more for their viewers, and the ratings, proclaiming they're offering content and quality? And then delivering it?

I think they would, and nonstop during my career, I've asked, demanded, petitioned, pleaded, pestered, cajoled, whined, even cried, for more good stories, fewer exclusives, often to a point where I've been told, "Enough, already! Shut up and read the goddamn news!" The joy of writing this book is that I'm not being told to shut up.

The few things bean counters, numbers crunchers, hawkers, consultants, and, especially, the just-out-of-college ad agency account executives would like even more to sell than The Big Exclusive, and would if they could without being embarrassed, are sex, murder, and stories about celebrities. And they would, if they could, use them to soak up one-third of a local evening news broadcast.

Nationally? An abducted child, preferably a little girl because of the likelihood of sexual abuse, is 'round-the-clock "news" on the twenty-four-hour channels. At least if she is white, she is. Reporters are directed by assignment editors to compete for standing room outside her home, cameras rolling in case a parent emerges and can be asked, "How do you feel?" If the response is choked-up or, better, teary, it will be run and rerun all day and night, to promote whatever newscast is coming up next.

If the child's been murdered and a "person of interest" is under suspicion, or even guessed by the media to be, the news offers endless pictures, many of them the same ones over and over again, of squad cars and lawyers coming and going between courthouse and jailhouse. It's amazing what news managers in their executive suites think they know about what news viewers in their living rooms want to see.

Executions, for instance.

Murderers usually are put to death a few seconds after midnight, an hour and a half after the end of the ten o'clock news, which often is extended fifteen or twenty minutes to include interviews about last-minute attempts to persuade the governor to prevent execution. Programming between 11 P.M. and midnight is sometimes interrupted every few minutes for up-to-the-minute "information" from outside the prison walls, where microphone stands are set up in the glare of mega-watt bulbs under a makeshift tent, at whatever cost, to wait for witnesses to talk about what it's like to watch an execution.

In Chicago, in addition to executions, there's nothing like a particularly grisly slaughter to energize the press corps into a frenzy of competition—the eight student nurses living dorm-style in a small townhouse on the southeast side in 1966. Seven of them were found strewn about their few rooms in pools of blood, stabbed and slashed to death. The one who survived had played dead and later told police of a madman, Richard Speck, who wielded the knife.

The media had equal access to the essential facts of what happened. The challenge to Chicago journalism was to unearth the elusive, unimaginable details. And that required a deftness honed hard by tricky old-timers during many years in the game.

Best of them all was *Chicago's American*'s Harry Romanoff, known as the "Jascha Heifetz of the telephone." At about five and a half feet, Harry seemed as wide as he was short. He had a bulbous nose under kindly brown eyes and a devilish but loving smile that, when necessary, turned terrorist. Watching him work, as I was lucky to do by hanging around the city desk, was an education unlisted in the catalogue of classes at Columbia, or any other university teaching journalism.

Harry's skills were sharpened in the foxholes, and they dropped my jaw. I took notes on the people he called, what he said, and how he asked questions. Some of the notes I memorized, others I kept on paper. And during my many years in the game, I squeezed from them techniques that earned me good stories. Exclusives.

I wasn't at the *American* in 1966, but those who were said that the moment Speck was accused of murdering the student nurses was the moment Romanoff shifted into his high gear. He dialed up a policeman involved in the investigation, identified himself as a deputy Cook County coroner, and asked for specifics about the wounds suffered by the victims—and got them, precisely.

Later, posing convincingly as Speck's attorney, he called the alleged killer's mother, asked for, and was given exclusively, details about Speck's childhood, his abusive father, his behavior problems in grade school, and his friends in the US Navy. (For better or worse, caller ID has diminished the effectiveness of a Heifetz of the telephone.)

There are many managers in the executive suites of the media, especially those responsible for policing the tactics used by reporters to compete, who decry Romanoff's ruses for getting information. In both print and electronics, lying is not a generally sanctioned method of ferreting out truth, but I'm not ashamed or reluctant to say there are times when I tell what I consider little white lies. Seeking information from public officials who are averse to yielding it, I've misrepresented myself. Sometimes it's the only way for me to find out what I believe the public has a right to know.

Let's say an assistant commissioner of the city Department of Streets and Sanitation is padding his public payroll, is aware that it's me calling about it, and suspects I may do him harm. He's not likely to tell me what he's doing, or answer a question that may help me track it down. But if I identify myself as a clerk in his payroll department, he may reveal what I need to expose malpractice. Fair enough, I believe.

Or, consider this: Residents of the Lawndale neighborhood have been calling on city hall for weeks to repair a badly damaged and dangerous street, and to replace a missing stop sign at a school. If I call city hall, identify myself as a reporter, and ask why no response to Lawndale's complaints, I'll be given an excuse that I cannot disprove. If I identify myself as a neighbor, I'm likely to be given an excuse that I can easily disprove, then tell a story about it on television that'll get the street fixed the next day, and the stop sign replaced. I believe the need for help in a neighborhood justifies my lying about who I am to get it—before a child breaks his neck on a pitted street or is hit by a car at a school crossing.

I learned a lot about newspapering in Chicago from Harry Romanoff and others at the *American*, one of whom was Luke Carroll, our managing editor, the big boss. He was hired by the paper after a distinguished career as a reporter and editor at the prestigious *Herald Tribune* in New York. He was a corporate executive who looked like it—tall, sleek, gray at the temples, charcoal suits, perfectly folded handkerchiefs, pin-striped shirts under perfectly knotted Ferragamo ties, tasseled loafers, and a sniff of East Coast arrogance. He bore a demeanor of the Hamptons decidedly more than the grit and grime of Alderman Paddy Bauler's "Chicagah [that] ain't ready for reform."

Mr. Carroll, which is what we called him, combined his journalism with his bottom-line efficiency, enough so to satisfy both the chiefs upstairs in the Tribune Tower who gave him his job, and the journeymen downstairs at the *American* who worked for him. He spoke both languages and knew how to blanket breaking news while conserving resources for news that was sure to break next. Uniquely, he valued and balanced substance and rubbish, thus bridging the gap between the internal conflicting forces that commonly afflict the media. Though most of us at the paper feared Mr. Carroll, we liked him and had genuine respect for his judgments, however harshly he imposed them.

Luke Carroll succeeded the *American*'s legendary Harry Reutlinger, a lifer who had started as a copy boy shortly after World War I and was the first reporter to interview Charles Lindbergh after the aviator's baby was kidnapped and murdered by Bruno Hauptmann in 1932.

Earlier in his career, Reutlinger helped crack the White Sox ("Black Sox") fix of the 1919 World Series. He did it the Romanoff way (except that he was before Romanoff, so maybe it's the Reutlinger way passed down to Romanoff). He asked a White Sox fan, "Who's the dumbest player on the team?"

"Easy," was the answer. "He's Happy Felsch the outfielder." Reutlinger went to Felsch's home.

"I just want to tell you your teammates have confessed," he lied.

Ballplayer Felsch, living up to his reputation, blurted out: "Well, those wise guys. Sure, I got mine, too. Five hundred bucks."

I say, good for Reutlinger the reporter, but it's something a managing editor cannot do. That kind of newspaper warfare is for the streets and alleys that company CEOs rarely patrol. Their workspace is on Moroccan rugs under leather chairs behind massive desks of glass and steel, where they make newspaper policy to be executed by their city editors commanding day-to-day and night operations on the rim.

My city editor at the *American* was John Madigan (Oscar-nominee Amy's dad), a tweedy man in his early forties, of curious but stern blue eyes, and lean and too-frequently mean temperament. He was a fast and smart Chicago journalism roughneck, whose hands were indelibly ink-stained, as we say, and all over everything he considered newsworthy. He told his reporters to "move out," and we did, to be thorough and accurate, and we were. To be fair, and I believe we were that, too.

More fair, in fact, than he was. Of Irish and Democratic heritage, he bowed too often to the Prince of City Hall. When Mayor Richard J. Daley positioned himself on an issue of partisan politics or social welfare, Madigan followed. That's not to doubt the sparkle of his résumé, which included time spent as a Washington correspondent. He was an unusually knowledgeable and well-sourced Chicago political scribe. Just too disposed to opinion, I believe, to be directing our coverage of things. (In their witty 1979 book *Who Runs Chicago*, *Tribune* reporters Michael Killian, Connie Fletcher, and Dick Ciccone, himself a city editor, dryly observed of Madigan, "It's nice to have an honorary member of the Daley family mingling with the newsfolk.") Firm opinion freely expressed is fine for columnists and editorial writers, not for a city editor.

Not long after I arrived at the *American*, in 1962, Madigan left, lured away by the promising dazzle of television and, it's fair to assume, money, which was more, likely twice as much, than he was paid by the newspaper. I say that with confidence because it was about to happen to me, too. Madigan's benefactor, and eventually mine, was WBBM-TV Channel 2, the Chicago station owned by CBS, which was aiming to distinguish itself in news.

At Channel 2 in '62, Madigan was a proficient multitasker. He wrote and delivered on-camera what is believed to have been the first editorial on Chicago television, three and a half minutes of the station's point of view on local and national issues. His editorials aired at the end of the 5:30 newscast. The concept was hailed by the *Tribune* as "courageous" and as possibly "a highly significant breakthrough."

It was and, in months to come, was imitated by other Chicago stations—a good idea, like the editorial page of a newspaper, designed to speed up or slow down the machinery of government depending on what it was or wasn't doing in or against the public interest. A problem was that unlike the newspapers, television had no op-ed page, so the editorials had to be less strident than those in print. They withered and disappeared.

John Madigan himself, however, was staying put. He was appointed news director of WBBM-TV, captain of a ship of some three hundred reporters, anchors, writers, producers, cameramen, soundmen, lightmen, copy editors, film editors, teleprompter editors, broadcast directors, floor directors, and stage hands in two big studios airing Channel 2 News two or three hours a day.

Madigan was in charge of it all, and in search of his kind of reporters, mirror images of himself, to bring aboard—intense, insatiably curious, fearless, irrepressible, persistent, pushy, and CHICAGO. He saw me fitting his model and called me one day to propose that I do what he did, trade in newspaper for television.

I was intrigued by his suggestion, though torn between the familiar that I loved and the unknown. TV news was gaining momentum, impact, influence, and stature. It was today instead of yesterday, new instead of old, fast instead of slow, restless and urgent. All in all, it was pretty appealing, and it offered added incentives of better pay and some celebrity.

So why not? I knocked on the door of scary Luke Carroll.

"John Madigan's offered me a job," I trembled. "Would you give me a leave to find out what television's like? Say, six months or so? What do you think?"

"I'm happy to tell you what I think," he said in so many words. "We don't give our reporters leaves of absence to find out what television is like. You want to be on television, you just get the hell out of here, and go be on television if that's what you want to do."

Mr. Carroll, like many newspaper people, especially those dyed in the wool, was contemptuous of TV. He glanced at the door as if to tell me to walk through it, which I did.

Thinking about Madigan's offer, a sports analogy came to mind. Newspaper reporters are like football players whose faces are hidden by helmets—anonymous. Television reporters are like baseball players whose faces are well known.

Admittedly, I'd always been a baseball guy.

5

New to TV: From JFK to Muhammad Ali

The moment I arrived at WBBM in the latter part of 1963, I began nagging John Madigan, as I had nagged Jack Mabley, and P. K. Wrigley before him. The conversation went something like this:

"When will you assign me to be a reporter?" I asked, and asked again.

"Not yet, Walter. You just got here. Hold on, okay?"

"But I left the newspaper, remember, when you told me you were looking for a reporter."

"I do remember that," he said, looking at me with what I took to be a certain fondness, but was not. "I also remember telling you I wanted a reporter who'd start as a writer. Now you're here, so do what I say, and you'll work your way up. It's not that I want to hurt your feelings," he said, his Irish bubbling up at my persistence, "but you're new at this game. You're a nobody, a little nobody. Remember that."

He was right about my being little, no doubt about it. I was five-foot-seven, 135 pounds. And a "nobody?" He was right about that, too. So I did it his way—slapped my mouth, drooped to my desk in a corner of the newsroom (the "some-bodies" got to sit in the center of the room), and wrote news for broadcast editors to judge, and for dressed-up, made-up, oh-so-envied anchors to read.

As impatient and self-assured as I was, and as angry as I was at Madigan, I considered the wisdom of minding my manners. I set myself to keeping quiet, writing and producing broadcast news, and, despite Madigan's scolding, working on what it takes to become a television reporter as fast as I wanted to be one. And I was understanding more about how different from each other television and newspapers really are.

Each has its own set of rules for covering and disseminating news and attracting the widest possible audience. Television news is in pictures; newspaper news is in words. Television is surface; newspaper is depth. TV condenses news, newspapers expand it. TV targets emotions; newspapers thought. Television is instant; newspapers come out many hours or a whole day after the fact. The news on TV is simple and easy to grasp; in the papers, it's often elusive.

There also are differences in news-gathering techniques. For instance, to cover city hall for *Chicago's American*, all I needed was a pencil, a notepad, enough speed to beat the competition to a telephone, and whatever it cost to use it. For Channel 2, where, six months after being hired I did become a reporter, I had to coordinate a three-man television crew (light, sound, and camera), set up in a quiet place with minimal visual distractions, then find an alderman or city official with enough ego and thirst for exposure to want to be interviewed, or enough fear of the consequences of refusing to be. And I needed to ask a relevant question that was answerable before the camera ran out of film, or a battery went dead, or someone knocked over a lamp or a sloppy spittoon, or before an el train outside a window scratched and screeched around a curve, all the while having to think about what I'd need to do when the interview was finished. How would I get the film to the developer, then to the studio and into the hands of an editor before a broadcast ran out of time?

The logistics at city hall were easy, the mayor's office being hardly a mile away from the Channel 2 studios on McClurg Court, a block from the lakefront at Ontario Street. The Illinois General Assembly, on the other hand, is in Springfield, some 175 miles away. Not easy.

Follow me:

It's a sticky summer afternoon, the assembly is haggling over a proposal to bail out the long-suffering Chicago public schools. The clock reads 5:30. The politicians are still at it. The rush hour is snarling traffic most of the way to Chicago. My cameraman, Don Norling, an old hand, estimates we'll need an hour to wrap up the equipment and pack the car before heading home. Can we make it in time for the ten o'clock broadcast, in which the executive producer is holding the first three minutes open for my story from Springfield?

"No," Norling says to me, comfortable that it'll be my fault not his, since I'm the one who decided to wait a few more minutes to roll on one more squirt of poison between the parties on the floor of the assembly's House of Representatives.

"Oh, Christ, I think you're right. We can't kill an hour getting out of here, we can't. Give me the film. I'll get it back."

"What are you, nuts? What do you mean you'll get it back? How're you gonna do that?"

"Put it in the can, Don. I don't know how, but I'll get it back."

This turns out to mean bounding down the great marble staircase into the rotunda, out the door and into the street to a cab stand, where I rattle a snoozing driver. "Can you get me to an entrance ramp to I-55 heading north? A busy one, please, as fast as you can. I need to hitch a ride to Chicago."

"Uh," he burps. "Whadja say?"

"How about you taking me to Chicago? How much would it cost?"

"Uh, Chicago? Uh . . . four hundred. Uh . . ."

I have to be there in three hours max. There's no way I have $400, and it'll take forever to find a telephone, call the newsroom, and no doubt be denied permission to agree to pay that kind of money. There must be a lot of people driving to Chicago. I'll try to find someone on the highway.

The best I can get from the cabbie is a shrug, and a $12 ride to the shoulder of I-55. Dressed in suit and tie, natty TV newsman, I thrust my right thumb into the traffic, which, of course, gets me nowhere. So I loosen my belt, arrange the can of exposed film into the small of my back and, with both arms and hands, wave frantically for someone, anyone, please, to stop.

A few minutes into that proof of my commitment to television news, before a state trooper can pass by and haul me off to where I certainly don't want to go, someone does stop, a Chicago lawyer, a lobbyist, to whom I explain what I'm doing and where I need to be by 9:30 at the latest. A nice guy, Channel 2 viewer, and political junkie on his way from the General Assembly to his home in the Beverly neighborhood on Chicago's far south side. He chauffeurs me and my can of film ten miles out of his way to the newsroom on McClurg, dropping us off at ten after nine.

That was a problem peculiar to television in the early 1960s, a reporter having to hitchhike his story 175 miles. Channel 2 had a couple of videotape machines as early as 1959, but we were still using film when I was covering the rancor in the General Assembly. Ten years later, when videotape replaced film, a story could be transmitted through the sky by satellite. No more shooting and developing and drying and splicing and projecting. Just push a few buttons, and we give you politicians live in your living room. Television news was not only whizzing by the newspapers but packing a more powerful punch.

"We smack 'em," a newscast producer at Channel 2 once bellowed at me. "Smack 'em in the face, and the heart. Let the newspapers drag on with what they think is important. We splash what's interesting."

What the good newspapers and television stations have in common, I believe, is what's more important than what we don't: a pledge to the basic principles and hard-rock standards of journalism—accuracy, objectivity, and fairness. They're important but often tough to meet through the blur of events, conflicting perceptions and opinions, and the fervor of arguments on both or several sides of the most momentous issues.

Consider the 2008 presidential campaign. Try being fair to candidates arguing about health care, the debt ceiling, federal spending, taxes, Iran, Iraq, India, Pakistan, and Afghanistan. And about campaign strategies and tactics. How can you be fair when not only the candidates, but their advisors and parties, and the talking heads on MSNBC and the Fox News Channel are accusing one another of deceit? What's fair to whom? In the 2008 presidential campaign, Barack Obama and John McCain were in constant dispute, as were the journalists following the campaign, over what "fairness" means. Stir into that mix the onus of assuring television news viewers (or newspaper readers) that our reporting, even if it conflicts with public perceptions, is accurate. Whew!

And double-whew on the pledge to be objective, which is an even more rugged standard to meet. To be objective, I'm expected to avoid nuances and have no feelings or opinions. That's ridiculous. There is no such thing as undiluted objectivity. What I must do as a reporter is get a grip on the nuances of a story, understand my feelings and opinions, accept them, and then suspend them from my work.

To illustrate my point, here's a story about a proposed tax increase a few years ago by the now former president of the Cook County Board of Commissioners, Todd Stroger. Through the prism of fifty years of covering local government and politics, I saw telltale signs of Stroger's intent to bloat his budget for political gain, the most obvious being his rearrangement of administrative positions and salaries. From the day he moved into his executive suite on Clark Street, he'd been stuffing the county payroll with his friends and relatives. Right off the bat, he hired three friends at a combined cost to taxpayers of $270,000 a year to handle his public relations, on top of a PR staff already in place. To his cousin on the county payroll he granted a 12 percent increase in salary. To pay for all that and other personal items, he proposed to more than double the county sales tax to the highest level of all major metropolitan areas in the United States.

The jobs and pay raises were being maneuvered by Stroger to feed his cronies at the taxpayers' trough. How brazen he was in spending our money recruiting troops for his political platoons. That was not fact, but my opinion.

My assignment on the story was to report the news, not what I thought about it. The story is not "President Stroger is hiking the sales tax in order to beef up his politics." It is "President Stroger is hiking the sales tax because, he says, Cook County is in debt and he has no choice." If I include in my report a statement by a member of the county board critical of Stroger, I must also include a statement supportive of him. Objectivity, Mr. Reporter. Objectivity.

You'd think that would be Journalism 101, which it is, or ought to be. Objectivity is a filter through which every story ought to pass, a cardinal rule of the road in journalism's book of directions, to be learned early on and practiced until automatic. It's a rigorous, difficult discipline that's crucial to our trustworthiness. It is not, however, applicable to every story. There's not a whole lot of objectivity necessary when covering, say, car crashes and fires (the staples, sadly, of local television news).

Back to my story:

After what seems an eternity, my first day in the Channel 2 News lineup as a reporter is a Saturday. My position is second-stringer, assigned to stand by in case a first-stringer is late coming in, or busy enough on a long-term project to beg off a story he deems too routine for his attention, or beneath his stature.

Weekends in Chicago are slow for news. City hall and the county, state, and federal buildings are closed, as are the courts and public schools. Maybe there's a parade in Lincoln Park, or a robbery somewhere, or a drive-by shooting. But that's about it.

News on Saturdays and Sundays is not only scarce, but mostly inconsequential. Broadcast producers are hungry for stories to fill thirty minutes, which is one reason why, as I say, our local staples are crashes and fires. Another is that they're cheap and easy to cover. And they're sometimes tragic and therefore judged by news managers to be especially compelling in the spirit of "there but for the grace of God go I."

As my first day moves from eight in the morning toward noon, here's how it goes—I'm the newsroom second-stringer, circling the assignment desk, wishing for something important or at least interesting to happen. Nothing does, so at three o'clock I'm on my way to a fire, a little one, a few puffs of smoke escaping from just three windows of an office building on North Michigan Avenue. Is this why I quit the newspaper to be a reporter on television? To chase a hook-and-ladder?

Two sirens are sounding, three hoses are being attached to fire hydrants, and, occasionally, a lick of flame curls lazily skyward. Nobody's hurt, nobody endangered, no story. Except that a fire is a picture that can fill time on the six o'clock news, which justifies the producer's decision to cover it. Also, it's just four blocks away from the WBBM garage, which makes it easy to get to, which is one of the highest priorities of television news—cover it, and still have time to cover another one.

At the scene I look for a white helmet, under which I know will be a fire lieutenant.

"Walter Jacobson, Lieutenant, Channel 2 News." Big Deal. "Can you give me a minute?" I sneak a peek over my shoulder to make sure the cameraman is rolling and has sound. If he isn't or doesn't, I give him a signal. Then go for it.

"Do you have her under control, sir?" (Dumb question. At six o'clock, when this'll be on the air, everybody will know whether it's under control.)

"I think we're OK . . .

"Everybody out? Looks like it." (I'm huffin' and puffin' from hustlin' to the scene.)

"Yep, thank God. Not many people in there. Saturday, you know."

My first television interview, done! Lead story on the six o'clock news. A minute's worth of smoke and fifteen seconds of the lieutenant and me. By 6:20, I've taken fifteen calls, at least: "Saw you on the news." "Was that you with the fire guy?"

The in-your-face presence and impact of television is colossal. Its audio-visual capacity to alert, inform, explain, and do good is incomparable. Among the things it does bad is to be so fast it gets reckless (declaring winners before polls close, influencing the vote). We're reckless about many things in the news—the weather, for instance. We're too fast to say four inches of snow are on the way, when we know how often four inches turn out to be one. As much as we help with urgently necessary information (school closings), we hurt with hurried misinformation (Florida goes for Gore).

Television news is useful when it exposes government malfunctions, useless when it dwells on Sarah Palin's wardrobe. It enriches with texture but cheapens with brevity. Our close-up pictures of satisfaction and joy are uplifting, but our close-ups of anguish and tears are intrusive, too frequently offensively intrusive.

Of that, here's an example:

On Friday, November 22, 1963, I'm spooling spaghetti for lunch at the Chicago Press Club in the Hotel St. Clair, a few blocks from the Channel 2 newsroom. The executive producer of our afternoon and evening broadcasts, Dick Goldberg, and I are talking politics between glances at one of several attached-to-the-wall TV sets, the one tuned to CBS. Walter Cronkite is on the screen. Odd for the noon hour, because his broadcast on the CBS network isn't until 5:30.

"Shh," Goldberg intrudes on my monologue. Twenty-five or thirty other reporter-types, producers, writers, and a gaggle of PR flacks at the other dozen tables in the room also are shushing. Something big is happening. The buzz stops as Cronkite seems to be saying that President John F. Kennedy has been shot by a sniper in Dallas, Texas.

The specifics are lost in the din of knives and forks clattering to plates, and chairs being pushed around by almost everybody in the room jumping up to the elevator, which takes forever to arrive to the twenty-second floor. Goldberg and I are running to the newsroom, juiced by that touch of self-importance a reporter feels en route to a big story. I'm thinking, what will I be told when I walk in the door? What'll I be assigned to do? I can hope, but I know it won't happen, that I'll be greeted with "Hey, Jacobson. You're going to Dallas."

I had years of work in front of me before an assignment like that. And besides, local television stations aren't much interested in sending reporters cross-country to cover news. It's too expensive. The networks do that. In Chicago, TV decision-makers look for local angles to big stories. If the president is shot in Dallas, local TV reports what people in Chicago are remembering about seeing him a long time ago in Morgan Park or Rogers Park, which eats up five minutes of a thirty-minute newscast. We interview someone in the city or suburbs who remembers having once talked to Kennedy, or someone who knows someone who once talked to him. I don't buy into that. To me, giving up five minutes of airtime on a local angle to a presidential assassination in Dallas is a waste.

The five minutes ought to be spent on providing information that's essential to understanding the story.

My assignment on the day President Kennedy was assassinated? Take a camera crew to the Chicago Theatre on State Street. Roll it on people coming out. They've been in the dark for the past three hours watching a movie. They'll have no idea the president's been shot. Tell them what happened, and ask how they feel about it.

"Close-ups, Walter, close-ups," roared the assistant news director as I lurched for the crew room. "Tight on their faces. They're not gonna know what hit 'em. I want shock and tears. Go in close on their eyes."

Which is what I did. And what I got was shock and tears. A lot of it.

Telling someone, cold and out of the blue, that the president of the United States has been shot in the head and is dead, then demanding to know "How do you feel about it?" That's not journalism. It's *National Enquirer*, a paparazzi attack. It's intrusion.

Looking back, I wish I had refused to be that intrusive, that grotesquely insensitive. But back then, it didn't occur to me to refuse. I was a second-string reporter competing for the starting lineup, and the story was huge. I didn't think about what it would be like on the other side of the microphone, how much I'd want to smash it, or at least turn away from it in disgust, and to give a finger to the cameraman.

(When I say cameraman, I mean *man*. In the early '60s, I went with a cameraman, a soundman, and a man to operate the lights. No women, at least that I can recall, behind the cameras, on the street, or in the studios. The unions wouldn't stand for it and barred Katies at the door. I can't prove that, and the machos'll deny it, but it's true. Oh, the streets of Chicago are too rough for women, they sniffed. The language on the streets is too nasty, or the equipment is too heavy or complicated. Truth is, the boys just didn't want to mix with women, at least on the job they didn't. As Cronkite used to say about a day in the life of America, "and that's the way it is" with the unions in Chicago.)

Sometime after the little fire on Michigan Avenue and the Kennedy assassination, I received my first assignment as an anchor—by accident. I was writing and producing a fifteen-minute newscast at noon on Sundays, prioritizing stories, placing them where I judged they ought to be inside the fifteen minutes, minus four for sports, weather, and commercials, and getting a script into the teleprompter for that day's anchor, Carter Davidson, to read. He was my hero in local television news, a thoughtful, articulate intellectual in the tradition of NBC's John Chancellor. And like Chancellor, his passport was filled with the stamps of countries where he had worked and I had once dreamed of working.

Carter, in his late forties, carried a look of distinction. He was, as I remember, just under six feet tall, a bit stocky, with light hair graying at the temples.

His glasses were steel rimmed, and he strode like he knew about things, which he sure did.

He had come to the station in 1960 from the *Chicago Sun-Times*. Prior to that, he was a foreign correspondent for the Associated Press in London, Paris, and in Berlin after World War II. When Israel gained its independence in 1948, Carter Davidson was the AP bureau chief in Jerusalem.

Astonishingly, WBBM, a *local* television station, hired Carter as a *foreign* correspondent. (Now there's a position that you won't find anymore, a local foreign correspondent.) In that capacity, he reported from Europe, Asia, and Africa, producing documentaries on Vietnam, Congo, and Berlin. Compare that to the year 2000, when my colleague Larry Yellen, a reporter with a law degree, had to plead with Fox News Chicago to send him to Florida to cover one of the biggest stories in the political history of the United States, George W. Bush versus Al Gore in the Florida recount.

But about that day I became an accidental anchorman:

To produce the fifteen-minute broadcast at noon, I arrive at the station at eight to read through the morning papers. On this day at eleven o'clock, Carter calls in sick. There are no other anchors or reporters around, and no way to stir one up in an hour. So it's clear that I am to be a substitute for a day, which may be problematic.

First of all, I've never been in front of a live camera before. I have no experience, none, with teleprompter or lights, microphones, floor directors, or commands in my ears from a control booth. You name it, I've never done it.

Second, because it's warm outside, I've come to work in shorts and a t-shirt. Not exactly appropriate dress for reading news on television. In a frenzy, I search unlocked lockers in the makeup room until I find a dirty blue shirt that's too big, and a wide, wide, ugly red-and-yellow polka-dot tie that someone must have left behind after an Art Deco costume party. Still in my shorts, which I hope will be hidden by the anchor desk, I tuck in the shirt and zip unzipped into the studio.

Third problem? The anchor desk hides my shorts okay, but also too much of the rest of me. The desk is up to my chest. At five-seven, I appear to be standing in a hole. The stagehands solve this one by stacking bricks, two under each foot. (Try standing like that.)

A fourth problem materializes two minutes before air when an engineer in the control booth runs me through a sound check. "Something's wrong," he says with some urgency. "I'm not getting sound. We have to rectal mike."

"Rectal WHAT?" Despite my panic at the clock ticking to launch time, I'm focused enough to reason that he's pulling my leg. "C'mon, guys," I play along for his fun of it. "You're messing me up. I got a minute and a half before—"

"Walter, cool it. You're not the first anchor to have to move a microphone. We need to get it off your tie. It's gotta go down. Drop your drawers."

"You serious?" I sputter it into the mic that's not sounding, still playing along with what must be an initiation thing. Forty seconds. "Okay, okay. They're dropped. I'll get behind the desk. Which camera am I—," as guffaws bounce off the studio walls.

That was the day the techs and I became friends, workplace teammates whose friendship I'd need many more than a few times over the next twenty years. As for the Channel 2 News at noon that day—it wasn't good. I stared into the wrong camera more often than into the right one, teetered on the bricks, and spoke before I was signaled to speak. When a light went on I blinked, and when the teleprompter stalled I tried to, I tried to . . .

I don't know what I tried to do. What I do know, and will never forget, is that I was terrified. All-in-all, a not very impressive performance, an ominous omen for the future.

But things have ways of happening. Due to Carter's reduced schedule, staff shortages and realignments, budget concerns, and my persistence, news director Madigan soon assigned me, until further notice, to anchor the Sunday noon news—write it, produce it, and read it. ANCHOR it!

I was now a CBS-WBBM-TV News anchorman, with perks and pitfalls ahead. What I liked most was almost everything. What I liked least was feeling Hollywood, knowing that what I wore and how I looked on the air mattered to the brass as much as what I said.

Having come to television from a newspaper and been at Channel 2 for just a short time, being assigned to anchor a broadcast in the third largest market in the country (behind New York and Los Angeles) was, for me, an extraordinarily lucky opportunity. I set out to do whatever I could to take advantage of it. One idea I had was to spend two of my fifteen minutes on a live, in-studio interview of someone prominent in the news or sports or the arts, or an expert on local, national, or international affairs. The guest was positioned next to me at the anchor desk, and we talked.

It worked, so I was able to convince the news director to expand the Sunday noon news to thirty minutes and allow me to interview a guest for half of it. I went after "A" names and lined up some big ones. Soon the interview portion of the broadcast was drawing some attention, and, of course, that helped me get even bigger names. Politicians and celebrities are happy to make themselves available when they know there will be an audience, whatever the size of it.

My first really big guest was Cook County state's attorney Edward Hanrahan, who had just orchestrated a raid on the radical Black Panther Party in an apartment on the west side. His police killed two Panthers, including Illinois deputy party chairman Fred Hampton. On December 4, 1969, Hanrahan was big news around the world; he came to Channel 2 for my Sunday noon news to talk about what happened during the deadly raid. My first television-news exclusive!

But an even better Sunday was when I hooked Muhammad Ali to talk about refusing to serve in the US Army. What a time we had. My wife and about-seven-year-old son, Peter, came along to watch. After the broadcast, all employees present followed Ali from the studio to the newsroom to see him bumblebee-buzz around the desks. Then the best: He needed a ride to his home, which was just a few minutes from where I lived. You can guess how fast I offered it.

Talking in the car, we somehow got on to the subject of parents. I said my mother had spent the night at my house and was still there. Ali asked to meet her. Guess how long it took me to agree to that? If I had been keeping a diary, I'd have written "Great Day!" My mom hardly expected to see the champ walk through the door. Standing not much higher than his waist, she trembled, "How d-d-d do you do, Mr. Ali?" He curled down to her size and kissed her on a cheek. The greatest day ever.

There are plenty of books that chronicle the history of the medium. You don't need it from me. But a few words about the early days of WBBM are in order, as the timeline of that station echoes the timeline of television and, in particular, television news.

In an excellent essay about WBBM Channel 2 News in the book *Television News in America,* Marjorie Fox notes that by 1944, WBBM's forerunner WBKB was broadcasting about twenty-five hours per month, using on-camera news performers. "One of the experiments involved two announcers in shirtsleeves in a noisy newsroom setting," writes Fox. (Hmm, I remember a similar experiment some thirty years later. Keep reading.)

As a seven-year-old in 1944, I didn't see those announcers. We didn't even have a television set in our house until I was twelve. News wasn't watched in those days; it was heard on the radio or read in the papers. My early memories of television involve amateur talent shows, a few soap operas, and wrestling. Lots of wrestling, in black-and-white and dotted by what we called "snow."

The schedule for news, says Marjorie Fox, was, "rather erratic." There was a program called *Today's World Picture,* which aired haphazardly at different times on different days. At this time, WBKB was an ABC affiliate broadcasting on Channel 4. CBS purchased it in 1949 and in 1951 changed its call letters to WBBM. The operation was moved to Channel 2, which began airing a local newscast from 6:15 P.M. to 6:30, followed by the national CBS news, later called *Douglas Edwards with the News.* It, too, ran fifteen minutes, the first regularly scheduled news program in Chicago television history.

By the mid-1950s, WBBM had added the *Standard Oil News Roundup,* anchored by Fahey Flynn. He was followed by a variety show, which was followed by *The John Harrington News.* In 1959, the Flynn and Harrington newscasts were merged into one—fifteen minutes at 10 P.M. Flynn did it alone.

On September 26, 1960, WBBM made history when it hosted the first-ever televised presidential debate. John F. Kennedy squared off against Richard M. Nixon in a studio a few yards down the hall from where Flynn did the local ten o'clock news.

The debate was a ratings smash and put to rest any doubts about the power of television to shape public opinion on the most important of matters. It's the live picture and eye contact that do it.

To those who say you need Kennedy-like looks to master the medium, I respond with two words: Fahey Flynn. He was just about the furthest thing possible from the stereotypical anchorman. As one colleague observed at a dinner in Fahey's honor: "Can you imagine any station manager today hiring a man who is five-foot-five-inches high, overweight, with a leprechaun face, wearing a bow tie, and bearing the name Fahey Flynn?" No.

But that's exactly what the powers that be did back in 1953. Actually, they didn't hire Fahey but shuffled him from WBBM radio to television. In his polka-dot bow ties and his neighborly voice, he began the broadcast with what was to become his signature, "How do you do, ladies and gentleman."

The thirty-seven-year-old Irishman from Michigan's Upper Peninsula quickly built an audience. And his broadcast's popularity was enhanced by weatherman P. J. Hoff, a balding everyman who illustrated his forecasts with cartoon drawings of Windy City characters, including the "Vice President in charge of looking out the window."

When in 1963, at age twenty-six, I switched from newspaper to television, from *Chicago's American* to WBBM, the Flynn-Hoff team had been Chicago's number 1 newscast at 10 P.M. for several years. Why? Fahey was warm and friendly, not severe on the air (or off). People liked him and believed and trusted him. And it didn't hurt that he occasionally went on the air in, shall we say, a tipsy way that made him all the more charming.

And it sure didn't hurt that he was rosy-cheeked, blue-eyed Irish in a market with a large Irish population and a city hall run by Irish politicians. And oh how he knew it, the potency of the ol' sod. He often talked with us about it in the newsroom.

There was another big kahuna at Channel 2, Frank Reynolds, our highest profile reporter and anchor of the 6 P.M. news. Frank was an entirely different personality than Fahey, wearing an entirely different look. Not much taller, but leaner, he was arched, starched, and ferociously serious, imparting substantive information (when the bosses weren't looking) for fifteen minutes. He was more "Mr. Reynolds" than "Frank." "Network material," is what we said about him.

Flynn read news—masterfully—from the teleprompter. Reynolds had news in his head. Flynn did almost no reporting on television, and he wrote very little of his own copy. He was an anchor. Reynolds was a combination reporter-editor-anchor who wrote much of his own copy. He was a bulldog journalist, and his broadcast on local news, like Cronkite's on the network, was formidable stuff. Or as formidable as he could make it without being put down and lightened up by management.

Also like Cronkite, Reynolds got himself fifteen additional minutes. His broadcast was expanded to half an hour, a change cheered by the newsroom because fifteen more minutes meant more time for reporters, writers, and producers to get in on the action. Frank insisted on fewer stories more in depth and got away with it—until news director Madigan ordered more stories less in depth. Madigan also instructed Frank to stop editorializing on the news, which he was in fact doing—not just with his words, but with exaggerated gestures and facial expressions.

Reporting on public officials making speeches, Frank's look said, "Oh, come on. Get off it." Watching Frank anchor the news, you knew what he was feeling—not right, not in my book. As I've said, except for an aside now and then, anchors and reporters ought not be expressing opinions on the news; that's for designated, and clearly identified, commentators to do.

Madigan also informed Frank Reynolds that management wanted fewer stories on the six o'clock news about race relations, especially about public protests against segregation. Writing about Chicago television news, the late, great journalist John Callaway reported that Frank told him, "I kept hearing [from John Madigan] that the man on the street was sick of segregation stories. My answer to that was, 'So what.'"

Unhappy with Madigan's design of his broadcast, and frustrated by the restrictions on his performance, Frank packed it in. He left our Channel 2 for Channel 7 and eventually for the anchor chair on the ABC national network at 5:30, as high as you can go, big as you can be, in television news. Good for Frank, good for journalism.

Fahey, good ol' reliable Fahey, stayed right where he was, on top of the local news heap in Chicago. No problems with management, or WBBM marketing or sales people, or with young hotshots bold enough to scheme to unseat him. Least threatening of all to Fahey Flynn was me. My voice was nasal, I took excruciatingly long pauses at wrong times, still flinched when the lighting changed, and was hopelessly inept at taking cues.

I was better as a reporter on the streets in the neighborhoods but occasionally had problems there, too. I still am haunted by one particular lapse in judgment. *Here's why:*

In an apartment on the west side of Chicago, three small toddlers are found dead in the family bathtub. The newsroom is tipped that it just happened and that a suspect is being taken to a police lockup. In a flash, the assignment desk has me and a camera crew on the way. (As I've mentioned, nothing stirs local news management like something gruesome, the more so the better.)

We assume the tip is good because it's from a cop who calls often and is almost always accurate. Owing to the nature of Chicago politics, the police and the press are mutually useful. (A policeman slips me a good story about city hall interfering with his work, I check it out, confirm it, and report the story quoting an anonymous source, and city hall backs off.)

Channel 2 cop tips are the best in town, so we're first to arrive at the lockup, at just the moment a frantic, deranged diminutive young man in handcuffs is being dragged upstairs by three tough and steamed-up cops. I'm right behind, trailed by camera, light and sound.

In order to score a really major scoop, all I have to do is ask the suspect a question and get his face on camera. But first I have to get the cops to slow down enough to let us pass them on the way up for a better shot. The stairs are narrow, wires all around, everybody shouting at everybody else.

"Why'd you do it?" I reach toward the suspect with my microphone wrapped in that CBS eye. His answer is silence, a stew of bewilderment and terror. Again, more aggressively, "Why'd you do it?" Over my shoulder to the cameraman, "You rolling?" Back to the suspect, mercilessly, "Whydyoudoitwhydyoudoitwhydyoudoit?" as he's pushed through a door that is slammed shut behind him. The media mob is arriving, instantly aware that I'm ahead of it, and that I've probably had an exclusive moment with the suspect. I snatch the film magazine from my cameraman, squeeze down the stairs through upcoming traffic, lock our treasure in the trunk of our car, and return to get the rest of the story, the police version of what happened—a domestic quarrel over money, after which the guy drowned their three children, one at a time.

We do have a major scoop, a big, big story for the top of the six o'clock news, including pictures of the apartment building, bodies in bags, the suspect, the cops, the stairs—and me, "Whydyoudoitwhydyoudoit?"

My first call the morning after "whydyoudoit" is from a psychology professor at the University of Chicago, inviting me to her class, "so I can introduce my students to a maniac." I ought to go, to teach myself a lesson, but I decline.

6

The First Mayor Daley

Murder always is big news in Chicago, and when it involves children, it's bigger still. But, what matters most in Chicago (next to the Cubs, of course) is city hall—not governance, but politics; not the hands of public service, but the muscle of money and votes. That's how it's been for as long as the Cubs haven't won a World Series (103 years). And that's why it became my goal at Channel 2 to be assigned to watch city hall, and to report what I saw.

In 1965, I had been at WBBM-TV just two years and already was drenched in city hall fact and fiction:

Fact: In the history of Chicago, Mayor Richard J. Daley is the boss of all bosses. Fiction: He may be clever, but he's not smart; this is a fiction that's been written and broadcast since the day he was sworn in, that his malapropisms expose a less-than-towering intelligence. For example:

Singing the praises of his city, he said, "We shall reach greater and greater platitudes of success." In response to the words of a critic, he said, "I resemble that remark," meaning he resents it. During the Democratic National Convention in Chicago in 1968, he told reporters, "The police are not here to create disorder, they're here to preserve disorder."

Mayor Daley talked the language of the "preecints," meaning precincts, which meant he was smart enough to get himself elected and reelected, and to govern Chicago, four times. He bossed us for twenty years, a reign eclipsed only by that of his son, Richard M., who also bobbled the language but was smart enough to get himself elected and reelected five times.

When WBBM decided I could handle city hall, I set out to challenge some things Daley did, and things he said (there it is again, as with my mother, that disdain for authority).

Richard J. was a four-star general in civvies when he paraded into a news conference two steps ahead of a phalanx of aides and department heads, and approached a wooden lectern low enough to make him high enough to boom his authority to a dozen reporters and half a dozen cameras squeezed into a pressroom on the fifth floor of city hall.

A scenario:

It's 1965. President Lyndon Johnson has just signed the Voting Rights Act. Local reporters need to localize the story, so we ask Mayor Daley about voting rights in Chicago—does he think there are problems?

"We don't have problems voting in Chicago," he puffs into a bank of microphones.

"But, Mr. Mayor," a *Tribune* reporter objects. "Chicago is famous for problems in voting . . . vote fraud . . . vote early, vote often . . . vote ghost. Everybody knows about Chic—"

"Who's everybody? They haven't been here, have they?" Mr. Mayor starts with a lilt, then picks up steam, and ends with a stare and a snarl. "They haven't been to a polling place in Chicago, have they? They ever been to a polling place? What do they know?"

When it's my turn: "I know voters who've been paid by precinct captains to—"

"Who's been paid?" His blue eyes are as light, bright, and cold as any I've ever seen. Like one of those cool mountain labels on bottled water. "What's his name, what ward? We'll investigate."

"Well, I'll ask. I'll see if—"

A surge of voices from the few rows of chairs, "Mr. Mayor . . . Mr. Mayor . . . Mr. . . . ." All the reporters, all at once, clamoring for his attention, which is just what he wants, so he can turn away from me toward one of the others, so I can't finish what I'm saying, which is that I'll see if I can get permission to bring in names of people who've been paid to vote, or not vote.

I'm cut short, but I've recorded two minutes of contentious Q-and-A to bring back to the newsroom for our six o'clock broadcast. The mayor is riled, and the broadcast producers love him when he is. And the redder his cheeks, the more wobbly his waddle, the better. It makes for good pictures, easy to promote on the air during the afternoon—"Mayor Daley Explodes at Our Reporter! We'll Have the Story at Six O'Clock!"

What's special about that news conference, for me, is that when the mayor says, "Thank you," and abruptly leaves the room the same two steps ahead of his aides and department heads, I linger behind, and record on-camera a personal assessment of what goes on between the Boss and the press. It goes something like this:

"Mayor Daley doesn't like being questioned about vote fraud. He says that in Chicago there isn't any, which he knows is ludicrous, no vote fraud in Chicago. He's not telling the truth, and he knows it. He asked me for names of people who've told me they've been paid by precinct captains to vote, or not vote. I'll get the names, with permission to give them to the mayor, and let you know what he says. I'm Walter Jacobson, reporting from city hall."

I return to the newsroom to screen, with our executive producer, my post-press conference remarks. His reaction: "Interesting, Walter. You're ballsy and provocative, and seem to be accurate." And no other station in town has a street reporter going that far beyond the information, adding so personal a touch. "Let's go with it," he says. "We'll see what happens. Maybe Madigan," the news director, "won't notice it."

On the six o'clock broadcast, I'm stepping over the line between reporting and opinion. There are no complaints, no hell being raised by management, or by our viewers. So here I go, peppering my reporting on politics with my judgment on who in city hall is talking truth, who's talking lies, and what it is that our politicians and elected officials ought to be telling us, but are not—careful to avoid saying things on the air that may cause the general manager to be frightened by what I'm doing, and tell me to stop.

News in the mid '60s was yielding abundant grist for me to mill, from Barry Goldwater defending extremism in defense of liberty to LBJ burning daisies in his campaign ads on TV. Chicago was described by the US Civil Rights Commission as the most segregated big city in America. An African American bought a home in a white neighborhood on the south side and was bombed out of it. Anger was busting out of the ghettos, and the bigoted, nasty superintendent of schools, Benjamin Willis, was thumbing his nose.

People in the neighborhoods were becoming increasingly, painfully, aware of inequities in our system of justice, of discrimination in public and private employment, segregation in education and housing. Activists were rising up to knock down walls. Selma, Alabama, was thundering into our living rooms on television; minorities in the south clamoring for the right to vote. Minorities in Chicago were demanding better assignments and more promotions in the police and fire departments, which were stubborn and pernicious bastions of discrimination not just tolerated, but licensed, by city hall.

Lawsuits clamoring for civil rights were crowding the dockets. Martin Luther King was rumbling into segregated Chicago neighborhoods, rattling realtors and residents on the southwest side, knocking on doors to the offices of government and the media. Mayor Daley and the city council were getting jumpy. The Civil Rights Act was passed, and in *Brown versus Board of Education*, the US Supreme Court ruled against separate-but-equal. In the mid-60s there were ticklish, perplexing, nagging, and embarrassing questions being asked, and it was, as it's always been and will be, up to reporters to demand answers. And when public officials are dishonest or hypocritical, it's up to us to say so, and to explain why.

Here's how:

Mayor Daley is on the north side breaking ground for a community project. The event is covered respectfully by reporters. When he pitches his last shovel of soil and is heading back to his limousine, I try to ask if he'll please confirm information I've received from a reliable source that a high-profile alderman is the target of a federal grand jury investigating alleged bribery involving a building permit. True or false, I don't know; but, I'm sure the mayor knows. As I begin my question, he moves, and I'm stopped by police. Left in the wake of his departure, I say into the camera:

"I followed Mayor Daley to his photo-op this morning to ask about a federal investigation involving city hall. He brushed me off—an indication, I believe, that he knew precisely what I was talking about. When the name of a Chicago alderman is spoken to a grand jury, there's no way Mayor Daley doesn't know about it. He just prefers to not talk about it. I don't think he ought to get away with that, do you? I'm Walter Jacobson."

I emphasized "Walter Jacobson" because my opinion ought to be attached directly to me, to avoid doubt about it's being an opinion; and it ought to have been declared and labeled as "commentary." But it was not. At WBBM-TV in the mid-60s, there were no declarations of commentary, or labeling of opinion. The pinstripes at CBS in New York didn't want commentary. They viewed it as needlessly controversial, words to be checked by lawyers, lawsuits to have to defend, hot politicians to have to cool down. But the company was benefiting from a splash of attention drawn by my opinions. Station executives were counting new numbers in the ratings, new viewers who seemed to want to hear me say that greedy, selfish, irresponsible politicians ought to be exposed and pressed to explain their actions, and to pay the price of bad behavior. A dilemma for the brass at CBS—let Jacobson continue expressing his opinions that are attracting viewers pro and con, and live with the fallout, or stop him before he becomes trouble. The nature of the business, the instinct of the people running it, was to avoid fallout. The safe thing to do would be to stop the commentary; the problem was how. What would Channel 2 say to the viewers and newspaper that surely would call to ask, "Where are Walter's commentaries? Why are they not on the air? Are you muzzling him? Is Mayor Daley telling Channel 2 what to do?"

How could Channel 2 answer those questions? One way would be to say there's not enough time on our broadcasts; another would be to say the station needs Walter for other assignments. Neither one would be believable. The easiest thing to do, and best for the ratings (always a priority) would be to look the other way that Walter adds his two cents to the news he covers. Two cents, for instance, on the conflict in city hall between the mayor and Alderman Despres, Mr. Scruples, lonely liberal in the city council, ultimate political outsider, always itching for a fight, scratching at Mayor Daley about the suffering of Chicago's underclass. Children of the ghetto, Despres howled, they're playing on floors littered with flakes of lead paint that taste like candy. "Brains are being fatally affected." He was right. During six weeks in July and August 1967, six young children died of lead poisoning.

With passion and a plea for help, he proposed legislation to compel the owners of buildings to clean up their lead paint. It dropped dead in a council committee, buried by Mayor Daley's lockstep majority. On the news at ten, I told the story and added a comment about "the bruisers in the city council" letting Despres know who's boss by slapping his proposal off their agenda.

"While the summer plods along," I lamented with my two cents, "paint peels from dilapidated walls and two-year-olds are dying. Kindness in the Chicago City Council? I don't see any! Walter Jacobson reporting."

Since there was no interference by management, I sharpened my tongue, and my style. My comments became more direct and—to the major players in government—more irritating. To WBBM-TV, and to CBS, I was becoming a complication. So what next? An invitation from the news director, John Madigan, to see him in his office.

Catch the mood:

Madigan is not happy. He's a ferociously loyal Daley Democrat, of the opinion that most young journalists on the payrolls of the press in Chicago are smart-ass, liberal, Ivy League, left-wing, revolutionary hippies—like me, for instance, one more cocky moppet who knows nothing, but thinks he knows it all, and is on Channel 2 News picking on Mayor Daley, accusing him of being dishonest, hiding public information and covering up corruption, telling Chicago to stop the mayor from ducking important questions.

Madigan likes my grit, but not my attitude. It's obvious why he wants me to cool it. He's uncomfortable about the dissonance I'm causing between the mayor and the station. He believes that reporters ought to report the news.

"Tell us what you see," he barks at me, "not what you think. We don't need to hear your goddamn opinion. You do understand me, don't you? You do hear what I'm saying," he says with enough clarity and finality to let me know to not talk back. But I talk back nonetheless. Or, I begin to.

"I hear you," I stutter. "Yes, I get it. Except, what if—"

"Jake, there is no what-if."

"I understand, but—"

"Maybe, you don't understand."

"I do, but let me say one thing. Okay?" Sensing his curiosity about what I may be thinking, not pausing for permission, I proceed: "If a story can be better understood with analysis, or if we can provide information the other stations do not, or add commentary that's insightful and provocative, and be more interesting, isn't there a way to do it? What if we super my name" (that's adding to the picture, at the bottom of the screen), "and say that I'm doing 'analysis' or 'commentary?'"

"We don't do analysis or commentary. You're not an analyst or a commentator. How long have you been here? A year, a year and a half? Do you think you're qualified to be a commentator? You, my friend, in case you forgot, are a reporter. Act like one, and we'll go from there. Cool it, Walter. Just cool it. Okay?"

I may not know when not to talk back, but I do know when enough's enough. He said, "Go from there," didn't he? That means, doesn't it, that maybe, in time, I will be doing commentary called what it is, or should be—closer look, through a prism of experience, at the workings of government, the machinations and shenanigans of politics?

Commentary certainly is not a new or particularly bold idea. Eric Sevareid is doing it on national television for CBS. Len O'Connor is doing it locally at Channel 5. Madigan himself did it here. But Channel 2 News is not about to feature a twenty-eight-year-old rookie, especially one who, stretching it, looks like he's twenty-two.

Madigan is careful not to say, or even hint, to me or anyone else, that he's being asked by city hall to censor me. He'll never admit it, and I'll never prove it, but I believe he's receiving mayoral messages, delivered not by Daley himself, which would be a dumb thing for the mayor to do, and he rarely does a dumb thing, but by trusted insiders with whom Madigan, more often than other news executives, shares prime rib at quiet bars and chop houses. "Hizzoner" is not threatened by my challenges on television, just displeased and occasionally annoyed, which is enough to stir his toadies into action on their own, hoping to be graced by a nod. They'll let Madigan know what the boss wants.

And it goes without saying in Chicago that whatever the boss wants he gets, with few exceptions. He's not only mayor, remember. He's also chairman of the Democratic Party, which bestows upon him the brawn to fill, or empty, most premier positions in city and state government. His is the prerogative to steer the course of government in any direction he personally believes is necessary—and, to firm his grip. If he would like Channel 2 management to understand that Walter Jacobson is too aggressive, the management understands it, clearly.

But why does the mayor care? Because he sees what we're all beginning to see in the 1960s, that television news is en route to becoming a force in electoral politics. Anchors, reporters, and commentators, on multiplying broadcasts, are ascending to levels of influence that, until now, have been the exclusive preserve of the newspapers. Madigan's in a position to stall the trend, at least at Channel 2—thus, my being invited to the conversation in his office, and instructed to cool it. I don't like what's happening. In fact, I abhor it, am ashamed of John Madigan. And I resent not having a choice, other than to quit. Not now. Not yet. Better that I do as I'm told.

An assignment I draw covering Mayor Daley is to get his reaction to a story in the papers about city employees loafing on the clock, sitting in the cabs of their trucks schmoozing, not a block out of view out the mayor's office window. The story includes pictures.

The first question at his morning news conference is about the loafing employees. And he is, as always, prepared for it. The pictures in the paper, he says, show what they show, and are being investigated. That's it, all there is for today. We could not get him to say more. Had I not been instructed to cool it, I would have concluded my report with a comment about city workers in the Daley patronage system wasting taxpayers' money, and the mayor being unwilling to talk about it, act on it, or even acknowledge it. But, I'm being cool, reporting the story, and adding only that "the mayor says he's investigating, but is not saying when he expects to complete the investigation, or what he will do when he does."

"Cooling it" and I don't get along. I think the mayor needs more heat in his kitchen, and that television reporters ought to turn it up, which we're not doing, in my case because Madigan isn't permitting it. A year has passed since he imposed his restrictions, and I'm still minding my manners, his manners. And the mayor's hegemony remains intact. But, for how long? Pile up the distress and frustrations of the poor, stir in their access to television, the disdain of the rich, and the blindness of boneheads in politics, and you have the makings of a storm that will rain wreckage, no telling the magnitude, on guarded offices in city hall, and in polling places citywide.

It's the late '60s. Television news is giving unparalleled voice to discontent, and adding pictures worth thousands of words. It is wise for power brokers to be wary, to brace themselves for more rigorous journalism that will invigorate civil unrest. They do see it coming and are enlisting, furtively, the assistance of reachable, susceptible news managers.

I suspect they'll continue to enlist, and get what they want, easy questions and minimal pursuit, at least for a while. Television news in the '60s is malleable. It's young, searching for ways to succeed, unsure of its mission, unsteady in making decisions. Do we do fifteen minutes, thirty, or an hour, shallow headlines or in-depth reporting, weather and sports or politics and budgets in Springfield, or pretty people in Hollywood? And how do we do it—solo anchors or teams, all men, all women, or both, good looks and good voice or Chicago news experience, happy-talk or serious? In short, what sells?

Not, it's decided, investigative journalism. Not now, anyway. It's too complicated. It involves hidden cameras, tape recordings, network standards and policies, and lawyers. And dealing with city hall's bellyaching or legitimate grievances or both. It's easier to leave the investigating stuff to the newspapers. Let them commit the resources; we'll take the stories off their front pages.

It seems to be a good time for me to break away, to take a year off to escape my private woe of having to cool it. I'll wait for Channel 2 News to value the combative political reporting that I believe is crucial to good governance, sustains viewer interest, and jumps the ratings. There is, and always will be, official malfeasance in Chicago for reporters to investigate—public records that contain information sufficient to expose a malignant patronage system that, according to the Chicago *Tribune*, has placed sixty-eight members of the Mayors Daley extended family on the city payroll. Since 1970, more than two dozen Chicago aldermen have been convicted of crimes including wire fraud, mail fraud, bribery, tax evasion, and extortion.

Investigative journalism and credible political commentary will, one day, detail the sins of patronage and the names and high government positions of the sinners who run it. I'll be among the reporters who try. But for now . . .

CBS sponsors a prestigious fellowship program at my alma mater, Columbia in New York, the television equivalent of the Nieman fellowships at Harvard. It offers a leave of absence, with pay, for a year at Columbia to work in any field on any subject except journalism, and to meet once a week with news icons like Walter Cronkite and Mike Wallace. The purpose is to allow a break in routine for up-and- comers to focus on things that may be useful later on. History, science, the arts, whatever strikes a fancy.

The fellowships are awarded to CBS newsmen and -women around the country who are demonstrating particular skills and promise for long-term careers in broadcasting. A chance to go back to school and, while I'm at it, escape John Madigan.

I apply for the fellowship and, unexpectedly, am accepted. Anything except journalism, right? I want to learn Chinese. If Chicago TV news doesn't work out for me, I'll go back to those dreams of being a foreign correspondent. At thirty, I have more time ahead of me than behind.

CBS helps me find a small house to rent in Englewood, New Jersey, just across the George Washington Bridge over the Hudson River, twenty minutes from Columbia. My wife, Lynn, and I pack up our Chevy and two children, Wendy and Peter, five and three, and leave Hyde Park for we know not what, except becoming one of nine, I think it was, of the company's designated hopes for the future. I enroll at Columbia's Oriental Institute, Lynn at the school of art history, and Wendy and Peter at preschool and nursery.

It's a year never to forget—not only Chinese, but lectures by internationally eminent academicians and congressional and White House insiders like Zbigniew Brzezinski, President Jimmy Carter's national security advisor; seminars with the elite producers, editors, anchors, and correspondents at CBS; and all of everything else New York serves up every day.

Although at semester's end, I'm a long, long, long, way from speaking Chinese, I truly believe that someday I will be CBS's correspondent in Peking. A little too soon, perhaps, I pitch the job—not by calling CBS, but by writing a letter to Lin Biao, minister of defense in the profane and brutal government of Mao Tse-tung's Communist China:

Dear Mister Minister:

I'm an American journalist who believes the road to lasting peace is winding through forests of misunderstanding too dense to penetrate, and that a tranquil world will remain beyond our reach until we learn to communicate. That's why I'm trying to reach you by mail, to appeal to you to help us all.

"I'm thirty-years old, a reporter for a television station in Chicago, on a fellowship at Columbia University, studying Chinese. I'm preparing myself for a day when our nations agree that to be friends we must talk, people to people. May I ask your permission to record the voices and feelings of your people, to bring to Americans your way of life? Please don't hold my nationality against me. The time is urgent. Thank you.

Sincerely . . .

My letter includes a brief recitation of what little I know about Chinese history, Chairman Mao, and the Cultural Revolution, the "Great Leap Forward" or "Long Live the Victory of the People's War." I tell him about my children, my hopes for their futures in a world not scarred by confrontation, and the sacrifices my family is willing to make for an opportunity to live, whatever number of weeks or months, on the mainland. (I thought my letter was pretty good, until I reread it while writing this book. Now, I see it as an overly dramatic and meandering plea of a very naïve young man. China, in 1967, was a closed society. Chinese citizens talking to the wrong people could be arrested and tortured. The minister of defense wasn't about to invite me to come visit, even though I wrote in longhand, figuring he'd like a personal touch.)

I can drop my letter in the mailbox outside Columbia at 116th and Broadway, but I know there is no mail service between the United States and China. I write to a friend from college who's working for the State Department in Egypt, asking him to find out where to mail my letter to Minister Lin Biao, and to please do so. He does, and I fancy that if I get invited to China, CBS will hire me as its man in China. But, there is no invitation. In fact, I get not a thank-you-for-writing, or even a postcard from the minister. Three months after I return from the fellowship to Chicago I do get, in my accumulated mail, free of charge, a subscription to the *Peking Review,* in English, a propaganda rag published by the Chinese government. My time to be a foreign correspondent still is not to be. But I will, one day not too far away, get to China.

Before going home from New York, and falling back in line at WBBM-TV, I try to use the CBS fellowship to open a door at the network. I call Don Hewitt, the famous cantankerous creator and executive producer of *60 Minutes*. Hewitt, I know, has never heard of me, probably not even of the CBS fellowship. He doesn't pick up the phone, but his secretary pencils me in for an appointment. "Ten minutes. That's it!" she says.

When I arrive at his office, Don Hewitt is sitting at a desk stacked with pictures of Don Hewitt and very important people. He's peering over reading glasses, already obviously impatient. "Whadda you want?"

"A job, please."

"A job? If I had one, why would I give it to you?" He's not being mean, just Hewitt.

"Because I don't want to go back to Chicago, and *60 Minutes* is the best there is, and I'll do whatever you need."

"Is there something that makes you think you're qualified?

"No, not yet. But, at some point, Mike Wallace wasn't qualified. And uh—"

"When you're as good as Mike Wallace, call me." Then a dismissive smile, and that's it. My job interview with *60 Minutes* is done.

The fellowship and my leave of absence are done. I'm to return to WBBM-TV. But I'm a big shot now, a CBS Fellow, so I must have some leverage, right?

I'll test it. Before we drive home, I'll call Madigan to tell him I'm thinking about staying in New York, but I'll return right away if he'll name me "Political Editor" (I'll go for the commentary later). It works. Maybe because Madigan is coming around, but more likely because the Democratic National Convention is coming up, the mayor and his machine have been prepping for it for months, and Channel 2 News will need political reporters with know-how, contacts, and good sources.

Whatever his reason, Madigan says okay, so, I'm going back with a title. From now on, when I'm on the TV screen talking politics, the words *political editor* will be there with me, giving me the latitude to make an assessment of what's going on in politics, and to express a judgment. For example:

"The mayor's not telling the truth on this one, and it'll come back to bite him, as it should." Or: "The aldermen are asleep, and need to be slapped awake." Or: "Based on that, I'd never vote for him, would you?" Good commentary, good for viewers, good for Channel 2 News, good for me.

The news itself in the spring of 1968 is not good. Robert F. Kennedy and Martin Luther King are shot dead. Violence erupts around the country, the worst of it in Chicago in the west side ghetto.

Blocks along Madison Street are torched and burning to the ground. Eleven residents, all black, are dead. Looting is out of control. Mayor Daley orders a curfew, prohibits traffic in the area, and instructs police to "shoot to kill arsonists," and to "maim looters." Chicago is aghast. Reporters can hardly write it down. "Shoot to kill . . ."

I go to Madison to walk the burned-out blocks and think to myself about what Daley said, "Shoot to kill." I've never heard of a mayor telling his police to shoot to kill. Summary execution?

A storm is building, and the mayor himself is shaken by what he said, so, in front of the city council, he explains what he meant: "It is the established policy of the police department—fully supported by this administration—that only the minimum force necessary is to be used by policemen in carrying out their duties, . . . but I cannot believe that any citizen would hold that policemen should permit an arsonist to carry out his dangerous, murderous mission when minimum force cannot prevent or deter him."

When I report what's happening, should I add a personal observation? Whatever my observation may be, the answer is no, not on this one. Don't add fuel to this fire. Chicago's angry enough now, and the convention's coming. Why say something that may further polarize and rile people? The ancient International Amphitheatre at Forty-Third and South Halsted is being spit-shined and lit up in the now-gone, but still stinky, stockyards. All hell is about to break loose. Again.

7

My Mouth Runneth Over

Mid-August is a steamy, sweaty time in Chicago. In 1968 the city is further sizzled by the hot air of politics—the Democratic National Convention! President Lyndon Johnson says he's not a candidate for the nomination. The war in Vietnam has worn him down. He wants out and gets out, and some ten thousand agitating activists are here to make sure he stays out. This leaves the party with poor Vice President Hubert Humphrey, who passionately wants in and has declared his intention to win the nomination, but doesn't know how to harvest the votes.

If he forsakes the president on Vietnam, he'll be abandoned by the party establishment and much of its rank and file. If he supports the president on Vietnam, he'll invite the damnation of a boisterous national movement set to storm the convention. We in the reporting pools can see it coming. Flames are being stoked to a blaze by Abbie Hoffman, Jerry Rubin, David Dellinger, and Black Panther Bobby Seale. These firebrands are being followed by our cameras and offered our microphones, as are Mayor Daley and the Chicago police, more than twenty-thousand strong.

"As long as I am mayor of this city," the Boss warns, "there is going to be law and order in Chicago!" Under the circumstances, not a wise thing to say, and that's how I describe it, standing outside the amphitheatre. My commentary is that Mayor Daley is provoking the protestors, revving them up for a war in Chicago (as Mayor Rahm Emanuel will do forty-four years later when planning NATO summits in Chicago). If Daley wants to impose law and order, then impose it. Why announce it? He has to know that television will deliver his challenge to the hotheads roaming Grant Park, which will cause him, his city, and his legacy unimaginable harm—a strong way to conclude my observation.

The mayor is acting unwisely in other ways: refusing the protestors a permit to parade near the amphitheatre, showing off his police in boots and helmets, armed with billy clubs and tear gas. His plain-clothed cops on the convention floor are roughing up television reporters, including Dan Rather, Ed Bradley, and Mike Wallace. And there's his bluster, all being broadcast by television into millions of homes. The whole world is watching. How can the usually astute Mayor Daley be so utterly blind to the realities of mass communication and the potential consequences of being portrayed as a bully?

His biggest blunder is his uncontrolled, red-faced outburst erupting like a volcano from the Illinois delegation seated directly in front of the podium in the amphitheatre. He's listening to US senator Abraham Ribicoff of Connecticut lecturing him on the chaos outside the Hilton Hotel on Michigan Avenue, and in Grant Park and Lincoln Park.

"Gestapo tactics in the streets of Chicago," snarls Ribicoff.

"Fuck you, you lousy motherfucker," Daley snarls back. Or, that's what some delegates say he snarled. And that's what it looks like on television. Other delegates, closer to the mayor, including his son (the future mayor) and his pack of politicians, insist he did not snarl "fucker," but "faker." The mayor is not near a microphone, and the media's subsequent, repeated efforts to read his lips yield no proof. Watching him on tape gets us nowhere. But news about it spreads, and the bottom line is that after three terms, thirteen years in office, he ought to know better than to snarl anything that anybody can hear.

How can Mayor Richard J. Daley of Chicago, brilliant strategist and king-maker of the Democratic Party, wizard of local and national politics, do things or say something, or appear to say something, so harmful to himself? That's not an unfair question, and I'm not the only reporter asking it. Chet Huntley and David Brinkley of NBC are asking it. So is CBS's Walter Cronkite and the columnists and editorial pages of the most-read, most influential newspapers.

Was it "fucker" or "faker"? It depends on what you know about the mayor. I don't say this on the air (even with bleeps), but I believe it was "fucker," for two reasons—one, he's fluent in that particular language; and two, he is so angry he can't control himself.

As big a story as the convention is, I'm on the air about it for just a few minutes a night. None of the Chicago reporters is on any more than that because the networks are committing most of their airtime to themselves, for gavel-to-gavel coverage and late-night pontifications. Conventions on television circa 1968 draw huge audiences, for whom the networks put on a show aimed at enhancing the image and boosting the ratings of their news divisions; CBS, NBC, and ABC are sparing nothing to succeed.

They've built glassed-in studios above the convention floor and set up an astounding array of communications hardware. They're bringing in planeloads of news managers, producers, directors, and writers, booking hotel rooms, and suites for the brass, and budgeting their meals, cab fares and late-night cocktails and dinners on Rush Street and in the bars of the most extravagant saloons.

And they're throwing sensationally lavish parties for political and financial big shots, money-raisers, lobbyists, hangers-on, and movie stars—and for their television anchors whom they're promoting like movie stars who are prancing around acting like movie stars, Mr. Cronkite chief among them.

"Excuse me. Who are you?" Sir Cronkite snaps at me as I poke my nose through a door to his anchor desk in the CBS "studio." It's an hour before the convention will be called to order, and I have temporary access to the floor and television workspaces.

"Walter Jacobson, Mr. Cronkite, WBBM Political Edit—"

"Who did you say you are? Who're you looking for? Would you mind?" he snoots, tossing me the back of his hand.

"Excuse me for interrupting [though there's nothing to interrupt]. I'm covering the convention for Channel 2 News," which is owned and operated by Cronkite's CBS. "I thought I'd introduce myself, and share some information I have about Mayor Daley and the Illinois delegation that may be useful to you."

Whatever it is, it's clear that he thinks there's nothing I may have that can be useful to him. So I poke my nose back out; and that's the way it is, Walter Jacobson and Walter Cronkite.

Too bad, because I could have told him that in the back rooms at that moment the mayor is twisting arms to dump Hubert Humphrey and bestow the Democratic nomination for president upon Edward Kennedy, senator from Massachusetts, youngest brother of the president who was assassinated in a Dallas motorcade, and younger brother of Senator Robert Kennedy, who was assassinated in a hallway outside the kitchen of the Ambassador Hotel in Los Angeles.

Too bad I'm being dismissed, because my information could be a Walter Cronkite–CBS News "EXCLUSIVE!" A scoop that could help his network move forward in the ratings, for which it is spending a fortune. Covering this convention is likely a bigger and more expensive job than covering a World Series and Super Bowl combined. The magnitude of it, the money and manpower invested, the rewards to reap are driving the anchors and corporate executives to distraction, causing them to be much too anxious and busy to think about their Chicago station, or its reporters.

Our Channel 2 broadcasts are being cut in half, sometimes down to five minutes. Our reporters are on the fringes, getting less air time than tear gas. What little we are getting, however, is better than none.

The reason we're getting any air time at all is that what's happening outside the amphitheatre, is as big a story as what's happening inside—thousands of Secret Service agents, Chicago police officers, US Army troops, and National Guardsmen are arresting about 650 protestors. Some of the police are swinging clubs at the protestors, and at reporters. On South Michigan Avenue near

Orchestra Hall, I hear a chorus of cops singing, "Kill the fuckers!" I hear it, but can't describe it because I can't see through the fumes.

Hundreds of people, many of them police, are being injured in what the distinguished CBS commentator Eric Sevareid describes during one broadcast as the "most disgraceful night in the history of American political conventions." A federal investigating commission will later call it a "police riot."

Is it in fact a "police riot"? The tumult is so pregnant with politics that an objective conclusion is impossible. Dan Walker, who is to chair the commission, is an activist Democrat who will use his postconvention celebrity to pound on Mayor Daley, and beat up Daley's "preecint" captains in a race for governor of Illinois.

A "police riot"? From my perspective on the battlefront, no more so than a "protestor riot." It's an everybody riot, and a turning point in the history of American politics—television news turning its cameras from the preposterous jargon of elected officials to the ad-lib bombast of their adversaries. Turning its reporting beyond the facts to commentary, shaping public opinion. It's what TV news ought to do—serve our viewers a helping of wit and (presumably) wisdom to incite their interest in current events, and stir debate over domestic and foreign affairs, and demand transparency in government. Think of what commentary could do with "Pay to Play" in government, steroids in sports, greed in city hall, and stealth in Mayor Daley's Democratic machine. Commentary on television could be like Mike Royko in print.

The Chicago convention riled the nation and primed it for "Royko journalism." If local television news is to sally forth, and if I'm to have a crack at commentary, I'll be ready. I typed up what I learned on the 1968 convention beat:

1. The prevailing business at a political convention is the exchanging of favors. In every muffled corner and stairwell, through aides and in furtive glances, politicians are making deals.
2. Nobody, but nobody, in politics trusts anybody.
3. Everything being done is motivated by a wish to gain access to the centers of power.
4. Lobbyists are highly reliable sources. Not only do they have information, but they're always willing to share it. (Remember: Sit at a bar, and be quiet. Feign disinterest and listen, just listen. What you hear may knock you off your stool—the names of congressmen and senators who are being bought, for how much.)

My desk in the newsroom is stuffed with enough notes, names, and telephone numbers to feed a year's supply of commentaries not only about government and politics, but about the personalities, competence, and ethics of the media:

- The clash of ambitions for more exposure (Cronkite versus Rather versus Mudd versus Wallace versus Schieffer).
- Competition for exclusive interviews. (Network anchors making deals with candidates and leaders of state delegations. "Come to me first, and I won't ask questions you don't want to answer." Same for correspondents competing for exclusive information. "Give it to me, and if you don't want to be known as my source, I'll report that you were unavailable for comment.")
- The mavens of network public relations nonstop pitching profiles of their luminaries.

Here's how that pitch is delivered:

A nubile public relations assistant shipped in from New York to Chicago drifts toward me in the lobby of the Hilton, where journalists are milling around waiting for a Ted Kennedy press secretary to swagger from a meeting. "You're a reporter, I can tell," she purrs, "Aren't you?"

"Yes, I am."

"Who you with, have you ever interviewed Dan Rather or—"

"No, I haven't. I've never met Dan Rather."

"Who'd you say you're with?"

I don't answer the question because I want to watch her work, and I know that if I tell her I, too, am with CBS, she'll flash her baby blues, and dance away in search of the newspaper or magazine writer she had hoped I was. Her mission is to get Dan Rather quoted in an article about convention coverage, or mentioned on the radio or in a gossip column—Dan Rather seen at the popular dining spots like Gibson's Steakhouse or Gene and Georgetti's. Achieving any one of the objectives could be her big break in her hunt for a celebrity-soaked career in public relations.

The 1968 convention is done and gone, but the battles between local politicians persist. As mayor and chairman of the Democratic Party, Daley struts his terrain as though both jobs are his for life, which they probably are. He has no trouble in the city council, none in the precincts or on LaSalle Street or in the legislature in Springfield or the bonding houses in New York. No trouble on the Gold Coast, or even in the ghettos. And although the public schools are bad, he has no trouble with them either.

If there's one itch the Boss needs most to scratch, it's the Chicago media growing restive and increasingly on the attack. Since the convention, we're not as reluctant as we had been to challenge his assertions. We are responding to tips on corruption and to calls about segregated housing, unequal education, police profiling, and abominable health care in the inner city.

In the newspapers and on television, publishers and station managers are less intimidated by building and zoning inspectors and the tax assessor. Columnists and commentators are taking off. Royko is unrestrained, on his way to winning a Pulitzer Prize in 1972.

Another clout critic, Len O'Connor of Channel 5 News (NBC-WMAQ), is ferocious. "Mayor Daley and his boys are doing things wrong," he intones unequivocally, buttressed by 230 pounds and piercing blue eyes. His cheeks are pink, his hair is white. And like nobody on the ten o'clock news in Chicago, if anywhere else, he commands the screen. A typical commentary might go: "It's about time His Honor straightens out. Or, gets out! . . . [pause] . . . and . . . [staring down more than half a million viewers, probably including the mayor] . . . and *I* [with emphasis] . . . am Len O'Connor."

Neither telegenic nor smooth of tongue, his voice high pitched, his bearing a perpetual scowl, O'Connor often garbles his words. But he never garbles his point. That's commentary.

My designation is "political editor." As imperceptible as it may seem, especially to those who believe the media is biased, there is a difference between a commentator and a political reporter, between what O'Connor does and what I do. He grabs the news and calls for action. I digest the news and try to unravel it. We both interpret and analyze, but I stop short of telling Mayor Daley what to do, like, "Get out!" I may mean for him to get out, but I don't say it.

Why not? Good question, to which there are several answers. One of them comes from a mayoral advisor who's been around the hall and the media since the Daley autocracy began in 1955: "You're a reporter or political editor, Walter, not designated as a commentator, so we [the mayor] can point out your bias, condemn it, and interfere," he tells me after hours. He's furrowing his brow and pretending to whisper. "It's harder for us with O'Connor. You try doing his bullshit, and see what happens. We'll cut your balls off."

"How?"

"C'mon, Walter. Don't be naïve. Think about it." I don't have to think about it. I know. I work for WBBM-TV in Chicago, which is owned and operated by CBS in New York, which grants only so much independence to its managers in other cities. The men (no women, yet) who run WBBM are forever on alert, fearful of corporate disapproval.

A message from Mayor Daley to the right friend in New York will be delivered to the right person at CBS corporate headquarters. And in less time than it takes Walter Cronkite to say "and that's the way it is," the message will be forwarded to McClurg Court in Chicago, in prose something like: "Jacobson's a problem for people who are important to us. What in the hell is he doing?"

Enough said. If I pop off like Len O'Connor does, I'm cooked. It's different for O'Connor, who works for WMAQ-TV in Chicago, which is owned and operated by NBC in New York but operated more independently of its network than WBBM-TV. An attempt by Daley to have NBC in New York interfere with O'Connor in Chicago will be met with word like "Call WMAQ in Chicago. Here's the number. Work out your problem with the general manager, Bob Lemon." And that, more likely than not, will be the end of it. When his ethics and standards of journalism are challenged, Bob Lemon at WMAQ doesn't flinch. I must be cautious, focus more on reporting, less on expressing my opinion, invest my time in soaking up what's in city hall and on the streets, tapping into sources, establishing trust in my commitment to keep a secret and my clout as political editor to get it on the news when my source wants it on the news. Those are big words in the neighborhoods—"clout," "trust," "secret." I work hard at them.

In Chicago newsrooms, the big word is "scoop." So I'm working hard on that, too, and doing okay. I'm the first to report a major development in the continuing story about State's Attorney Hanrahan's 1969 raid on the Black Panther Party, during which Fred Hampton and Mark Clark were killed. First, also, with news about Cook County sheriff Richard Elrod preparing to admit, publicly, that he lied in describing his hugely controversial role in the Weatherman riots in October of '69.

I expose a link between a prostitution racket and members of the Tenth Ward Regular Democratic Organization. When the county Democrats select a candidate for schools superintendent, I reveal his participation in race riots ten years earlier; he's dumped from the ticket. When my old pal county assessor Parky Cullerton holds a dinner to bloat his campaign kitty, a cameraman and I join the crowd, get pictures of real estate developers, and I say on our news, "This affair is a must if you own property." I tell a long and painful story about a black man unable to buy a house for his family of nine in a segregated neighborhood on the southwest side, and I wrap up the story with, "He'd have the house by now, if only he were white."

My plate is full, my mouth runneth over. And I sense there's trouble ahead because my "analyses" run right up to the edge of commentary, to the line of discomfort.

Sure enough. In 1971 the hints begin. The executive producer of our ten o'clock news tells me: "We're too full, tonight. I'm holding your report for tomorrow at six" (when fewer people are watching). An assignment editor says, "We're short on reporters, today. I need you to cover opening day at Wrigley"—hints from above, I know. I try to ignore them, continue to push the envelope. Until I'm summoned to the company summit. I'm frightened, but mostly angry. It's time to test a fortune cookie I recently opened. Its prediction is that I will soon be involved professionally with a person of great inspiration.

8

From Reporter to Commentator

Before heading upstairs, I call WMAQ Channel 5 and ask to speak to Bob Lemon, the general manager. I've talked with him at events, but never for more than a minute or two. He's a disarmingly friendly but serious man in his early forties, of light and kindly features, a comfortable smile, and eyes that say, "You can talk to me." At about six feet, he's trim and fit and wears short his recently graying hair. He looks more like a high-school therapist, tennis coach, or a LaSalle Street banker than a Chicago TV station manager pacing a newsroom that's making big stories out of small confrontations and bad weather. He's fiercely independent, and, as the cookie said, he's "inspirational."

"I think I'm on my way to being fired," I tell him.

"What do you mean, on your way to being fired? Why would you be fired?" He's genuinely puzzled.

"I'm causing too much heat, most of it from city hall. I know I'm going to get it. Can you use another commentator?"

"If you're fired, call me."

"Thank you. I sure will."

Our news director at WBBM no longer is the mayor's man John Madigan. He's Al Mann, summoned from a station in Minneapolis to execute orders from our general manager, who's executing orders from New York. He knows little about journalism, less about Chicago. I see him as an unprincipled, boorish, deceitful bully who's worse for Channel 2 News, and particularly for me, than Madigan was.

He's about to tell me my time is up. All these years since, I can't recall our exchange verbatim, but here's a try: "We don't have analysis and commentary on our news, Walter. That may be what you want to do, but not here. I need you to resign, but not in anger. Okay? I'll put out a press release that you want to pursue other opportunities in journalism, okay?"

"Okay, Al, but when the papers call, what would you like me to say?"

"They won't call. Our release will say you're leaving because you need time 'to work on a freelance article you're writing.'"

"Sure, Al, whatever you think."

What *I'm* thinking is how can this man be so stupid? Didn't he find out before he came here how focused Chicago is on politics and the media? There's no way the papers won't see this as a story, a good one. They'll call, all right, the minute they hear about it.

"Let's see if I have this right," wonders Ron Powers, television critic for the *Chicago Sun-Times*. "Walter Jacobson was not 'fired' from his job as Ch. 2 political reporter. And he did not resign 'in anger.' Jacobson simply decided that after seven years as a leading television news analyst, he had better quit so he could devote more time to a freelance magazine article he'd been wanting to write. So Jacobson handed in his resignation to news director Al Mann, who accepted it 'with regret.' That's the composite official version of how Chicago's best young broadcast news analyst came to forsake WBBM's tree-shaded hide-away on McClurg Court. One yearns for a sense of conviction in the above version, but one's instinct, built over years of crafty observation, analysis and hard thinking, whispers that certain elements of the narrative just aren't there."

The headline in the *Chicago Journalism Review* reads, "The Invisible Hand of Spiro T. Agnew," referring to President Nixon's vice president, who's informed the world that journalists are "nattering nabobs of negativism." The story under that headline:

"Was WBBM-TV responding to the Agnew syndrome when it eased political editor Walter Jacobson out of his job? The question can't be answered defini-tively but there are enough unsettling aspects to Jacobson's departure from the CBS station to cause concern among anyone interested in televised news. . . . Jacobson appears to have been a competent and popular reporter who violated three Agnew strictures: he made waves, he reported stories that the political es-tablishment preferred not to hear, and he tried to interpret the news. . . . TV news needs more, not fewer reporters who doubt and question what they hear. And, contrary to the prevailing mood at WBBM, it needs people who can interpret the news, lest a station pass on to its viewers the unvarnished lies of public figures."

Maybe Al Mann, counting on not being in the papers, feels better when he reads George Tagge, political editor of the *Chicago Tribune*: "Memories crowd in as we hear of Walt Jacobson's departure from WBBM-TV. We recall Walt march-ing with the pickets around the Statehouse and singing, "We Shall Overcome.""

No, George, not true. And after writing that, he's re-remembered his memo-ries, retracted what he said, and allowed as to how he must have mistaken me for someone else.

The *Sun-Times* adds this: "News in Chicago . . . does require the interpretive and explanatory abilities of a Walter Jacobson. We are too complex a city to allow the kind of coverage that results when somebody throws a press release into the air and the broadcast reporters descend like pigeons in Civic Center Plaza." Channel 2 must "reverse what appears to be the beginning of a recession into journalistic blandness"?

Maybe it must, but there's not a sign that it will. And even if it does, I won't be around to be a part of it. I'm moving to Channel 5, hired by Bob Lemon to be political *commentator* number 2, behind number 1 Len O'Connor. He's on the flagship ten o'clock news; I'll be on the six o'clock and on weekends doing commentary that's labeled "commentary." It's a big break for me, joining Lemon's team. I'm happy to back up O'Connor, to substitute for him at ten, do research for him if he wants it, carry his water. Anything. I'm onto the path, into the footsteps, of the best in the business.

(Pause for a word about clichés—"carry his water," "onto the path," "into the footsteps." Critics deem them unacceptable. Clichés are maligned by books on good writing, shunned by copy editors of television news. They have a bad reputation. But the criticism is often undeserved. A cliché speaks the language of regular people. Contrary to conventional wisdom, a cliché does not interrupt communication, but facilitates it. Information by anchors and reporters is dished so fast, is so obscured by pictures and buried in prose, that by the end of most broadcasts, our poor viewers can remember only sports scores and weather. Describe politicians as "peas in a pod" or "playing the same tune" or "scratching my back and I'm scratching yours" or "walking the plank" or "preaching to the choir," and we may be flunked by professors, but we'll be understood by an audience. Clichés are so useful, it's too bad we go to great lengths to avoid them.)

It's 1971. I'm clearing out my cabinets, and boxing things to move to WMAQ's big spread in the Merchandise Mart, largest office building in America after the Pentagon. I'm thinking of others who've been recently, recklessly fired by WBBM, or have been leaving in disgust: the research director Judy Wise, news director Bob Ferrante, reporter Carole Simpson, anchormen Bill Kurtis and Fahey Flynn. Kurtis has become a CBS News correspondent in Los Angeles. Fahey has crossed Michigan Avenue to Channel 7 ABC-WLS-TV to sink Channel 2 in the ratings.

In the files of colorful Chicago media stories, Flynn's departure from WBBM is about as good as it gets. For twenty years, he was the most popular anchor in town, telling us what was going on in our lives, and assuring us there would be a tomorrow—until beckoned one day by management, and told his bow tie was unbecoming to an anchorman and to take it off. He did, and kept it off for two years until, as he said, "feeling naked" caught up with him, and he asked if he could please put it back on.

The know-nothings at Channel 2 said absolutely not, and, as he importuned, they fired him, figuring it couldn't hurt because a clause in his contract prohibited him from going on air at a competing station for a year. What they were not figuring, arrogance trumping reason, was that when they broke the contract, they nullified the clause. So, very quickly, Fahey Flynn, and his bow tie were on the ten o'clock news on Channel 7, partnered with Joel Daly, a magna cum laude graduate of Yale, a lawyer whose hobbies included yodeling and singing country western. Inside of a year, just one, Flynn increased Channel 7's ratings by more than 100 percent, dropping Floyd Kalber at Channel 5 into second place, the Flynn-less Channel 2 deeper into last.

When I get to Channel 5, the Flynn story is ripe for a commentary; but to be honest, I haven't thought of it. I enjoy reading about it in the papers, but in my new job I'm all politics. Dan Walker, of the Walker commission that called the '68 convention a "police riot," is running for governor. Mayor Daley is building his booty for a run for reelection. Jesse Jackson is beginning to kick up a storm over segregation in the public schools. Soon there will be Watergate. There's a lot going on, about which I am now free, and encouraged, to comment.

I've been assigned a small office, about twelve-by-twelve, into a chair on rollers behind an old metal desk next to a two-drawer filing cabinet under a fluorescent light bulb. Hardly top of the line, but everything about it is perfectly fine with me. What matters is that I'm here, and that Channel 5 seems pleased.

Across a carpeted narrow hallway is Johnny Morris, sports anchor, former wide receiver for the Chicago Bears. He's not much taller than I when stretched to five-eight, but three times bigger, a brick. He was a hard-nosed player with a soft streak inside, warmly profane with a winsome sense of humor. He's a practical joker who's nice about it, even when he pours water on my script while I'm reading it so that I can't separate the pages. Pretty funny, I have to admit.

Morris knows his sports and is confident and comfortable in the studio, unlike Paul Hornung, formerly of the Green Bay Packers, who briefly anchored sports at Channel 2. Hornung was Hercules in the studio until the lights went on and melted him into mush. It wasn't the heat, but fear of the camera that cramped his career on the news and left us dumbstruck at how in the world that could happen to a guy who had been so fearless on the football field.

Outside my space and up the hallway twenty steps is the appropriately large, big-windowed office of Len O'Connor, with a spectacular view across the river and south to the end of his city. Standing up to the glass, I can see east and west, and wonder how often Commentator number 1 gets an idea just by looking out his window. He can't tell what people down there on LaSalle and Randolph, in and out of city hall, are doing, or whether stoplights on Wacker Drive are working, or where people west on Lake Street or Roosevelt Road are going to lunch. But I'll bet he can feel what's going on, hear the city speak, and sense its heartbeat. And ponder things to say about it.

On my first day at Channel 5, awestruck and with respect and some trepidation, I introduce myself to Len. I feel awkward, but as gruff as he is (it doesn't go deep), he puts me at ease. "Glad to have you here," he says. "Now, behave yourself. No mistakes." After that, I often walk the hall to peek around his half-opened door to guess how far away in thought he is, or how busy at his typewriter. If the coast seems clear, I knock once, wait for his wave, and enter with a question.

"Did you ever actually meet Paddy Bauler?"

"Meet him? Of course I met him. Used to talk to him once a week, the crafty son of a bitch. Used to give me my best stories."

"Is it true that he said, 'Chicago ain't ready for reform?'"

"Yes, it's true. And Chicago still ain't."

Sometimes I stay for a few minutes because I know he likes to reminisce, and I love to listen. He'll soon write a book about what he knows. The title will be *Clout*, and I will review it for the *Chicago Tribune*, writing in part, "O'Connor has played the game long enough to know that you don't learn about Chicago politics by getting a press card and tape recorder, and calling somebody up on the telephone and asking for an interview. If you want to know what the politicians are doing, you find out where the politicians are and you go to them. And you don't settle for the words that pour out of their mouths. You look at the expressions in their eyes."

The move by Fahey Flynn and his bow tie to Channel 7 is the talk of the media and in the executive tiers of local news. Wearing matching blue blazers, Circle-7 logos on their pockets, Flynn and coanchor Daly, Bill Frink on sports, and John Coleman on the weather are reporting in a new form called "Happy Talk." Their light give-and-take takes them to new heights in the ratings. Floyd Kalber on our Channel 5, doing the news as if seated on Mount Olympus, is reaching new ratings lows. Channel 2's just plain out of it.

In the early 1970s, anchors are being changed so fast it's hard to remember who's on which channel. The ratings are changing so fast the ad agencies don't know from where to pitch clients. The bean counters are so confused they don't know what they don't know. Corporate pecking is kicking in. When there's trouble, the guy on top blames the guy below who blames the guy below him until there's nobody below to blame. Then off with their heads, all over all the pecking orders, until a station's in disarray and cooked for five or six years.

That's what's happening at Channel 2. When I was in the middle of it, it hurt. Not anymore. Now, I'm a commentator happily anticipating an assignment with Len O'Connor to cover the 1972 Democratic convention in Miami. It promises to be a great story, and it is.

Leading up to the convention, Mayor Daley is accused of all sorts of Machiavellian politics, causing him and his Illinois delegation to be denied credentials, replaced on the floor of the convention by the Reverend-Jesse-Jackson–Alderman-Bill-Singer delegation of ragtag, independent, unexpectedly savvy liberals. One of the most revered and feared Democrats in the land is ousted from a Democratic convention, Richard J. Daley is sent packing to his hotel.

WMAQ Channel 5 gives me substantial, substantive air time in Miami. For what more could I ask? I see myself working at the station forever.

I can't be more mistaken.

9

From Commentator to . . . Anchor!

Home from the convention in the fall of '72, I'm at my desk in the Merchandise Mart when my direct line rings.

"Walter? It's Van Sauter." Van Gordon Sauter, a name from the past, prominent in Chicago during his years as a reporter for the *Daily News*, and then news director at WBBM Radio. He's back in town to take over Channel 2 News. I don't know him well, so I'm surprised to hear him on the telephone. "How about our getting together?" he asks.

"Sure, Van. It'd be great to talk to you. Anytime."

He's just resigned his prestigious position as director of special events for CBS Radio News in New York to come to Chicago to lug Channel 2 up from the dregs of terrible ratings (barely half the audience Flynn-Daly has on Channel 7 or Kalber has on Channel 5).

Why does Van Gordon Sauter want to get together with me? To ask what I know about Channel 2, about the local news scene, the mayor's chances of being reelected next year? You never know in this business why somebody wants to get together with somebody. He can't be thinking about bringing me back to Channel 2, can he? He knows why I was fired by 2, and he can turn on his television any evening at five o'clock, and see how happy I am as commentator number 2 on Channel 5.

Stranger still, he says let's meet not for lunch or dinner, but for a drink later at night, not downtown, but anywhere else. And he'd like to bring along his general manager, Robert Wussler, whom I've never spoken with, or ever even met. I feel like I know him, though, because of who he's been at CBS: executive producer of CBS News, coverage supervisor of space shots and two presidential campaigns. Sauter says they'll pick me up at my home in Lincoln Park.

And they do, arriving at about 10:15 in a limousine. We're in my neighborhood, so they ask me where we can get that drink. Four Farthings, I say. It's a cozy little bar and restaurant half a block away. We walk. I'm baffled.

"Nice place," says Sauter, sitting down at a small, round oak table in a quiet corner of the room. The bar is an antique of old carvings in dark wood, twenty feet long, at which four or five neighbors, familiar but unknown, are sitting on stools on a wood floor.

"Farthings has been here forever," Sauter says. "I used to come in two, three times a week." A pause, and then: "We'd like you to come back to Channel 2 to work with us."

Just like that, out of the blue. "Come back to work with us."

I'm stunned. "Why? What do you want me to do?"

"Anchor the ten o'clock news."

I'm even more stunned. "Anchor the ten? Are you serious?" Silence, glances all around. "Guess you are serious, or we wouldn't be here. Right?" Now I pause. "I'm not an anchor. You think you're in trouble now? Make me the face and voice of Channel 2 News, and you'll be in trouble forever, or gone before you can get me on the air."

"We're going to make you a star," says Van.

A shooting star, I think. Off into nowhere.

Wussler isn't saying anything. Starched into a gray suit, he's just listening, but looking serious enough for me to take him seriously. With a Budweiser and popcorn, Van's doing the talking.

"We want to team you with Bill Kurtis at ten. And we have plans for a six o'clock you'll love to hear. What you've always wanted, Walter. An hour. You and Kurtis for an hour. Chicago news, in depth."

"Have you talked to Kurtis? What does he say?"

"He's in Seattle on a story. We're going there tomorrow. Think about it."

The big question in my mind, that I believe should be in the minds of Sauter and Wussler, is: Why me?

Chicago is major league, World Series, Wimbledon, the Olympics of local television news. Anchors here are professionals. They come not from Peoria, but from Denver, Dallas, Cleveland, Miami. Sometimes they come from backup anchoring in New York or Los Angeles. They know how to handle the teleprompter (what to do when it suddenly goes backwards or blank). Professional anchors know the control booth and floor directors, and what to do when that thing in the ear screams conflicting instructions that have to be followed, in an instant.

Before anchors make it to Chicago, they know when to turn to which cameras, and how to vamp (ad-lib) when a live shot goes down. They ooze confidence. They're in big markets because they've made it in smaller ones. In other words, they are precisely the opposite of me.

So then, back to the question: Why me? Bob Wussler finally speaks. He says it's because he wants to make Channel 2 News different from itself and from other stations in the market.

Maybe he can, I think. He's the first CBS-WBBM-TV general manager to come from news, not sales. He's not yet forty-years old, sent to Chicago to manage a station that's performing so poorly, and is so low in the ratings there's nothing he can do to make it worse. His assignment to Chicago will include time and money with which to experiment, and the latitude to try almost anything.

Wussler's idea is to have two anchors who are newsmen, not newsreaders, in a newsroom reporting news, focusing on issues impacting Chicago. Sauter wants anchors of distinctively different personalities who relate to each other and the camera. Kurtis as the reporter. Me as the analyst. Bill the mature and fatherly figure. Me the saucy young kid, even though I'm four years older.

Think about it, says Van. I *am* thinking about it; I'm consumed by it. Leave Channel 5 after just two years? Walk out on the best job I've ever had, or can hope to have? Turn my back on a station and staff that are so good to me? I won't do that, not even to become a foreign correspondent for the *New York Times*, let alone an anchor across the street.

I'm part of the Channel 5 team, I like the people, and they like me. The work is good, and when Daley runs for another four years, it'll be better, and even better than that when he wins. When Len O'Connor retires, I'll move up to commentator number 1. Give all that up to go back to the same struggles in that awful station that fired me, and that nobody's watching? To read about burglaries and fires on a teleprompter (in my high-pitched nasal voice, versus the dulcet tones of Bill Kurtis and Fahey Flynn and Floyd Kalber)? Compete in a game I'm unlikely to win? A baby-faced Jewish anchorman in an Irish town, where people attach to their anchors as they do to their parents and priests? As I said at Four Farthings, Van's crazy to ask. Now I say, I'd be nuts to say "Yes."

And what about Kurtis? He, too, had been fired by WBBM, fifteen months after I was. Some of his history: "For nearly two years," writes the *Chicago Tribune*, "Channel Two stayed with Kurtis, hoping he'd pull off a miracle, but doing little to personalize his image. By then, the station had entered fully into its rudderless phase."

Bill was bumped from the ten o'clock news and told he was finished at WBBM-TV. He moved to California to be the CBS News correspondent covering eleven states for Walter Cronkite's evening broadcast. He reports daily on the Charles Manson trial and is so good on air that he's being talked about as a possible heir to Cronkite's throne. Can Sauter and Wussler lure him off that track? I don't see how, but I ought to call him to find out.

"I don't think so," he confides. "Things are going pretty well for me here. I like the network, and the assignments are great. And the Cronkite thing . . ."

"I don't want to talk you into Chicago. I'm going to say no to Sauter, too. But aren't you better positioned for network anchor as an anchor in Chicago than as a correspondent in LA? Is there a way for you to find that out?"

"I don't think so."

"Well, who knows better for you than you? Trust your gut. We have to keep in touch."

"Yes, I agree."

"Meantime, I don't see any harm in letting Sauter pitch, do you?"

"I don't either."

"Then let's say if either one of us thinks about catching, let's talk."

We both decline the offer, and that's that. Until Wussler and Sauter come at us again, and again, with all that stuff they know we'll listen to: an hour show, less junk, more substance, live interviews, documentaries on the side, interpretation and analysis.

"Whoa! Stop right there! 'Analysis?'" I ask Wussler. "Do you mean no commentary?"

"We'll work on that."

Now, I know that anchors are on top of the heap in television news. They are tremendous investments and, therefore, coddled like babies. What anchors want, they get. What they want to do, they do. What they want the broadcast to be, it is. In quarrels with management, anchors usually win, if not by agreement, by force. On the street and in restaurants, anchors are celebrities, turning heads and treated like princes. And they are paid like kings. Wussler is offering to more than double my salary, from $25,000 a year to $55,000.

All that fame and fortune notwithstanding, there really is no way I'll go anywhere if it means losing the commentary. I've spent ten years making it reliable enough for a regular place on an evening news broadcast. Not for a million dollars, not for anything, would I ever even consider walking away from the commentary.

"We'll work on that," says Wussler, again. Is he really interested in hiring an anchor to do both, read the news *and* do commentary? And even if he is, will the corporation permit it? Can he guarantee my role as a commentator? Dubiously, suspiciously, I ask him that question.

"I'll have to work on it," he repeats over another beer. "I'll try. Give me a few days," during which my "No" feels like it's becoming "Yes."

In four days, Wussler says okay. "You do commentary on the ten o'clock news," up against Len O'Connor on Channel 5.

Bill's "No" also is becoming "Yes" because he can stop scattering himself all over the West Coast, and back and forth to Hawaii, Las Vegas, and the Rocky Mountains. "Yes" for Bill because it will serve him well to respond to an SOS from CBS in New York. Maybe it will advance him a step toward an anchor chair on the network. In fact, he's insisting on it, and in fact Wussler's already nudged CBS into committing to Bill some network anchor time.

So, early in '73, the deals are done, the announcements made, "Bill and Walter in March." Reaction in TV land is bouncing off studio walls, and the newspapers are all over it.

"Despite what you may have seen in the ads," says the TV critic Johanna Steinmetz after we debut, "the star of Channel Two's new look in news is not its newsroom. Nor is it Bill Kurtis or Walter Jacobson. Starring at Channel Two News is shirtsleeves. White shirtsleeves, blue shirtsleeves, yellow shirtsleeves, striped sleeves, checked sleeves . . . the start of a push by Chicago's CBS-owned TV station to gain parity in news ratings with Channels Five and Seven. For extra panache, Walter Jacobson wears his shirtsleeves with a vest, affecting the look of an old-time country newspaper editor. I half expect him to lean back and let fly with a wad of chewing tobacco as he starts his analysis."

That's Steinmetz's word, "analysis." It's also Sauter's. But our agreement is "commentary." "Not to worry," says Van. "We're figuring out how to get my commentary on the air," which is to say how to get approval from New York.

CBS policy expressly prohibits the mix of anchor and commentary. Anchors don't do commentary, and commentators don't anchor. The bulldog media columnist in the *Sun-Times*, Robert Feder, who never takes fluff for an answer, and is editions ahead of his competition, and so much more insightful, asks Wussler why he's permitting his anchor to do commentary. Feder writes, "Wussler believes he has nothing to lose."

Feder's style, rare in contemporary journalism, is to ask a question, and listen to the answer. He invariably gets more that way than other reporters. Here, thirty years later, in astonishingly frank detail, is what Wussler will say to Feder about adding commentary to my role as anchor:

"CBS did not appreciate it. The corporate attitude of CBS, including Mr. [William] Paley and Frank Stanton, was their subjective feeling that they did not want their news people editorializing or doing commentary. They wanted a complete separation of church and state. However, I was in the fortunate position of having taken over a television station that had fallen on very difficult times. . . . At ten P.M. WBBM was in fourth place, behind even Cubs baseball.

"There were people at CBS who were ready to swap the station altogether for another one in Houston or Phoenix. So risk taking was a little easier to do. Quite frankly, I slipped it by them. I just told them I wanted to hire this guy who'd worked at WBBM previously and who I felt was one of the few personalities then in Chicago who lit up the screen whenever he came on. I sold them on Jacobson as Mr. Rough-and-Tumble, and Kurtis as a gentleman.

"After four or five weeks on the air, somebody [from CBS] in New York called and asked, 'Is Jacobson doing commentary?' I said 'yes.' They said, 'By whose authority? That really flies against company policy.' I told them I had done it by mine. My argument was that Chicago is the kind of town where news, viewpoint, commentary and editorializing are very important. More important than, say, in New York or Los Angeles, where people are less passionate about local politics and local issues."

Wussler knew what he was talking about. New Yorkers are distracted from local politics and issues by the marquees of Broadway, and the important and dapper diplomacy at the United Nations, and the international ramifications of transactions on Wall Street. In Los Angeles, it's Hollywood. Dat kinda glamour and glitz don't make no waves in Chicagah. Our celebrities are the Cubs, the mayor, the aldermen, and the newspaper columnists and television anchors.

My argument is that commentary can be a force for good government and, at the same time, entertaining. We just have to figure out how to do it in a way that won't agitate the corporate brass in Manhattan. We could be unaggressive with it, tread gingerly, treat our subjects delicately. But that would defeat its purpose.

Let's be brawny but keep it off the anchor desk where it may be mistaken for news. Let's put it somewhere else, out of the studio, in the newsroom. How about setting up lights, making space for a camera in front of my work desk in a corner of the newsroom, moving the typewriter into a place where I can talk over it, clean up the mess in the bookshelves behind me, and clearly label what I'm doing.

"Walter's Perspective," commands Van Sauter, a news director who knows Chicago and the value of political commentary. "We'll put that title and your signature on the screen, and keep them there until you're finished." And one more thing. "I think," says Van, "we need to do something about the way you look, too young to be telling people what to think, and the mayor what to do."

He's right. I do look too young. (I'm thirty-six.) I don't project wisdom. Compared to Len O'Connor, with his white hair and craggy cheeks, his girth and knowing eyes, unequaled commanding presence, I look like kindergarten.

"Maybe," Van speculates, "glasses will help."

"Glasses? You mean regular glasses, eyeglasses? I don't need glasses—"

"We'll get you clear glass in a narrow, metal frame. Age you up a bit, make you look profound."

"You're jesting. What'll I do, lift them from my desk, wrinkle my brow, and point 'em toward the camera?"

"No. You'll wear them. No problem. They'll be clear glass."

I'm sitting on a dark leather couch in his office, which looks like a library at Harvard College. Like Len O'Connor, Sauter is of commanding presence, big and strong, but of the style of an intellectual, in beard and corduroys and topsiders sans socks, and he puffs a pipe. Next to four TV monitors—Channel 2 the large one in the middle—is Molly, Van's talking parrot in its cage: "Loretta" (that's Van's secretary). "Loretta, Loretta" (and not much else), it squawks.

Not a feature is fake. Van Gordon Sauter is how he looks, and thinks; he's renaissance. "I like it," he says. "Glasses'll work." "Walter's Perspective" on the arrogance and abuse of power, racism in housing, sexism in the work place, failures in education, corruption in government, shenanigans in politics and in sports, and wasting of taxpayers' dollars. An example:

A woman is unnecessarily strip-searched by Chicago police. She files suit against city hall, and, after lengthy negotiations, says she'll settle for $20,000 and an apology. The boys in the hall know very well the police were wrong, and that in court, she'll win. But, macho-macho, they fight her in court, and lose, and are ordered to pay her $120,000 plus legal fees. I say, "How good for the lady who suffered the indignities. She's getting $100,000 more than she asked for because the lawyers in city hall told her to bug off. The mayor doesn't apologize, she gets $120,000, and we get the bill, $100,000 dollars down the drain."

Between Kurtis's stature as an anchor, my insolence as a commentator, and our working newsroom, Channel 2 is making a splash. Nothing quite like it has been done before. Not in Chicago, not likely anywhere else—a giant space, in the middle of which is a six-person anchor desk, a chair each for Kurtis and me, one for Brent Musburger on sports, and space for three more chairs for guests we bring in during the broadcast to talk with us about breaking news.

Behind and around us are two dozen writers' and reporters' desks under typewriters, newspapers, wire copy, broadcast copy, notepads, rolodexes, and telephones. And a horseshoe assignment desk, manned by a constantly moving crowd of news managers and staff. There's a weather corner with maps and machines, and editing booths, blackboards, cameras, and TV monitors attached to walls and hanging from the ceiling.

It's all live, and often spontaneous; it changes midparagraph when one of us is handed a page of information about a late addition to a story already told. Even the telephones on the anchor desk are live, and we use them, which adds to the display of disseminating news as it happens. I finish a report about Eleanor "Sis" Daley, the mayor's wife, and problems with a police captain I've identified as her cousin, and hear in my ear, "Pick up your phone, it's the wife." On the prompter is my page, but Kurtis reads it while I listen to a quite unhappy Mrs. Daley.

"Walter, you've got it wrong," she says, surprised she's been put through. "He's not my cousin. He's not related to me." She tells me I misidentified him. I can't check it out, not now on the air. But I can give her the benefit of a doubt:

"I'll report you've called, Mrs. Daley, and I'll call you back when we're off the air."

I hang up, turn to Kurtis on a two-shot, wait a few seconds for him to finish what he's reading, and say to him, "That was the mayor's wife, Sis Daley. She's pretty upset. She says the captain I named is *not* her cousin." Then I turn into my camera and continue, "She says he's not related, that the captain's name is Cartan.

Her cousin's name, she says, is Curtan. If I made a mistake, I'm very sorry, and I stand corrected. If there's more to the story, I'll follow up."

Then back to Bill on the two-shot. "One of the good things about news-anchoring this way is that we can update immediately, and correct mistakes." The plus for news viewers is an inside look at how we work. As the station's promotions are saying, "Channel 2 News. It's Not Pretty, But It's Real."

Chicago is tuning in to check us out, and staying tuned. And we're getting an inordinate amount of attention.

From Gary Deeb, columnist at the *Chicago Tribune*: "There's a happy, aggressive, freewheeling spirit at WBBM-Ch. 2 these days, and they're doing it without Muzak in the hallways, Babbitts in the executive suite, or the superficial gazes of alleged newsmen re-rehearsing the moronic byplay that passes for 'spontaneity' on some local newscasts."

From Ed Planer, news director at Channel 5: "I'm fascinated by the fascination with Walter. . . . The thing I equate it with is the small town where everyone knows the kid with the freckles and fishing pole."

From Ron Powers at the *Chicago Sun-Times*: "As news director of Channel Two, Van Gordon Sauter has proved to be one of the shrewdest and most capable executives in Chicago television . . . done amazing things to give credibility to a badly disorganized news department . . . from doormat to dark horse."

That's some of the good attention. There's also bad.

From Dick Kaye, political reporter at WMAQ-TV: "Jacobson can't cut it as an anchorman. . . . Kurtis has tried and failed as an anchorman . . . not going to help Channel 2 News."

From Don Rose, Chicago's best-known political guru: "Among polished journalists in town, Jacobson is viewed as a performer. His stuff is frail."

From my former boss John Madigan, now a radio editorialist: "The success Jacobson has had as an investigative reporter acting on tips from the disgruntled has been tainted by his outrageous and demagogic commentary, usually weighted with innuendo and guilt by association."

My response? I say the more critics the better, as long they're watching. The "numbers," as we call them, the ratings, are moving our way on both broadcasts, at six o'clock and ten. The money, the manpower, the focus on local issues, our big working newsroom—with some luck—is paying off.

Luck that comes in the shape of a Minicam, a strange little device that Wussler and Sauter brought with them from New York. No bigger than a breadbox, and only twenty pounds, it's about to revolutionize television news; it is small enough to be carried almost anywhere in any weather to take pictures in any amount of light and send them live into living rooms.

Channel 2 is the only news in town that has one. So when el-trains crash or a chemical leaks into a residential neighborhood, we're showing live pictures of the damage. When Mayor Daley is taken to a hospital, we're with him. Our viewers are watching violence in the streets and craziness in city hall as it's happening.

That's a big break, and we're taking advantage of it, using the Minicam as often as we can. It cost us $110,000. It's earning us a lot more than that. People are buzzing, "Have you seen the Minicam?" The other network-owned stations will be getting them, but not for seven or eight months. Meantime, growing numbers of people are watching us, including elected officials who don't like what they're seeing, chief among them Governor Dan Walker. He's unhappy about things I'm saying in my commentary, called "Walter's Perspective"—that he ought to report the names of his campaign contributors, stop spending tax dollars on his politics, and be more honest in his campaign ads. He's running for reelection, I say, and thinks if he wins he'll have a head start in the next presidential campaign, which is where he thinks he's cut out to be. "He has little patience for criticism," I add, "particularly on newscasts that are reaching the voters."

Walker's not going to take it anymore. He's hired a high-powered law firm to write a letter to Neil Derrough, CBS vice president and general manager of WBBM-TV: "Jacobson fires from behind the cover of his Perspectives at Governor Walker or any other person or idea that happens not to please him . . . to sway the public's decisions by slanting the news of Governor Walker. . . . We are entitled to have furnished to us on a continuing basis copies of each broadcast in the future and your assurances that this unfair practice will cease forthwith."

And there's a demand in the letter that the governor get equal time on air "to counteract the position advocated by Jacobson." That's an obvious attempt at intimidation, and the governor is taking a beating for it. "Gov. Dan: Walking Small in TV Feud," bellows a *Tribune* headline; "Walker's intimidation exposed," says the editorial page of the *Sun-Times*. "We do not think WBBM should cave in to the threat. Television needs more, not less, hard hitting commentary to cut through the half-truths and obfuscations of politicians who commandeer its air time."

Amen to that. Neil Derrough—successor to Wussler, who, in 1974, one year after teaming Kurtis and me, returned to New York to head CBS Sports—doesn't cave in to anybody. He informs the governor, in person and in response to questions from reporters, that WBBM's treatment of Dan Walker has been more than fair. To make his point, Derrough cites an eight- month period during Walker's administration that the governor's been on our air sixty-six times, saying what he wants to say about himself, his government, and his politics. "We are fully prepared," Derrough snaps, "to defend Walter Jacobson's commentaries."

It's clear that Dan Walker is not so much refuting my specific criticisms as he is in stopping the commentaries. If he thinks what I say is inaccurate or unfair, he can call a news conference and say so. But if he does, he'll have to explain himself, which will generate more talk about it than there already is. He doesn't want that to happen.

It's amazing, the governor thinking he can muzzle a reporter; more amazing that his press secretary Norton Kay and his chief deputy Victor de Grazia think it. They're old hands at politics and the press. Don't they know that a politician who tries to muzzle a reporter in Chicago will find himself up against all reporters? Stupidly, they parade their arrogance into a meeting with Channel 2 executives and a CBS lawyer from New York.

They come away with nothing. Zero. They withdraw their demands for copies of the commentary, and for equal time. Derrough says to the press, "We had a very sincere, gentlemanly meeting . . . no deals, no compromises. . . . I have no intention of gloating or trying to rub their noses in the dirt." He doesn't have to. The governor and his wise men are rubbing their own noses in the dirt.

How do they figure on getting away with it? I speculate they are so egocentric and wrapped in the culture of power that they don't consider consequences. When you step out of the real world into the swirling never-never land of politics, you lose perspective on what's doable, and what's not, especially on what's not. When you're a governor believing you have a chance to become president, your problems with the media multiply.

Dan Walker expects not to be told "No," and he very rarely is. If he wants to intimidate a reporter and a television station in Chicago, he assumes he can do it, and he has no one at his side to tell him he cannot (I specify Chicago because reporters here are trained in the streets; we know how to duck and dance around a "no comment" or prevarication, and where and when and how to strike). Walker, not having a naysayer nearby, is engaged in enormously risky business.

If Otto Kerner, when he was governor of Illinois, had had a naysayer, he wouldn't have been convicted, several years later in federal court, of bribery, tax evasion, conspiracy, and perjury, and wouldn't have been sent to prison. Jiminy Cricket would have told him to stay away from Marjorie Everett of Arlington Park, the queen of horse racing in Illinois who gave the governor valuable racing stock in exchange for choice dates and expressway exits to her track.

A naysayer would have stopped state auditor Orville Hodge from embezzling more than a million dollars of the taxpayers' money, with which he lavished upon himself a personal fleet of four Cadillacs, a Rolls-Royce, and two jet planes (if you're going to steal money, don't spend it on something as obvious as a Rolls or a jet).

If Paul Powell, Illinois secretary of state, had had a naysayer, he would not have stuffed $800,000 of ill-gotten gain into a shoe box in a closet in his hotel room. Naysayers were nowhere around Governor Rod Blagojevich, either. At his trial in 2011, his lawyers contended their client was innocent because no one around him ever told him that his schemes were wrong or illegal.

On the national scene, US senator Gary Hart wouldn't have had an affair, denied it, or challenged reporters to prove it. President Bill Clinton (maybe) would not have messed with Monica Lewinsky, and then said on television he "never had sexual relations with that woman." President Nixon would not have denied Watergate.

My point is: Public officials (Eliot Spitzer, Anthony Weiner) ascending to high office on the wings of admiration are given to delusions of magnificence, to a degree that they recklessly grant themselves immunity, or what they think is immunity, from the focus of journalists who ascend to the heights of our the profession on the wings of investigative reporting. It is stupefying that a president of the United States can be smart enough to win the office, then dumb enough to throw it away.

Just like Otto Kerner and Richard Nixon, Dan Walker was lunkheaded enough to believe he could intimidate the media. How did he not know, or at least be advised, of the public fuss he'd cause?

10

Heat from Jesse Jackson

Never underestimate the determination of a reporter in pursuit of a scoop. I know that because of the work being done by my legmen in our corner of the newsroom. In 1976, I have three assistants digging for stories for "Perspective," and shoveling up some very good ones: city workers filling potholes for three hours in the morning, breaking for lunch for two hours, dumping what's left of their asphalt into the Chicago River, then signing out at 2:30; city inspectors charging into a corner newsstand and ordering the owner to install a sink and toilet because, they declare, the candy and gum she's selling is "food"; an alderman congesting traffic by making a street one-way in order to provide more parking for a friend's restaurant; firemen using a hook-and-ladder to hang a sign outside a bar that one of them owns; the Department of Streets and Sanitation paying taxpayers' money to a private trucker (the best precinct captain in a north-side ward) to spread salt while city trucks stand idle in a parking lot.

Our stories come from anonymous letters or telephone calls, or from me or my legmen on patrol. We're always on patrol, almost always with a camera in a pocket, sometimes in disguise. Members on my team average about thirty years old, are pursuing jobs in investigative journalism, and are being paid an average of $20,000 a year. In four or five years, they wear out or move on. In addition to exposing waste, corruption, and hypocrisy in government, they scrutinize city, state, and federal budgets and payrolls and analyze court decisions in our hunt for judges on the take.

Because of the trouble I'll be in if I make a mistake in a commentary, I choose my assistants very, very carefully. When they've been through my boot camp, they go places—the Washington bureau of CBS News, *60 Minutes*, competing local newsrooms, an anchor chair in Chicago radio news, TV news management, an executive suite of a major newspaper. They are uniquely competent young journalists committed to accuracy; they are thorough, fair minded, and tireless.

One of the best stories we've dug up, I'd say the most controversial, is about Reverend Jesse Jackson preaching paucity from the pulpit while house-hunting in the suburbs. I'll tell you the story, but first a word about how hard it is working a story on Reverend Jackson—in battling the Chicago media, mainstream and ever-so-white, Jackson almost always counts on winning; so the harder he's hit, the stiffer he defends. The more he yelps, the more his friends and supporters do too, the more access he has to news executives. He takes his grievances directly to the top and doesn't walk away until satisfied it's redressed.

Now, here's the story:

The reverend is looking at a place for a second home near Libertyville, forty miles northwest of the Chicago, a twenty-five-acre estate that's priced at $295,000. He hears my commentary about his house hunting and doesn't like it. Not one bit. He calls Channel 2 management demanding equal time, and being the man in Chicago most feared by the media, he gets it—on the set with Bill and me on the ten o'clock news.

"That was a racially motivated report," Jackson says of this "Perspective," "designed to keep the black in his place. I had just a casual look at the home near Libertyville. I had no intention to buy. My wife and five children live under tremendous pressure. I want to get away. I want to have a hideaway. I need one, but I cannot afford one. It was just a casual look. I had no intention to buy." He is steaming. "I've visited the White House, but I don't plan to buy it."

"I reported on the air your statement that you're not buying," I respond. "I said it twice in the commentary."

"Then why did you use the story at all?"

"Because you are a prominent and interesting person. What you do is news." Kurtis and people working in the newsroom are becoming uncomfortable. The Reverend Jackson:

"There are two bad aspects to your story. One is that I might be taking money that doesn't belong to me, and the other is that there's something weird about a black man even looking at property like this. I can't say for sure whether the story of the estate would have been used if I were white, but I'm inclined to think it wouldn't have been. I can't just laugh off a story like this. It does a lot of harm. I will not be circumscribed by anything Walter says."

As Jesse Jackson draws more media attention, he's causing us increasing consternation over how to cover him. Other public figures, when caught by reporters in a hypocritical or dishonest moment, take their medicine in print and on television, wince, and apologize. Not Jesse Jackson. He turns his bad moments back onto the reporters. He declares us the bad guys who don't understand what's necessary for him to do, or what God's calling on him to do, or the difference between right and wrong in the world.

If we're critical of Jesse Jackson, or allow others (the mayor, for instance) to be critical, we're racist, which is a hard rap to beat. Therefore, we lean over backwards to Jackson, which, in addition to being bad journalism, enrages the white middle class. So we're stuck, trying to be fair to everybody without being able to determine, fairly, what's fair to whom.

My story about the reverend looking in Libertyville is accurate, but that doesn't matter because he's saying I'm unfair. I don't know of a public opinion poll on the dispute, but I have no doubt that African Americans in Chicago, the news viewers he's aiming at, believe him more than they believe me.

I have a theory about Jackson's demand for equal time. It's that he sees my commentary as an opportunity for political gain and is seizing it. In order for minority politics to be a force, it must have a charismatic leader to rally around, and an enemy to rally against.

Jesse Jackson is loaded with charisma. For an enemy, he's been rummaging around—and has come up with me. His strategy is to take advantage of my high TV profile and the skyrocketing ratings at our station. Claiming mistreatment by the media, especially the white media, is a sure-fire way to rally people 'round. His public clash with an anchorman stirs emotions, energizes his base, and adds to the momentum of black power in Chicago politics, which, in seven years, will elect the first black person to the mayoral suite on the fifth floor of city hall.

His anger at me is boiling into hate that he'll spew during a speech at Operation PUSH, linking me to Revlon cosmetics, a company he says discriminates against blacks. "What is the kinship of Walter Jacobson and the kinship of Charlie Revson?" Jackson asks rhetorically. "Same national origin and same race." Then he ties me to Israel: "The same people, that's his people, are selling gunboats to South Africa to kill black people."

That's crossing the line, I think. What does my being Jewish have to do with a commentary about him looking for a home in the suburbs? Nothing, except that he knows, as we all do, about strains of latent anti-Semitism in black America. Tap it, spill it on me, and he gains adherence to his cause against the white media in Chicago. He is stirring suspicion, diminishing the credibility of a reporter who's taking on Jesse Jackson. His aim is to stop me, and to swell the power of his personal politics. But using race, religion, or ethnicity to do it doesn't work. It bites back.

Vernon Jarrett, Chicago's most prominent black journalist and an activist himself, writes about Jackson and me in his column in the *Tribune*. "This is the first time that I have heard Jackson vent his spleen with wild, unsupported charges against a white newsman," he writes. "I have several special objections to that kind of invective unless it is supported with at least a modicum of evidence. Jacobson's Jewishness does not automatically mean that he agrees with everything Israel does, nor does it ipso facto follow that he deliberately shielded—or even knew of—the Revson controversy. If Jackson has collected any evidence to support his charges against Jacobson, he should go to the Federal Communications Commission or to the management of CBS. Jackson is on very good terms with the managers of most white media. They love him and promote him."

Having had his equal time on my house-hunting story—and more time at Operation PUSH—he does not go to CBS about my kinship "and the kinship of Charlie Revson" or about Israel and my "people selling gunboats to South Africa to kill black people." He knows the absurdity of that kind of talk, and he knows CBS knows it. He'll save his call to CBS for a time when he has better goods on me. Also, he's not about to reactivate the ire of Vernon Jarrett, whose voice in the inner city is as impactful as his is.

Don't press your luck, Reverend. Don't overdo it. Play your cards. None of which is to say that Jesse Jackson is on the wrong side of the critical issues of his time, of all time. On the contrary, he preaches the right side of the racial divide, and of equal opportunity, freedom of speech, minority representation, independent politics, poverty, the environment—you name it. We're much more on the same page than off it, and we will become friends. Occasional combatants on matters of reporting, but friends nonetheless. Not come-to-my-house-I'll-come-to-yours friends, but, as in sports, less stubborn and aggressive off the field than on.

The next time I bump into Reverend Jackson, neither politics nor the media is on the agenda. We will be at a memorial service.

On December 20, 1976, I'm in Boyne, Michigan, skiing with my children. Off the mountain at the end of our second day of the four we planned, shivering from an all-afternoon snow, maybe eighteen degrees and no sign of sun for tomorrow, we shelter ourselves by a fire in the lodge. Halfway through hot chocolate, I'm called to a telephone. It's Jay Feldman, news director, speaking from what sounds like a chaotic somewhere. "Daley's dead. We have to have you back."

My God, just like that. Daley's dead, of a heart attack at age seventy-four. Suddenly, nothing's the same. That's it, period. He's out of my life, before I can meet him for lunch even once, or sit with him for five minutes in private in his office. Before I can know him well enough to hurt.

I don't have deep, aching feelings, but a memory, clear as if it's now, of when I was at the *Chicago Daily News*, Jack Mabley's first assistant, my first job on a Chicago newspaper, Mayor Daley's first election. Most of my life has had to do with him. Can I get along without him? What do I do?

First thing, is to get back to Chicago. Pack up, check out tonight, and be at the airport at seven-thirty tomorrow to wait for a chartered flight home. Wendy and Peter (we left Mom home for some R & R) don't understand why we have to leave. Why is work more important than children?

A fair question, which I'll be answering to them and myself until they go to college, and until Julia and Genevieve, my second family yet to come, go to college. "My work is not more important than you are. It's just that sometimes there are emergencies, and I have to be there. I love you. Buckle your seat belts."

On my way back to Chicago to coanchor continuous live coverage of what happens when Chicago abruptly becomes what it is not, I strain to remember things I've read in books about Mayor Daley's first five years in office, and what I've learned on the beat about his last sixteen, which have just ended in the bruising cold of a week before Christmas. Broadcasting live, nonstop, means having to have things to say when others don't, or when Frank Sullivan, the mayor's press secretary, reads a condolence from President Gerald Ford, or when the city faces the consequences of a precipitous halt in government, and politicians begin to jockey around the emptiness that comes with it. When the interviews run out of words and the producers begin repeating the pictures, it's time for the anchors to talk—we call it "vamp"—about what we know, without a script, without stumbling or making mistakes.

One thing during his two-decade reign Mayor Daley did not do was prepare for it to end. Even after his stroke two years earlier, a mild one but a warning of impending trouble, and blood pressure too high, and his magnificent Democratic machine wrenching, and his friends being licked in Cook County and statewide elections, the Boss did not plan ahead. He had to know he couldn't go on forever, but he resolutely refused to bestow his blessing on an heir apparent.

So the piranha politicians are coming to the surface to chew one another up. There's no need anymore to camouflage ambitions, or temper swaggers, or even to be cautious. Just go for what you can get. Suddenly, the mayoralty and the chair of the Democratic Party are vacant, and every ward healer wants them, or one of them, or a piece of each. Their gnawing, in public no less than private, is unrestrained. Alderman "Fast Eddie" Vrdolyak versus Alderman Ed Burke vs. Alderman Wilson Frost vs. Aldermen Richard Mell and Michael Bilandic, rapacious in their lust for the holy grail left there on Daley's desk not one day ago. Chicago is up for grabs.

The facts of Mayor Daley's life, from election returns and balanced budgets to zoning inspectors and his box at White Sox Park, are indisputable. His successes and failures are debatable, to be defined by the judgments of history. His private feelings, joyful and sad, can be defined by no one outside his family, possibly by no one even inside his family, least of all by journalists. His feelings were his alone. To get into his head was doable, into his heart was not.

I know about things he did for, and to, people, but not about why. I tried a few times to get through to his emotions—and, on occasion, to share mine—but was rebuffed. The closest I came was during a telephone conversation about a job.

Background:

My wife, Lynn, an art historian interested in architecture, reads about a vacancy on the staff of the city commission that deals with landmarks, and she applies for an interview. Six weeks pass, she's not been called, and has seen nothing in the papers about the vacancy having been filled. I call the commission as a reporter and ask about current projects, and whether the staff is sufficient to handle the load. My questions are answered by the press office. Several major projects underway, and, yes, the staff is sufficient, but always, of course, we can use more.

"Interesting," I say. "Maybe there's a story there."

"Anytime, let us know. We'd love to take you around. Thanks for calling."

There is a story there—a good one about how the commission decides what it wants to landmark. Who are the major players making the decisions? What are the politics? What developer may be paying which politician how much money for what kind of favor? For sure there's a story, and maybe I'll get to it; but truthfully why I'm calling, but do not say to the press office, is to find out about that vacancy on the staff and whatever happened to Lynn's application.

I suspect, instinctively, that politics is involved, but I don't want even to appear to be looking for a favor for my family. Why not call the mayor's office directly to try to talk to him about it, and if he comes to the telephone, which I'm sure he won't, be honest. Does the fact that an interview with Lynn Jacobson is being stalled have anything to do with me? A secretary asks me to hold, and in five seconds, the mayor's on the line. I'm stunned. I've never talked to him on the telephone. Richard J. Daley, the boss of everything, is saying, "Hi, Walter. What can I do for you?"

"This is a personal call, Mr. Mayor. Thanks for picking up."

"Anytime. Always."

"My wife has applied for a job, hasn't heard in six weeks." And I tell him what I think is going on—that the commission is playing the patronage game, or it has been advised that having Walter Jacobson's wife on staff on the inside may not be a good idea. So she's out.

"We don't do that here. There's no patronage. We hire people to work for us who are qualified. There's no patronage," the mayor says.

"My problem, Mr. Mayor, is not that she's not being hired. That's between her and the commission. I have nothing to do with it. My problem is that it's wrong for me to be the reason."

"I don't know the reason, but it wouldn't be you. Chicago doesn't work that way." Then he goes on for forty-five minutes (that's not an exaggeration), practically nonstop about how Chicago works—public parks, bond ratings, fighting crime, cleaner air, garbage collections, middle-class housing, streets and sidewalks. The good things. Then he says he has to run. "Nice talking to you."

He had no way of knowing I'd be calling. He came to the telephone without notes and rattled off statistics, history, and his philosophy of governance like a college professor. And he's the guy with less-than-towering intelligence? I'm very impressed and say no more than, "Nice talking to you, too. Have a nice night. Goodbye."

Three days later, Lynn is called in for an interview and gets the job. Politics and patronage at city hall? No doubt. Proof? None. During twenty-five years of watching, tailing, quizzing, praising, believing, doubting, disliking, loving Mayor Daley, that was the only time I talked to him on the telephone, which I made sure had no impact on my subsequent reporting or commentaries on him or his administration or his chairmanship of the Cook County Central Committee.

My feelings about him, his personal side? He was a deliberative, cautious, yet very likeable man with a soft sensitivity and comfortable sense of humor. I didn't realize how deeply he affected me on a personal level until I went to Ireland to visit the home of his ancestors in Old Parish, Dungarvan, County Waterford—not so much to *know* as to *feel* a few chapters of Daley family history that are unavailable in books and tattered news clippings.

I talked to no more than four or five people, but walked the countryside, stopping at eating places for brisket and boiled potatoes, cabbage and a taste of Guinness stout (ugh). No signs of the family, except for a pointed direction here and there, which invariably led me nowhere. It was an emotional experience for me. I felt connected to Mayor Daley in a way I could not at a news conference. Unexpectedly, it made me more comfortable criticizing him in my commentaries. City hall is one thing; Dungarvan is another. If Mayor Daley didn't like reporters, he'd always love Dungarvan. How could I not love him for that?

11

Madame Mayor

As far as I know, in his twenty-one years as mayor of Chicago, Richard J. Daley never felt the need to go to a television station to defend himself. His successor felt it. Mayor Michael Bilandic spent seventeen bizarre minutes live on camera telling me, Bill Kurtis, and our viewers that I was wrong in reporting hanky-panky involved in a substantial rate increase granted to Chicago taxicab companies.

Here's a brief history and the underlying politics of Bilandic's extraordinary appearance:

December 1976. Mayor Daley is dead; the city council maneuvers his Bridgeport neighbor Alderman Michael Bilandic into office as acting mayor and schedules an election for the two remaining years of Daley's term. Bilandic wins it and soon thereafter declares his intention to run in the next regularly scheduled election.

(Had Daley lived and hinted at a successor, it would not have been Bilandic, the soft-spoken son of Croatian immigrants, who until age fifty-four was unmarried and living in his family home with his mother, brother, and sister. Mayor Daley much preferred Jane Byrne, the feisty Irish American daughter of an Inland Steel executive. Widowed in 1957 at age twenty-three with a one-year-old daughter, Byrne taught school and became involved in Democratic politics. In 1968, Daley tapped her as commissioner of the city's Department of Consumer Affairs. Of all his lieutenants, he trusted her the most and depended on her to help him correct mistakes, the few he admitted making, and to keep him informed about what his enemies, and his friends, were up to. And contrary to what most people think, Daley valued the perspectives of women. "I guess I'm old-fashioned," he once said. "I still believe that the hand that rocks the cradle rules the world."

So he names Byrne cochairperson of the mighty Cook County Democratic Central Committee, the machine; and in the machine's clubhouse in the Blackstone Hotel downtown, he tells his army of city and suburban committeemen that they'll henceforth be jumping not only to his commands but to those of Ms. Byrne. They can't believe it and don't like it. Byrne can't believe it either but loves it, especially when she hears him tell his sons, Richard, Michael, John, and Bill, that they, too, better believe it, and behave accordingly.

Naturally, lady Jane of the Sauganash neighborhood on the northwest side begins having fanciful notions about a surge to center stage of Chicago politics and government. She's being mentored by the master, and her résumé sparkles—member of the Illinois Commission on Women and the Democratic National Committee; chairperson of the DNC's Resolutions Committee. Why *not* think about one day being mayor—an easy thought, but a labyrinthine journey.

When the general dies, the troops in the Blackstone strip Jane Byrne of her party leadership. But she remains commissioner of consumer affairs and sets out to reach for the top in a run against Michael Bilandic. Janie, as Daley called her, has a lot going for her. She is a very smart, unusually articulate, fiercely independent woman who is charming and has a wonderfully edgy sense of humor. And she understands that politicians don't leap anywhere in Chicago without the media. She works tirelessly at ripening relations with reporters who can do her the most good: the columnists in the newspapers and the commentators on television. With channel 2's ratings sailing, that includes me.

Byrne tells me that Mayor Bilandic "greased the way" through the city council for the taxicab companies to increase their rates by 12 percent. She's kept a diary about it, from which she writes an eight-page interoffice memorandum about secret meetings in city hall: "I believe [the rate increase] was fraudulent and conspiratorial, and should not have been granted . . . the increase was greased. . . . I sincerely believed Mayor Bilandic was going to run things straight. . . . I do not think he did." A memorandum like that, by the city commissioner who regulates cab rates? True or false, it's dynamite. She gives me a copy.

"When can I go with it?" I ask, knowing I have the makings of a very exclusive story.

"I've already given it to the US attorney . . ."

"You know, don't you, that if I go with this, Bilandic'll look for a way to fire you.

"You can go with it whenever you like."

That has to be right away, before somebody beats me to it. Our next broadcast, tomorrow at six o'clock.

We lead with it. I show the memo on the air, read parts of it, explain that it's the first scandal directly involving Mayor Bilandic, and report that I tried to reach him for a comment, but he was unavailable. Good story.

I go home for dinner. Thirty minutes into a pizza, the phone rings. It's the executive producer, breathlessly. "Jake, Bilandic just called. He's coming in to be on the ten, live."

"You're joking. There's no way. No mayor's ever done that. Hear of a charge like Byrne's made, and come in live to talk about it. You believe he'll do it?"

"I believe him. We're clearing the top of the broadcast and killing commercials. He can talk as long as he wants. We've called the papers. I expect a gang in the newsroom."

It's 9:20. I have forty minutes to get back to the studio, go through my notes on the Byrne memo, get made up, think about how to deal with the mayor live on the set, on a hugely complicated story that can cost him his job. At ten minutes to ten, he arrives with his entourage and his wife, Heather. With two minutes to air, he's seated on my right (Kurtis is to my left) under what to him must be blinding lights and enough heat to cook him faster than I can with questions. I look at him and say, "I'm uncomfortable."

"Why?"

"Because you're the mayor, and you're sitting right next to me, and in a minute I'll be saying things that are damaging to you. And I've got to do it directly into your face."

He chuckles. I can feel his breath. We begin with a recap of what I reported at six o'clock—the memo and Byrne's having taken it to the US attorney. I ask him if Byrne is lying.

"She's mistaken . . . incorrect."

Why is she turning on him like this? I ask. Has he instructed his attorney, as Byrne says, to ask the *Chicago Tribune* to hold off on negative stories about the taxicab rate increase? Will he take a lie test? I press him hard but get nowhere. He ducks, or filibusters with a monologue about what a good job he's doing. I interrupt with questions about specifics in Byrne's memorandum.

He says, increasingly annoyed, "Wait a minute. Let me finish."

Jay Feldman, the news director standing off-camera, out of the mayor's sight, twenty feet away, signals me to back off, let him finish. I do, then start again—does he think the US attorney ought to investigate? What does Byrne mean by "greasing the way?" What's he planning to do about all this? Will she be fired?

I'm astounded at how little he's saying about anything. I figured he'd be prepared to answer questions, and to criticize me for revealing the memo, and to rail on her for falsely condemning him. None of that. He's calm and comfortable, unrattled, confident, and not disapproving of Jane Byrne, almost like he doesn't want to provoke her into something worse. This goes on, without a break, for seventeen minutes, and he seems pleased with himself.

But if he's okay now, he won't be tomorrow, when he wakes up to the *Sun-Times* on his stoop screaming, "Jane Byrne Memo Accuses Bilandic of Fraud in Taxi Deal," a front-page, four-column headline over pictures of the mayor and the commissioner, and an excerpt from her memo: "I am writing this memo to make a record of all the events leading up to and including meetings,

secret meetings, . . . relating to the taxicab increase voted on by the City Council.
. . . [T]he information and data that I have attached should certainly verify
my charges." Inside the *Sun-Times* is the full text of the memo, a picture of
Bilandic on our broadcast next to a headline saying, "Mayor on TV for Cab
Memo Denial."

For Channel 2 News, the story can't be better. Our numbers are soaring,
up an unprecedented 9 percent from what they were before Byrne-Bilandic.
"Class ultimately wins out," says the *Tribune*, "and the performance of WBBM-
Channel Two is a textbook example of that theory. Channel Two is the class
act in Chicago television news. The station verified that status with its impressive work as it first 'broke'—and then fleshed out—the Jane Byrne–Mayor
Bilandic controversy."

That's frosting on the cake. What matters most to us in the newsroom, and
to the other stations in Chicago, is that management is sacrificing advertising
revenue to report news, and is extending a local newscast into network programming for whatever minutes are necessary to tell the story.

To Byrne and Bilandic, what matters most—if it's not all that matters—is
the upcoming mayoral election. What will be the consequence of the media
exposure of Byrne's memorandum? If, because the party machinery is working
for him, the mayor is not panicked, he is seriously concerned. His standing in
public opinion polls is sinking; hers is climbing. As predicted, he fires Byrne.
And as suspected, a few months later she announces her candidacy for mayor.

As it turns out, Bilandic now has a bigger problem than the taxicab memorandum. Winter blizzards are crippling the city. For nearly a month, Chicago's
thoroughfares, side streets, and parking places are unplowed and inaccessible.
There's simply too much snow to remove, and too little planning to deal with it.

Everything is stopped, except the frustration and anger jabbing at people's
patience, and into Bilandic's campaign for mayor. Chicago's the city that works,
isn't it? Not in snow like this, it isn't. Never have I seen the city, all of it, as still
as it is. We can't move, which, for days, is a big story in the news, especially on
television, thanks to the pictures. So big that all hands are needed on deck, but
the cameramen, most of whom live in the suburbs, are calling in to say there's
no sense even to try.

I'm scheduled to anchor at ten o'clock, so I have to try, and ought not have
too serious a problem. I'm in Lincoln Park, just a few minutes away. But, as I
open the door into snow above my knees, I know I'm not on easy street. I have
ninety minutes to go thirty blocks. There are buses, cabs, and cars all around,
but they're in the snow going nowhere. I walk it . . . no, trudge it, and do make it.

Question is, will Bilandic make it through the last days of his campaign?
The snow's too much for the city to handle. The guy at the top takes the heat
and, in this case, may get a very cold shoulder.

At six o'clock on February 27, 1979, the polls open to a beautiful morning sun, another blessing for Byrne, because in Chicago elections, good weather bodes well for an underdog candidate challenging the machine. It will ease Jane's job of getting her people out to vote, which means the Regular Democrats, ward committeemen, and precinct captains will have to march more of their people to the polls to defeat her. But they can't do it. The machine's grinding through internal conflicts and media exposure to a halt. Jane Byrne will beat it (by just twenty thousand out of eight hundred thousand votes) to become the first woman to have her hands on the buttons of power in city hall. Chicago politics will never be the same.

Nor will television news. As the Democratic Party falters, so does WLS-TV Channel 7 News. The Democratic Central Committee is losing its troops, Channel 7 News its viewers. Byrne has dumped Bilandic, Bill and Walter are dumping Flynn and Daly. Just six years after Bob Wussler and Van Sauter put us together, Channel 2 News at ten o'clock is fixed in first place. Thirty-one percent of the people watching television, 1,050,000 viewers a night, are watching us.

It's been fourteen years since Channel 2 has been on top. Channel 7's "Happy Talk," the shamefully silly lightweight banter that was introduced as news in Chicago in 1968 and then copied around the country, is out, its numbers no longer sustained by its prime-time lead-ins, *Starsky & Hutch* and *Charlie's Angels*.

News that's news is in. As Kurtis is saying to the press, "We've made broadcast history at this station. Think about it. In the midst of "Happy Talk" and all that nonsense, we went to work and actually covered the news in a responsible fashion. And now we've become number 1. You know, when we started doing this in 1973, it was almost unheard of for a TV station to break a story, to score a real scoop. We mostly followed what the newspapers reported."

Now, the papers are following what we report on malfeasance in local government and politics, and Bill's international scoop on Agent Orange, the deadly herbicide and defoliant sprayed by the US military onto South Vietnam, killing or disabling half a million Vietnamese. We're being encouraged, both of us, or at least permitted by our management, to travel for news—Bill to Vietnam for two weeks before the fall of Saigon in 1975, to Northern Ireland to cover the sectarian warfare, to Rhodesia as it was falling apart, and to Kenya and Tanzania for reports on the plight of black rhinos. Me to East Germany for stories on the underground fighting a Communist regime, and to Eastern Europe and China to report on life behind the iron curtain.

Those dreams of being a foreign correspondent, they're coming true. The letter I wrote twenty years ago to defense minister Lin Baio, and the several more I've written since, finally answered, I've made it to Shanghai, with a television crew, the first local TV news crew from the United States given visas to visit China.

We're prohibited from traveling much beyond Shanghai, and Canton, a few small villages and a commune, and we're almost always accompanied by a government official in a Mao jacket, in a minivan driven by a government driver in a Mao jacket, neither of whom speaks much English. But we're in China, hardly believing what we're seeing. And eating—the monkey I saw in a cage a few minutes ago. At the next table, dog for lunch.

The Chinese are still third world, not yet awakened from the slumber imposed by Mao in 1949, but they're stirring, and their ancient culture is magnificent. In sign language and smiles, in parks and school classrooms in Shanghai, and on walks along the shore of the Huang Pu, where men and women in their eighties and their slippers are doing tai chi, we talk. It's the most exciting experience of my professional life.

For the words and pictures we'll bring home, Channel 2 will give us an hour of air time. And we'll win awards. Thank you, Nielsen (the ratings keeper), for the numbers you've been posting for a year that have given me the clout to get the company to send me and a crew to China. And to East Germany and Poland.

There are more people of Polish ancestry in Chicago than in any other city in the world except Warsaw—a million Polish Chicagoans, a quarter of the white population. How obvious a destination Poland is for a series of reports from the inside. I ask about it and am told to go ahead, into an adventure that will include time in the notorious Auschwitz concentration camp, through the barbed-wire entrance under a sign that reads "Arbeit Macht Frei" (work will set you free), and into the barracks to see the suitcases, clothing, shoes, and hair of the prisoners, and the immense cement shower rooms the Nazis used as gas chambers, the ovens and chimneys of the crematoria, where the atrocities of the Holocaust come to life and tear at our hearts with enough ghastly history for a series of personal commentaries on the ten o'clock news.

The trip to Poland also includes a bad decision I make, my biggest and worst mistake in fifty years of journalism. So big, and so bad, it's hard for me to talk about it.

Roy Smalley, shortstop, my best friend on the Cubs. Author's collection

Queen Elizabeth at the Museum of Science and Industry on her first visit to Chicago. This was my first big assignment for City News Bureau. That's me in the white jacket. (Mayor Richard J. Daley, his wife, "Sis," and Governor Stratton are at left.)

Author's collection

Daily News columnist Jack Mabley and his "legman"—my first job.
Author's collection

Interviewing Martin Luther King Jr. in 1966. He was living at 1550 South Hamlin at the time. Author's collection

Ambushing President Nixon at O'Hare airport. Author's collection

For me, transitioning to a computer was slow and agonizing. Author's collection

The good ol' "Front Page" days. Author's collection

Carol Burnett stops by the anchor desk to talk. Personal collection of Evan Harris; courtesy of WBBM-TV

10:19:07, sports with Johnny Morris, former Chicago Bear wide receiver. Author's collection

With Bill Kurtis on *The Ten O'Clock News*. It must be something I said. Author's collection

Interviewing Mayor Jane Byrne, who was as tough as they come. She knew how to beat us at our own game. Courtesy of WBBM-TV

My all-time favorite picture—my son, Peter, and Muhammad Ali. Author's collection

Chicago's Emmy Award winners. Channel 2 News owns the market. Author's collection

Graffiti in Pilsen neighborhood. Author's collection

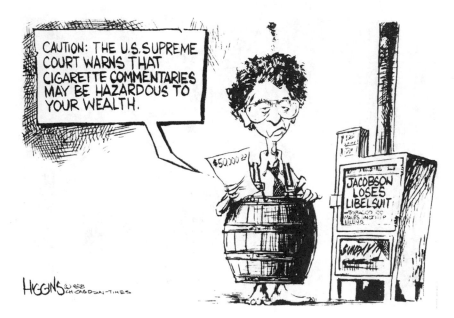

Sun-Times cartoonist Jack Higgins's take on my being convicted of libeling Brown and Williamson Tobacco Corporation. Courtesy of Jack Higgins, *Chicago Sun-Times*

THE PEOPLE WHO QUIT SMOKING CIGARETTES BECAUSE OF WALTER'S "PERSPECTIVE."

THE PEOPLE WHO QUIT SMOKING CIGARETTES BECAUSE OF CIGARETTES.

GUESS WHO GOT CONVICTED.

Another Higgins cartoon. You guessed it—I was the one who got convicted.

Courtesy of Jack Higgins, *Chicago Sun-Times*

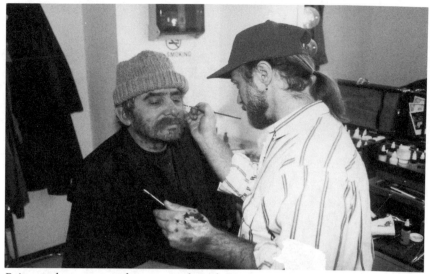

Being made up to go undercover as a homeless person. Courtesy of WBBM-TV

Posing as homeless—the story was a ratings bonanza for Channel 2, then again for Fox. Courtesy of WBBM-TV

Mayor Washington at home in Hyde Park. Off the record, the conversation was fun and lighthearted; on the record, he was strictly business, no messin' around.
Courtesy of WBBM-TV

With Bill Kurtis in Oak Woods Cemetery, where Harold Washington is buried. In the days when news was news. Courtesy of WBBM-TV

Disguised as a waiter, unmasked by Mayor Richard M. Daley at a private party.
Author's collection

With President George H. W. Bush. We had more access to "41" than to "43"; "41" didn't think we were out to get him. Author's collection

Chicago billboard in the days when local TV news had money to burn. Author's collection

Walking with Joseph Cardinal Bernardin at his Gold Coast mansion. A truly wonderful man. Courtesy of WBBM-TV

Interviewing John Wayne Gacy on death row. He was convicted of torturing and murdering thirty-three boys and young men. Courtesy of WBBM-TV

A few moments of R & R with Bob Sirott on WTTW. Personal collection of Evan Harris

With Bill Clinton, who was out of office but still bigger than life. Author's collection

CBS brings us back. An experiment in age and experience versus youth and good looks—Bill's sixty-nine, I'm seventy-three. Maria Ponce Photography

12

Bill Kurtis and the Golden Age of TV News

Lech Walesa is guiding the anti-Communist Solidarity workers' movement in Poland. He's an international symbol of freedom, a superstar hero in Chicago's Polish neighborhoods. In the fall of 1978, I'm scheduled for an interview with him on the same day I'm to meet with Karol Cardinal Wojtyła, the archbishop of Krakow. The archbishop is less known by Chicagoans, not in the news, and not as big a catch as Walesa. However, since the death, two weeks ago, of Pope John Paul, the cardinal's name has been mentioned, though not prominently, as a possible successor. I'll ask him about the selection process, and for his opinion on who will be the next pope, and why.

But Walesa's people tell us there is only a certain time when he is available. There's too little time to interview both him and the cardinal. So, while working in Warsaw, we gather after dinner to choose: Lech Walesa or Cardinal Wojtyła?

The choice is mine, and I say let's pass on the cardinal. Walesa is more current, and front-page. We drive north to Gdansk, where Walesa is waiting for us outside a shipyard. He and I talk for thirty minutes, the crew wraps up, and we're on our way back to Warsaw. Tomorrow, to Chicago, satisfied with what we're bringing home to edit, thinking a job well done.

That is, until the next morning when I walk into the newsroom and see commotion around the monitors, on which white smoke is puffing out of the chimney above the Sistine Chapel in the Vatican in Rome, signal to the world that the church has selected a new pope—the first non-Italian in more than four hundred years, the first Polish pope in history, Karol Jozef Wojtyła, archbishop of Krakow, now Pope John Paul II.

Oh, no. NO. How could I have done it, blown my chance to speak to the man who was about to become prince of the Catholic Church? I could have been the only reporter in the world to have known what Pope John Paul II was thinking, how he was feeling on the eve of his coronation. Ay Yi Yi! Well, sometimes things break your way, sometimes they don't. Having a scoop like that in hand and dropping it is bad news, as we say, as bad as it gets.

The good news (I try not to forget) is that WBBM-TV News is about to own the market. According to the *Sun-Times*, "Channel 2 can securely see itself as Chicago's most popular news operation." In the *Tribune*, "It now appears that Kurtis and Jacobson could be at the beginning of . . . a news dynasty. The Channel 2 audience triumph represents a genuine watershed in Chicago TV history." After scrambling for six years, we seem to be the proof of our pudding that in Chicago and suburbs, there's a thirst for news that is what it's called, and that the managers of the stations understand.

Channel 7 has been wooing us both, Kurtis and me, not just to heal itself, but to wound Channel 2. I'm not privy to what the general manager of Channel 7, Phil Boyer, is saying to Bill, or how often they're talking, but I know Boyer knows my contract's about up, and he's called me a dozen times to persuade me to cross town. And he's telling the newspapers, "I'd love to have Walter at my station. I wouldn't be doing my job if I didn't go after him."

Television news is a take-no-prisoners business. There's a lot of money being made and lost in shuffling anchors. Research shows that it's not the stations that capture viewers and ad agencies; it's the personalities. Secret negotiations abound. Snoops are enlisted to find out what managers, lawyers, and agents are telling, or not telling, each other. Plans are pilfered, dirty tricks abound.

In my case, for example, Channel 7, figuring it's not likely to entice me away from Channel 2, is trying to wound me at 2. It's running an ad in the newspapers that appears to be about the harshness of my "Perspective," and the negative attitude I have about the way city hall bullies people. There's a picture of Fahey Flynn in the ad, smiling, which is fair enough since he's the nicest and most friendly news anchor in Chicago. The ad is promoting a series of reports by Channel 7 on how to beat the blues. It says: "Take positive action against negative thoughts. To make yourself feel better, it is important to reduce the number of negative thoughts you have."

Next to the picture of Fahey is a blackened silhouette of a face that can, with minimum imagination, be seen as mine. Foul, cries a TV critic, wondering if Channel 7 is "using subliminal advertising in a bid to turn viewers against Channel Two anchorman Walter Jacobson. The message, coupled with the silhouette's amazing resemblance to Jacobson, could be a sly effort by Channel 7 to portray rival anchorman Jacobson as a negative, melancholy personality."

If that's what the people at Channel 7 are up to, I have to commend their skills at being malicious without getting caught. Subliminal advertising is a clever and successful strategy for sending messages below the threshold of consciousness. If it works in television news as it works in movies, as our marketing department believes Channel 7 intends it to work, it'll hurt. Who wants to watch a nasty news anchorman?

Phil Boyer, 7's GM, is asked about it and tells the press, "Believe me, I didn't even think of the similarity between Jacobson and our caricature. It wasn't done on purpose. Take a closer look. The chin line is totally different [than Walter's], the glasses aren't quite right, and I don't think Walter's hair is that well styled." I've taken a closer look at the silhouette and see the resemblance. Can't miss it. But it's not affecting the ratings. There's no dip in our numbers, no spurt in theirs. I'd say that if anything, it's good for us, because now it's a controversy. News viewers are reading about the silhouette and Boyer's insistence that it's not a likeness of me and, I'll bet, turning on Channel 2 to check it out for themselves.

In fact, I know that's happening because of all the calls and letters I'm receiving: "Oh, yes, it does look like you. Those nasty people at Channel 7," or "No, it doesn't look anything like you. What're you doing, calling the newspapers to whine about it? You're a creep, Walter. Get lost."

This is not the first time WLS Channel 7 has gone subliminal. Ten years earlier, when it trailed Channel 5, it tried the tactic on Floyd Kalber, whose eminent stature and commanding voice ruled the roost, seemingly invincible. The marketeers at 7 went after Floyd's supremacy with a strategy to depict him as an antique. They created a commercial that ridiculed a haughty, unlikable character who matched Floyd's perceived severity and boldness, or, you might say, his touch of arrogance—an intentional, obvious swipe at Floyd's popularity.

Being on top makes Bill and me water-cooler talk and, for those who don't like us, easy targets. I'm the bigger target because my commentaries are provocative, and sometimes annoying. Bill rarely makes judgments on the air. His work is that of a seasoned network correspondent. He's calm, cool, and respectful, trusted and loved by all. I'm audacious and often a pain in someone's ass, excitable, hot, not trusted and loved by all. Not by any means. But I'm a reason to tune in Channel 2.

By the measures that matter, Bill Kurtis is just flat-out good, like Walter Cronkite. Good enough for CBS News in New York to have its eye on him for a network anchor assignment; I believe that one day CBS will take him from us despite the damage it may do to WBBM-TV in Chicago, its own station. That's definitely something to be concerned about, but what good will it do for me to wring my hands?

We have good things going for us, and opportunities to make them better. If we're careful, maybe we can, as the papers are saying, build a dynasty. Fahey did it, Floyd Kalber did it, dynasties each for a decade. We're working on it, trying to redefine local television news, trying to set new standards for coverage, interpretation and analysis, winning good-journalism awards. Keep in mind, however, that some of our gains have less to do with what we do than with, simply, timing. In a business churned by cycles, it's our turn. After ten years of NBC-WMAQ, and ten of ABC-WLS, it's time for CBS-WBBM. And we're on our way, with a little help from WLS (Channel 7), which, as the 1970s draw to a close, is in free fall.

During just three "sweeps" periods (more on "sweeps" later), the station has lost a disastrous 8 percent of its audience. Its "Happy Talk" numbers are bad because its broadcasts are vacuous and because management has decided, in its infinite lack of wisdom, that the average news viewer in Chicago isn't interested in news, turns it on at night for sports scores and a weather forecast (as often wrong as right) and gossip on who's cuddling whom in Hollywood. Channel 7 seems to be saying to itself that the *National Enquirer* is a popular publication, so let's be the *Enquirer* on our news at ten o'clock. Let's dumb down our newscast enough so that dumb people choose us as their primary source of information.

The Channel 7 anchors, costumed in those pale-blue blazers with 7 in a circle on the hanky pocket, are yapping foolishness, tossing crumpled paper at each other, and serving up the fluff they figure will ease their viewers into slumber at ten-thirty. A case in point—on a night of new developments in the Jonestown tragedy in Guyana, which is the lead story on our ten o'clock news, and on Channel 5's, the performers on Channel 7 lead with four minutes of Heather Bilandic and her husband, Mike the mayor, having a baby.

Channel 2 is by no means perfect in choosing lead stories, but we do weigh the significance of events, placing in our lineup fewer dancing bears, more scrambling politicians. We're trying to respect not just our viewers, but our profession. In investigative reporting, news in depth, and stories that impact on life, are hard. Channel 7 is soft, and there's enough of a difference to make a difference. Channel 2 is winning numbers. Channel 7 is being scorned, which we read as an invitation to do more of what we're doing to widen the gap, spread the word that a good broadcast can be a successful one. It's hard for me to exaggerate how much that means to us.

I'll sign up for three more years, until 1982, and, while I'm at it, why not ask for an increase in pay. Bill and I don't talk money, but the newspaper columnists are reporting that he's at $300,000 a year. I believe that's accurate, because about me they're on the nose at $140,000, which is more money than I ever dreamed of making, much more than reporters are being paid by the newspapers. I'm an anchor on television, where money's not a problem; it runs like water (Katie Couric topped out at CBS at $14 million). I try for $300,000, settle for $250,000.

One justification for seeking a salary like that is tenure; in television, there's precious little of it. Here today, gone tomorrow. Ratings dip, anchors dive, and when we go down, sunk not by bad journalism but the whim of a fickle audience, we lose both income and the stature that's necessary to get paid somewhere else. Like football running backs, when we're down we're out. The scariest part of it is that a plunge in the numbers may have less to do with the newscasts than with primetime lead-ins.

National surveys confirm the assumption that after their favorite shows at nine o'clock at night, a whopping number of viewers stay tuned for the news that follows at ten o'clock. If *Dallas* on Channel 2 at nine has fewer viewers than *Charlie's Angels* on Channel 7, woe be to me. This will become dramatically evident in 2009 when NBC will install Jay Leno in the primetime hour preceding local newscasts. As a result of Leno's low numbers, NBC affiliates will lose some 30 percent of their local news viewers.

I better make that $250,000 now, lest tomorrow it be zero. The salary is grand, no doubt about it, one of the highest in the country for a local anchorman, but I'll work for it. No doubt about that, either. Or about the good assignments I'll get. Or the help from Mayor Byrne.

By "help" I mean she's doing things that make for good commentary—dealing with sexism in Chicago politics, out-maneuvering the late mayor's son, Richard M. Daley, and beating up on the politicians in the city council and the Democratic Party. "Since Byrne's become mayor," says an old-world boss, "I've taken more Gelusil than I took with Daley and Bilandic combined." She's popping-off into people's faces, saying what she thinks, giving me reason to refer to her as "Mayor Popcorn." We can always, always, count on Jane Byrne to make news that's worth comment.

I like that about her, and she's taking a liking to me, so we're developing something of a friendship. It's distanced by our conflicting obligations and mutual suspicions, but close enough to lead us to trust each other, or at least to know each other. She says she thinks I'm objective enough for her to be honest. I think she's honest enough for me to be objective.

In addition to that, occasionally we're having fun with each other, she as mayor, I as reporter. On a blustery day, for instance, she unveils her program for snow removal, featuring a cartoon character for public service announcements on television. "Skippy the Snowball" is its name, which is causing reporters to ask, "Why Skippy?"—the nickname that has stuck with me since I was a reporter for *Chicago's American*. Is she popping-off at me?

"No," she says. "Of course not. 'Skippy the Snowball' is a symbol. He's perky and puffy. You know, skippy."

Next morning, it's in the papers, good news for both of us. She's joshing a reporter, which boosts her image. I'm a reporter being joshed by the mayor, which may boost our ratings—a poor man's Dan Rather being joshed by President Nixon at a convention in Texas in 1974. "Are you running for something?" asked the president in response to one of Rather's questions. "No, Mr. President. Are you?" The exchange was the story of the day and is told as an example of what can make a reporter conspicuous, and hike the ratings of his broadcasts.

I'm getting ahead of myself, but here's an example of Her Honor's media savvy: In 1981, following a surge of inner-city gangbanger violence, and to get a handle on the nature of it, Mayor Byrne moves, unannounced, into the Cabrini Green public housing project and stays there with her husband Jay McMullen (former city hall reporter for the *Chicago Daily News*) for twenty-five days. All the projects are bad; Cabrini is one of the worst. It's a war zone featuring the Gangster Disciples on one side of Division Street, and various rivals on the other. The gangs maintain arsenals of clubs, knives, pistols, rifles, grenades, you name it, anything they can use in combat over Chicago's lucrative drug trade.

In a period of just three weeks, according to police, more than thirty people have been shot at Cabrini, more than ten of them killed. I say "more than" because the police don't have a precise number; they don't patrol the projects enough to be precise. "I'm shocked," speaks the mayor, "not only by the violence, but by the lack of media attention." Cabrini Green is a junkyard of ugly, desolate, terrorized, scarred, and very dangerous buildings not a fifteen-minute walk from $10 million mansions and $300 dinner tabs along the Gold Coast. Twenty thousand poverty-stricken Chicagoans are crammed into Cabrini, ten or eleven children imprisoned in two-bedroom spaces called apartments, in which battalions of cockroaches roam free.

When the mayor, her husband, and the policemen in the adjoining apartment leave, I move into Cabrini Green with a camera crew. That attention she wants and has every right to expect? She's about to get it—pictures on television of the quality (*quality?*) of life, the gangs and, most tragically, the children of Cabrini, in a series of first-person reports on our ten o'clock news.

I sleep in the project only three nights, but my home is nearby, so I've been to Cabrini many times, mixed with the residents, and exchanged stories with the bangers. One of the really good things about being a television news anchor, especially a commentator, is that it opens doors. Because they see so much of us, news viewers bring us into their families. They know us and love to talk to us. And I love to listen because that's the key to our game. Listening.

I couldn't have come along in this business at a better time to listen to talk about Chicago being dunked into a sudden, remarkable watershed. Daley the Boss is dead, and with him have gone twenty-one years, almost a generation, of government and politics by fist, which has made good news and bad—good about buildings and business, bad about race relations and equal rights and opportunities. Good news about law and order, not so good about power to the people.

Byrne, the fist-buster, is commanding monumental change. She's dancing like a butterfly, as Muhammad Ali would have it, stinging like a bee, which for the Chicago media, especially television, is picnic time—pictures of Ms. Mayor in pinstripe suits and bows at her neck that she can't bear to wear, close-ups of the glint in her eyes when she punches the departed Daley's boys, and the sly smiles on her face as she dares them to punch back. And the more determined they are for another round, the more she's enjoying it, the more we're enjoying reporting it. For what more can we ask than ringside seats to the brawls and intrigue of Byrne versus Daley II, Byrne versus aldermen, Byrne versus firemen, Byrne versus Jesse Jackson, Byrne versus TV versus the newspapers.

The mayor and I exchange jabs at news conferences, and in one-on-one interviews. I believe her scrappy independence is good for Chicago, and I like watching her in action. I also like her personally but bug her nonetheless on the issues, and with questions that touch off her Irish, and lead to a Jane-and-Skippy show. She has a show running with Channel 7's political reporter Hugh Hill, too, often wrangling with him during news conferences.

Mayor Byrne knows, much more than Mayor Daley did, about engaging reporters, and which of us is likely to say what about things important to her. When she's sitting on a story she wants told, she knows when and how to leak it to where it will do her the most good. She's up-to-date on which political reporters are watched by how many people, and what each of us thinks about a given issue. She's pretty sure about how the different TV stations will play her story. And if she's not she'll ask, and I'll tell her, as best I can in my interest, how much play it will get on Channel 2 News. She bets on what I say.

This is how it works:

At 5 P.M., I receive a call from one of the mayor's aides who says that Matt Bieszczat, an insider alderman who, during the Byrne administration, is now an outsider, "is refusing to meet with Mayor Byrne. He describes her as a 'blonde bitch who doesn't know what the [bleep] she's doing.' I know how the mayor's gonna shut him up. Your kinda story, Walter. Do you want it?"

"Of course I want it; for when?"

"Tonight at ten."

"You're kidding. Check it out, confirm it, and write it between now and ten o'clock?'

"You won't have a lot to check on this one."

"Okay. What is it?"

"We've done some research on Matt and can tell you . . ."

Reporters rarely received calls like that from Mayor Daley's people. Or, I never did. Daley didn't trust us enough. From Byrne we're getting calls with stories she'll embellish one day in a memoir—about great opera tenor Luciano Pavarotti insisting he ride in a police squad car, not a limousine, to one of Byrne's political fundraisers, and about Pope John Paul II's visit to Chicago.

"When he bowed his head to pray," she says, "I noticed that he would also peek at the people in the crowd to check their reactions. In his white robes and gold sash, he was dressed as the highest-ranking member of the Catholic Church, but when he sat down and crossed his feet I saw that he was wearing brown loafers and white socks. John Paul looked like a regular guy, a Sunday sport who's just come in from a day of golf and thrown his papal robes over his casual clothes."

Daley was more stern than Byrne; she's more entertaining. I admire her knack for compelling us to appreciate her style. And I'm not alone. She's enticing journalists nationwide, drawing them here from everywhere to watch a woman beat up on the Daley Democratic machine, especially in the heat of the 1980 presidential primaries.

Senator Edward Kennedy of Massachusetts is aiming to deny incumbent president Jimmy Carter the party's nomination for a second term. The Chicago boys are for Jimmy Carter, Byrne is for Kennedy, and she's on her way to the Democratic convention in New York to seize the Illinois delegation for her man by flexing mayoral muscle exactly as Daley did when city patronage was his to dispense.

I follow her, to report back on how she's doing—not well. Kennedy's counting twenty-six Illinois delegates, Carter 153. Jane Byrne doesn't have enough clout, not yet, not after just one year in office. But she's becoming the objet d'art of American politics, to the delight of reporters from Chicago, because we're the ones with access.

I know her, and more about her, than the out-of-towners do, and can get her on the telephone faster than most of them can, and get off the phone with more information, which enhances my value to WBBM, and to CBS News. In covering politics, access and inside information win the ratings that win the money that keeps management content with whatever we're doing. For now, the ratings are ours, and they're making management rich. CBS in Chicago is banking some $70 million a year, maybe $20 million of it profit.

"If we establish a success in Chicago," Bill Kurtis predicts, "we'll set a course that'll make a station a winner by building a reputation for presenting news rather than entertainment. We'll start a trend that will cross the country."

Nobody's debating him on that. Channel 2 News is off and up in the right direction, moving fast—until the roof begins to cave in.

13

Brown and Williamson versus Walter Jacobson

The mailman comes to Channel 2 twice a day, not carrying a bag over his shoulder, but pushing a two-by-four-foot canvas container on wheels through the delivery entrance on Erie Street. He checks in at the security desk, rolls his cargo up to a wall of cubbyholes outside the newsroom, and sorts the envelopes by name. Twenty-five or thirty of them go into "Jacobson," a double-size slot, where they pile up until I or my assistants—doing the legwork I did for Jack Mabley at the *Daily News*—spread them in a space between us, to be opened by whichever of us can stay off the telephone long enough to read. Not much of the mail has ideas we haven't thought of, or interesting angles to on-going stories in the news, or details of a person or family being stomped on by Washington, Springfield, or city hall.

But every now and then there comes what we wait for.

For example:

In the fall of 1981, in a hand-addressed envelope postmarked Lexington, Kentucky, comes a letter to me, scrawled and unsigned. "I've heard of your commentaries about the tobacco industry," it says. "I'd like to help you do more. I know of a confidential report on cigarette advertising in the files of the Federal Trade Commission that reveals tactics by the industry to addict children to tobacco."

The letter describes what it says is specific information the FTC has about the Brown and Williamson Tobacco Corporation, which sells Viceroy cigarettes. If I can confirm the existence of a federal report like that, I'll have a mighty good story—maybe not Watergate, but good enough for me. And not too problematic. I won't have to confirm that Brown and Williamson is trying to sell cigarettes to children, just that there's an FTC report accusing it of it.

My assistant, Michael Radutzky (who will go on to be a senior producer at CBS's *60 Minutes*), tracks down the report, which says that Brown and Williamson has asked one of its agencies for advice on how to market Viceroy to young people. It also says that Brown and Williamson has accepted the advice, "adopted many of the ideas" the agency recommends, and "translated the advice on how to attract young 'starters' into an advertising campaign."

Here are some of those ad agency ideas: "For the young smoker, a cigarette falls into the same category as wine, beer, shaving, or wearing a bra . . . a declaration of independence . . . striving for self-identity. Therefore, an attempt should be made to present the cigarette as an illicit pleasure . . . a basic symbol of the growing-up maturity process."

I include those words from the FTC report in a commentary about the tobacco industry peddling cigarettes to children. At the end I say, "That's the strategy of the cigarette slicksters, the cigarette business, which is insisting in public, they're *not* selling cigarettes to children. They're not slicksters, they're liars."

A television commentator telling a million people watching Channel 2 News in Chicago that Viceroy executives "are not slicksters, they're liars." That's it! Enough is enough! The tobacco industry isn't going to take it anymore. It will fight back. Brown and Williamson will sue for libel, demanding $17 million from me and CBS.

I've imagined the scenario a thousand times—a meeting in a wood-paneled, marble-floored, liquor-cabineted corporate conference room; two or three tobacco big shots, salt-and-pepper hair, gray suits, white shirts, rep ties, and (fake) gold cufflinks. A Scotch in a hand of each. None of them is smoking (they reserve the death sentence for the children they're aiming to addict).

"That little fucker in Chicago," I imagine one saying to another. "Let's nail him." Which is precisely what they do. They hire Martin London, one of the toughest, smartest, most aggressive corporate lawyers in the country, onetime counsel to Jacqueline Kennedy Onassis, and to Spiro Agnew, vice president of the United States under Richard Nixon, who resigned when convicted of federal tax evasion.

Channel 2 hires Don Reuben, equally tough and smart, one of the most aggressive criminal and First Amendment lawyers in the country, counsel to *Time* magazine and justices of the Illinois Supreme Court. It's a good match, until Reuben clashes with the general manager of Channel 2 and is dismissed. He's replaced by Tom Morsch, a senior partner at Sidley and Austin, an elite Chicago law firm. He's less experienced than Martin London, and, in courtroom style, exactly the opposite.

London's a street fighter, a bully and bombastic. Morsch is a peacemaker, elegant and reserved. He's afraid of London. He's in over his head. I'm the one who ought to be afraid, not Morsch, but I'm not because I believe Brown and Williamson is biting off more than it can chew, that it can't swallow me if I've done nothing wrong. The law says that to libel is to knowingly report an untruth with "malice aforethought," and I didn't do that (I don't do that). What I reported is true—that the tobacco industry hunts young people, aiming to hook them early, keep them hooked and buying the same brand forever.

But as confident as I am of my innocence, I'm becoming increasingly uncomfortable. When the case comes to trial in 1985, jury selection is difficult, and I read concern in Morsch's eyes. I sense a dislike of me among prospective jurors, one of them a man in his thirties who obviously is enjoying my predicament. Maybe in "Perspective" one night, I said something unkind about a relative or friend, and my being on trial is his chance to get even.

Also in the jury pool is a severe-looking woman with gray hair and steel-rimmed glasses. She's the next to be questioned by the lawyers and is staring at me as though she'd like to slap my face, which makes me think, uh-oh, maybe all the prospective jurors are hiding in wait to put me in my place. The selection process is tedious, because it's not easy to find people in Chicago who don't know of—or don't have strong feelings about—me. I've been anchoring television news programs every night, twice a night, and been a controversial commentator, for twelve years. Those who clearly like me, mostly African American and Latino, are quickly dismissed by Brown and Williamson attorney London.

The competing Chicago television stations are delighted by it all, figuring the trial may bring down Channel 2 News, or at least disgrace it enough to deflate our ratings. Their strategy, however, is, for the most part, to ignore the trial to avoid stirring interest. What if Channel 2 wins?

Not so the newspapers that can boost circulation with stories about me in the docket. They're having at it. At the *Sun-Times*, Robert Feder, distinguished and, by far, the most-read and -respected television columnist in Chicago, views libel as a gravely serious charge that could end my career and permanently damage not only WBBM-TV, but CBS. "It is a huge story," he says. "The number one anchorman in the number three market in the United States facing embarrassment, shame, ridicule by his peers, and what could be millions of dollars in fines . . . not a huge story? Are you kidding?" The *Sun-Times* is splashing news about the trial, and pictures of me, on its front pages.

The commentary at issue in the trial, which I read on the Channel 2 News on Wednesday, November 11, 1981, began:

> Ask the cigarette business how it gets its customers, and you'll be told, over and over again, that it's HARD [my emphasis] to get customers, that the good old days are gone forever. The good old ads for cigarettes cannot be used anymore. Old St. Nick pushing Lucky Strikes because "Luckies are easy on my throat." The cigarette business can't count on THAT anymore . . . or "More doctors smoke Camels than any other cigarette." The business can't count on that anymore, either. Nor can it count anymore on television. Pushing

cigarettes on TV is prohibited. Television is off-limits to cigarettes. And so the business, the killer business, has gone to the ad business in New York for help, to the slicksters on Madison Avenue, with a billion dollars a year for bigger and BETTER ways to sell cigarettes. Go for the youth of America. Go get 'em, guys . . .

My conclusion that the tobacco executives are "liars" is, I believe, what caused me to be a defendant in a libel suit being reported cross-country, and that has since become the subject of lectures in law school.

The *Merriam-Webster Dictionary* defines libel as "injuring a person's reputation by means of something printed or written or by some visible representation that gives an unjustly unfavorable impression of a person or thing." My language in the commentary was unjust? I believe not.

It is a fact, isn't it, that the tobacco industry is peddling poison? Cigarettes are, are they not, killing people? A cigarette advertisement using the word "recess," and picturing a boy and girl, just off their bikes in front of a fountain smoking cigarettes, is designed to attract young people, isn't it? So what's unjust about my comments that tobacco is harmful and that when the tobacco CEOs say they're not going after young people, they're lying?

(About a dozen years after that commentary was on our ten o'clock news, the CEOs of the largest tobacco companies in America were summoned to congressional hearings in Washington and questioned about their marketing strategies. Under oath, they acknowledged their efforts to target children. This means, to me, that in fact they were lying when they previously insisted they were not targeting children. The federal courts and the national press scorched the tobacco industry for its blatant attempts to conceal the devastations of addiction. "The tobacco companies have engaged in deceitful and harmful behavior for many decades," the *New York Times* scolded, "and cannot be trusted to reform." A US Court of Appeals found big tobacco companies guilty of racketeering and fraud as part of a "prolonged campaign to deceive and addict the public . . . false statements and suppressed evidence to deny or play down the addictive qualities and the adverse health effects of smoking." The courts also have found "volumes of evidence" and "countless examples of deliberately false statements" made by the companies to avoid restrictions on the sale of cigarettes. And Congress passed a law to prevent the tobacco companies from selling cigarettes near schools, and from adding to cigarettes tasty flavors that appeal to children.)

Meanwhile, back in the federal building at Jackson and Dearborn, a jury is being chosen. Court is being called to order. I'm beginning to realize how serious this is and am agonizing over what it may be doing to me. What I may have done to myself. Apart from whatever verdict there may be, how much damage is being caused by the day-to-day publicity? Certainly, it's not doing me or WBBM-TV any good.

Kurtis and I, everybody at Channel 2 News, have worked so long and so hard to get where we are in the ratings, and to earn CBS an inordinate amount of respect (and money). Can those two and a half minutes of mine spoil everything? One commentary out of more than a thousand in seven years, can it undermine the trust we've built in not only Channel 2 News, but in local television news coast-to-coast? TV stations everywhere are viewing tapes of our broadcasts, talking about how we're doing them, and trying to turn some of our magic into their own. They'll be following the testimony, and the attention being paid to it by the Chicago press.

After jury selection, before the trial begins, the day before opening arguments, I meet with my WBBM general manager at Sidley and Austin to talk strategy. Do the lawyers think that on the first day I ought to be in the courtroom? Or will it be better for me to be in the newsroom, or on the street, working—to send a message to the jurors that I'm sure of the truthfulness of my commentary and that I'm not about to be intimidated by Martin London?

If I'm not on the air with a commentary, will Channel 2 viewers think I've been taken off and interpret my absence as an admission that I committed libel? The lawyers advise me to go to work instead of to court. So I do—and am clobbered by the newspapers: "Cigarette companies have been under fire in this country for years" writes Tom Fitzpatrick, Pulitzer Prize–winning columnist, in the *Sun-Times*. "Marriages and friendships break up over smoking habits. Fistfights break out in restaurants over cigars. One would think Jacobson can't lose. But he can certainly blow it if the jury gets the idea he thinks he's too important to attend his own trial."

Not good.

The next morning I'm in my seat at the defendant's table, appropriately dressed in suit and tie, and paying attention. In the *Sun-Times*:

> Channel 2 anchorman Walter Jacobson has had a change of heart about being a no-show at his own libel trial—thanks to *Sun-Times* columnist Tom Fitzpatrick. Jacobson showed up in court, [and] he's expected to spend a lot more time in the courtroom than in his Channel 2 newsroom—or more than he and his lawyers originally planned.
>
> Two spokesmen for the station told us Jacobson hadn't suddenly changed his mind about attending, and that Fitz's admonition had no effect on their strategy. Then we talked to Walter. "Sure I respect Tom Fitzpatrick," he said, "and when I read his column I did feel an urgency to spend more time at the trial. When Tom Fitzpatrick says something, I listen."

There I go again, contradicting my bosses. I'm a loose cannon, I know it, and I'm trying to be careful, and to pick my moments. It's hard for me to clam up or to lie to the media. I can't (I don't) have a double standard. When I'm the reporter asking a question, I expect an honest answer. When I'm answering a reporter's question, I expect myself to be honest. What's good for the goose is good for the gander, right? (There goes one of those underused clichés.)

The truth is, yes, I'm in the courtroom because of Fitzpatrick's column. Every journalist in town knows it. My bosses know it. In fact, they're the ones who decided I'd better, "change my mind."

On my way to court each morning, I'm slower getting up and out than I am on my way to the newsroom. The hours in front of judge and jury are monotonous, the testimony weighted by legalese. I'm angry at the lawsuit, chafing at being a defendant, and furious at Martin London for his theatrics, and his flagrant accusations that I wrote, and Channel 2 aired, the commentary to spike the ratings.

"Walter Jacobson has defamed the Brown and Williamson Tobacco Company," London rages, "and we demand justice!" He's pointing at me all the time, and bellowing that I made things up, that I lied, and set out to destroy the company. After hours of his calumny, sometimes I just close my eyes and float my way into nothingness, or doodle on a notepad. Other times, I think about my children, Wendy and Peter, and how much this must be hurting them.

I've asked. "It didn't hurt," Peter remembers. "I heard you griping on the telephone about London and the judge. Your language was really bad. But you never seemed upset enough for me to be afraid. My friends didn't care. Those who knew about it, thought you did the right thing. I was in an airport when I saw you on a front page, surrounded by cameras and reporters. I thought you're the one who's hurting, and I looked around to see if anyone was looking at me looking at you. But, at home, I don't remember you feeling bad. I think you were protecting us. I wasn't worried about you."

"Same for me," says Wendy. "I never thought you were in trouble."

"Weren't you embarrassed?" I ask. "Wasn't Peter?"

"No, we weren't. You didn't seem fazed by it, so we weren't. Nothing seemed to faze you. Nothing fazes you, Dad. You show your feelings when you're railing at somebody on television, but you don't show them to us. That's you. I don't know if it's good or bad, but when you came home from court, you acted like what happened in court that day didn't matter much to you, so it didn't matter much to us."

At the end of my two weeks at that defendant's table, the jury finds me guilty of libeling Brown and Williamson Tobacco. On my way out of the building, off the elevator, I step into flashing lights and dozens of cameras and television and radio reporters. The scene is like what you've watched a hundred times on the news at the end of a mobster's trial when he gets off the elevator, wrapped in coat and fedora, dodging reporters to a waiting car. Except that I don't dodge. I stop cold, paralyzed by the crowd confronting me.

Would I do anything different if I were writing the commentary today, I'm asked by three or four reporters all at once. "No," I insist with too much haughtiness, "I wouldn't do anything different." And later, to Feder of the *Sun-Times*, I say that Martin London is "an angry, flamboyant bully who was brought in here to intimidate me, and he convinced a jury of eight people with his histrionics in court that I did something I did not do. In all the years I've been doing commentaries, I never, ever, knowingly put something false on the air. Never."

And on and on I go (shut up already!): "There was not an attempt in that courtroom to get to the truth. Nobody said to me, either London or my lawyer or the judge or jury, 'Will you kindly stand up here, and tell us what happened.' Every time I tried, London cut me off." I'm learning the hard way how unwise it was for me to be talking as I did off the elevator. At London's urging, describing me as unrepentant, the jury sets the penalty for libel at $5 million from CBS, half a million from me personally. An appellate court reduces the penalties to $3 million from CBS and $50,000 from me, which will be covered by CBS insurance.

It's hard to say how our ratings are being affected by all this, but neither WBBM-TV nor CBS is particularly bothered by it. Or, they don't seem to be. Nobody in the newsroom, or in the big offices upstairs, is calling me to task. Managers are not imposing restrictions on my commentaries, or even examining them more rigorously before air than they used to.

As unfair as I think the verdict is, and as much as I hurt, my guilt appears to have no impact beyond the front pages of the newspapers. And even that's not too painful, because after the headlines—"Jacobson Guilty"—there are media portrayals of me as the good guy. David versus Goliath.

The *Chicago Lawyer* magazine, for example, publishes a five-page article under the headline "The Wrong Verdict." The publication reports that interviews with jurors "indicate that they did not understand the threshold issue of whether Jacobson's derogatory broadcast about Brown & Williamson Tobacco Corporation was a fair and accurate summary of a government report." The magazine has interviewed six of the eight jurors (two declined) and "found all to be seriously confused about the issue. Some did not realize that the report said Brown & Williamson had translated the marketing firm's advice into an advertising campaign."

More impactful, due to a picture being worth a thousand words, are the editorial cartoons—a drawing of people in a park, fit and healthy, one of them jogging, under the words "The People Who Quit Smoking Cigarettes Because of Walter's Perspective." Next to it, a drawing of tombstones in a cemetery, under the words "The People Who Quit Smoking Cigarettes Because of Cigarettes."

A headline over Tom Fitzpatrick's column shouts, "Walter Is Paying for Being Walter." Martin London, a true barrister in the nastiest sense, maneuvered the jury into believing that with malice aforethought, I distorted facts in order to damage the company's reputation and its capacity to make money. He confused the jurors. It's a mistake to believe that our system of justice gets to the truth, or that it even tries to.

I learned from the experience how hard it is for me to muzzle my frustration and anger at being powerless to defend myself against false accusations, and to steel myself against the onslaught of a curious press. I was on the bad side of a good story, the subject instead of a reporter covering it.

Will I lose my job? Is my journalism finished? Luckily, the answer to my own questions is "No." But since the trial I have tried to be more sensitive to the fears and misery of people being prosecuted in federal court, even the disgraced former governors George Ryan and Rod Blagojevich.

14

A New Mayor, a Controversial Minister, and an Old Nemesis

C hicago, of course, does not come to a standstill during a four-year battle between me and the tobacco industry. In 1983, Mayor Jane Byrne is voted out of office after a single term. Harold Washington is in, elected to be the first African American mayor in Chicago history.

What a story! He emerges from a three-way free-for-all in the Democratic primary—Byrne versus Washington versus Daley, Richard M., the son, who splits the white vote with Byrne, while Washington runs off with the black vote complemented by just enough white votes to win. The totals are 30 percent for Daley, 33 percent for Byrne, 37 percent, and the keys to the fifth floor, for Washington, the son of a precinct captain, a track star, the only African American in his Northwestern Law School class (1952), former state legislator, and member of the US Congress.

"Harold, Harold" is what greets him where he goes, which isn't very far very often from the liberal-independent lakefront, or the University of Chicago in Hyde Park, or the south-side-west-side inner city. He's fresh air to reporters, inspirational to minorities, hope to the poor, scary to the rich, and a stranger to the rank and file in city hall, who stoke fires in the council, and add to his appeal to reporters.

As we counted on Mayor Byrne to surprise us with things unexpected, we're now counting on Mayor Washington to interest and entertain us by inflaming the establishment. He doesn't disappoint, so he's a breeze—and a storm—to cover. For me, less breeze, more storm, which begins to gather on the day he takes the oath during a spectacular inauguration under the big roof over the east end of Navy Pier. Not a good day for me.

I'm assigned, along with Harry Porterfield, Channel 2's only African American anchor, to host live coverage. On a TV monitor, we look not unlike anchors at a desk at a political convention. It's impossible for me to exaggerate the significance of the event.

Four thousand people have gathered at the pier to watch Washington take the oath, and who knows how many more are watching on television. As the VIPs are taking their places on-stage, too many of them unhappily, and the hoi polloi their seats in the crowd, Harry and I are doing play-by-play. His focus is on what this means to Chicago's black community and to African Americans nationwide. My focus is on the politics. Who's here from where, and why. Who's not, and why. Who's closest, and furthest, from the mayor-elect, and why is that.

The seating invites observation ("Look at the look on Jane Byrne's face.") and speculation ("I don't see Alderman Burke or Vrdolyak. If they're on the stage, they're way in the back, where Harold stuffed them, or where they choose to be?"). The ceremony is an emotional, tearful, heart-thumping moment in the peppery history of Chicago politics.

"In our ethnic and racial diversity, we are all brothers and sisters in a quest for greatness," speaks Harold Washington, he of warm and searching eyes and tangible smile. "We will not rest until the renewal of our city is done. I reach out my hand, and ask for your help."

"Will he get it?" I ask Harry, then answer my own question. "It depends on the damage he can do to the aldermen in the council who won't give it."

The broadcast is going well for us until the Chicago Children's Choir sings "Lift Every Voice and Sing," the black national anthem, after which I turn to Harry to tell him, and Chicago and the suburbs and my management and fellow reporters, that I don't know the music. I ask Harry, poor guy, "What is it?"

What's my coanchor to do with a shallow, brainless, insulting question like that? The only thing he can do—look not too shocked, and, as gently as possible, tell me it's the black national anthem, which is telling thousands of African Americans who are watching television, and thousands more who will hear about it tomorrow, that Channel 2's anchorman and commentator, Walter Jacobson, has never heard the black national anthem, and doesn't even know it exists. Think of the ramifications of that: Walter is just plain stupid, or he couldn't care less. It's the beginning, I think, or at least an omen, of some bad times ahead.

For the politics of our new Mayor Washington, it's a good omen. Not yet one day in office, he already has a high-profile media foil—a white reporter who doesn't give a wit about the black national anthem. In the sport of Chicago politics, television news bats clean-up, enormously influential in shaping public opinion, especially about elected officials. Harold Washington, like mayors everywhere twenty-four-seven, tries to maximize or minimize the impact of news, depending on what reporters and commentators are saying about it.

When I'm rough on Mayor Washington (which I ought to be, which all reporters ought to be, rough on all mayors), it's in his interest to maximize my words in a way to raise questions about my credibility, especially among African

Americans. Spread the message that I'm a honky, as he does at a luncheon of the Chicago Television Academy in the packed ballroom of a downtown hotel.

After delivering a speech about how reporters are covering his new administration, he opens up for questions. I rise, but before I can ask it, he reminds me, and the audience, of a "Perspective" I did about work being done in his apartment in Hyde Park.

I had followed a tip to take pictures of a man in painter's pants carrying a bucket and brushes into the mayor's building. Then I said on the air, "We've been given information that painters employed by the city are up there doing some decorating." And I said I called the mayor's press office and was told the decorating was being done by the mayor's friends, whom he was paying personally. I concluded by saying, "Ask [city hall] who the painters are, and you are told that the information will be provided. But it's not. You are told that your call will be returned, but it's not. So what we have is a brand new mayor, and the same old story."

A report in the *Tribune* about the academy lunch noted that the mayor "lowered his head toward Jacobson and scowled. Jacobson looked stunned, took a step back, and tried again to ask his question. The mayor would have none of it. 'I'm talking about when you accused me of having city workers paint my home,' he snapped. 'You're not honest. You don't have the wherewithal to do [your] job. You're the bottom of the barrel.'"

I'm unnerved, that's for sure, but I respond: "That story I did was about how a reporter can't get information out of city hall." His response to my response, to a now stilled banquet hall: "You gave the impression I got city employees to come to my apartment and paint my apartment at city expense."

When the luncheon ends, and as he is leaving the hotel, Mayor Washington is surrounded by reporters, I among them. Asked about the bottom of the barrel, he twinkles, turns to me, and says, "Walter, you're okay," and to the crowd, "Walter's the best thing since Campbell's soup."

"So then, why," I ask, "did you call me 'the bottom of the barrel?' And in front of all those people?"

"I was just kidding." A reporter who was there, an independent producer for WBBM, is quoted in the *Tribune*: "Walter stood his ground. But, I'll tell you, when I do a story on the south side now, I hate to say I'm from Channel 2. They all think Walter's a racist."

Fear of this causes me to be more tentative than I ought to be in reporting and commentary on government and politics. Harold Washington, mayor—like Barack Obama, president—ought not be treated more tenderly than white politicians. But because I fear, as my station managers do, the weight of being labeled racist, my instinct for self-preservation kicks in, even subconsciously, which leads me sometimes, I admit, to lean over backwards in search of more good things than bad things to say about him.

That's a problem in black-mayor–white-press relations. In "Perspective" and investigative reporting, I had better blind myself to color. Although black elected officials in Chicago are more sensitive to criticism, I believe that's not a reason for holding them to less stringent standards of behavior that white ones.

My times with Mayor Washington are more knotty than they were with Byrne or Daley—Byrne and Daley combined. Washington's press secretary, Grayson Mitchell, tells the newspapers that he catches me in "factual errors about every two weeks," and the mayor himself often says, "Jacobson doesn't know what he's talking about."

Although WBBM research on me finds my most loyal viewers in Chicago's minority neighborhoods, the heat I get from ethnic politicians burns hot because it's tinged with accusations of racism. A disagreeable "Perspective" about a minority public official almost always triggers a chorus of snarls.

Example: When I comment about state senator Richard Newhouse, an African American running for mayor, I run afoul of the *Chicago Metro News*, which circulates on the south side. My opinion, expressed delicately on our ten o'clock broadcast, is that state senator Richard Newhouse starts out with two strikes against him—his marriage to a white woman may lose him black support, and his position against the Equal Rights Amendment may cost him the votes of liberals and political independents. The *Metro News* hollers, "Walter Jacobson, anchorman on CBS television news, recently proved again his usual white, Jewish racist self, . . . using the media to brainwash people. He never comments about his sex relations with black women and his sneaking back north in the morning."

Also drawing a fierce reaction is my commentary about a death threat received by A. T. Tsoumas, state director of financial institutions. I report he's being guarded by a security detail of twenty-three state troopers; I question the necessity of that big a force. The National Greek Press accuses me of endangering Tsoumas's life, and describes me as a "miniature Goebbels," reichsminister of propaganda in Nazi Germany.

When I report some internal feuding among Harold Washington insiders, Reverend Jesse Jackson kicks up another one of his tornadoes. He says I'm displaying "poor taste." And he says, inaccurately, that I have "not walked on a South Side or West Side street in recent history, and he has not put a foot under a black table to eat. He has no credibility."

A safer place for me in black Chicago will come years later where I would never, ever, expect to find it—in the living room of Louis Farrakhan, commander of the Nation of Islam, a Muslim organization of some thirty thousand members headquartered in Chicago. Having succeeded Malcolm X and Elijah Muhammad, Minister Farrakhan is known in America, and feared (by whites), as a strident advocate of separating the races, of blacks living in a country of their own within the United States. Farrakhan had been dubbed by the media, most noticeably by the tabloids in New York, as an anti-Semite who preaches that Judaism is a "gutter religion." His Mosque Maryam on Stony Island between Seventy-Third and Seventy-Fourth Streets is the nation's flagship house of worship.

In the mid-1990s, Farrakhan is first on my list of interviews that are hard to get. I've asked for access so many times that his son, who's his chief of staff, and I have become telephone buddies. But the answer, always the same, is a polite "No, thank you." Until the minister decides, one day, to invite me to his home, a big (I'd guess fifteen thousand square feet) and strong construction of yellow stone surrounded by a forbidding wrought-iron fence in an integrated neighborhood walking distance from the University of Chicago.

Why has he changed his mind, I wonder. Maybe he just tired of my pestering. Maybe, but I doubt it. More likely is the clamor by the media that he's anti-Semitic.

I suspect he thinks that if he explains his "gutter religion" remark to me, a Jew, and that if I listen and seem willing to understand, he may be able to put it behind him. My camera crew and I are buzzed through a gate, stopped at the front door, greeted by three outsized men in suits, white shirts, and black bow ties. We are warmly, if suspiciously, led into a foyer, where we are frisked, instructed to remove our shoes, and motioned into Farrakhan's living room.

Two stuffed chairs facing each other on a lush white carpet are waiting, microphones on the armrests. A grand piano, couch, plants, lights, cameras, technicians—and tension—fill the space. I'm about to get a major scoop. His three lieutenants are about to watch their minister being grilled by a reporter they expect to be difficult.

Some history: I met Louis Farrakhan two years earlier at a news conference following one of his speeches. After the conference, we spoke for twenty minutes and, because of his lack of pretense, how earnest he is, and the degree to which he's been demonized by the press, I liked him. Or, maybe it was he just took a liking to me. Maybe he trusted me. Whatever it was, we enjoyed those few minutes together, and I asked him if he'd sit down with me for an on-camera conversation. "Sure," he answered. "Someday."

"Is that a promise?"

"Yes, it is."

Well, he's keeping it, stepping into the living room, dressed in a dark suit and, like the legions at his rallies, a bow tie. He's comfortable. So I am, too. We talk for an hour, about the Nation of Islam, separatism, his childhood and parenting, his love of classical music, his mother encouraging him to play a violin, his lessons, practice, and performances. I'm surprised to hear how much he enjoys playing solo in front of small orchestras. I enjoy answering his questions about my life.

I know he knows I'm looking for an opening, through which to pounce on "Judaism, the gutter religion." When it comes, I ask:

"You are often portrayed by the media as an anti-Semite . . . being anti-Semitic. Are you?"

"No, Walter. I'm not anti-Semitic. I'm not anti any religion."

"But you've called Judaism a 'gutter religion.'"

"As I've said so many times, that was taken out of context."

"What do you mean by 'out of con—'"

"As a Muslim, I revere Abraham and Moses, like all the prophets who Allah sent to the children of Israel. I believe in the scriptures brought by the prophets, as expressed in the Torah."

"Why, do you think you—"

"Over centuries, the evils of Christians, Jews, and Muslims have dirtied their respective religions. We have received a message from God to purify us from our evil that has divided us, and caused us to fall in the gutter."

I don't need to press him beyond that. I'm not up to discussing God, or religions of the world. Certainly, not with a minister. This isn't a debate. I'm here to record what Louis Farrakhan says, however he wants to say it. And to get a peek at his private side. We talk about his being a Cubs fan, my having been a Cubs batboy, and about the Bears, and what he does in his downtime. I tell him he has to take more of it, to not work so hard. He laughs and says he'll try.

We're relaxed, and having a good time. I'm thinking, Oh, my God (speaking of God), do I have a good one! The producers'll run five minutes of this on our ten o'clock news, every night for a week, and we'll turn it into a sixty-minute special report. This is very interesting, exclusive stuff. Even CBS News will want some of it.

As the interview ends, I say something about food—does he like to eat out—which prompts the minister to lead me into his kitchen, cameraman following. He introduces me to his cook and housekeeper, who reveals that he's home most of the time, and that his diet consists largely of fresh fruits and vegetables. Clearly, I'm on a roll, and I think I can get away with a comment about how fit he looks, and asking him a question about exercise. What if I ask if he has a workout room and, if he does, will he permit us to take pictures of him lifting weights. He may say okay.

But enough's enough, except that I do have to ask one last thing—will he show me just a little more of his home, to which he says "by all means," and he takes us to a small garden atrium topped by a skylight about twenty, maybe thirty feet up. We talk about peace and quiet, at the end of a very special day for me, and for Channel 2.

I'm in a hurry to get Farrakhan edited and onto a broadcast before he remembers making a promise to another reporter who may beat me to it. I have to presume the Nation of Islam wants "gutter religion" put to rest, and is doing what it can to spread the minister's gospel that he is not an anti-Semite. (Based on my time with him during and after that interview, and on encounters yet to come, and on my confidence that he can't get something by me, I believe Louis Farrakhan is not anti-Semitic. I'll take flak for that assessment, for failing to push harder on the subject, even for giving Farrakhan air time. All I can say is that I base my judgment about the man on our time spent face to face. I've interviewed thousands of people over the years, and I think I've learned how to determine if someone is being straight with me or selling me the Brooklyn Bridge. I respect the right of others to criticize my assessment, but that doesn't mean I have to change it.)

I'm eager to get the interview on the air also because it's not just a good story, but a story about good in the inner city, about a minister preaching hope instead of gangbangers selling dope. Pictures of a black man in a beautiful home, playing a violin, instead of in a paddy wagon on his way to jail.

That's good news on television, of which we have not nearly enough, and must have more. Our daily menu, stuffed with violence (if it bleeds, it leads), is stereotyping black Chicago as a colony of crime, in which killers and thieves are involved in every imaginable disorder. A night doesn't pass without pictures on Channel 2 News, and all the other channels, of an African American in handcuffs or on the lam, or on a stretcher or in a coffin, a victim of violence by a neighbor.

Except for white cops, faces in crime scenes on TV are black. A story about a burglary, and the story following it, and the one after that—are they so informative that we *must* tell them? Yes we must, I am told, because crime is news, and we can't suppress it, and we need to warn the neighbors, and if the other stations tell it and we don't, they'll get the ratings and we won't.

I say no, it's not a must. We ought to be conscious of the consequences of reporting black crime; and when it's not urgent, we ought to set it aside, do what we can whenever we can to arrest the polarization that we are inciting. Our interviews, editorials, and commentaries bemoan the divide between white and black, while we, ourselves, are widening it. Because I'm an anchorman, I have to read those unnecessary stories and show the pictures. Over the years, when I complain about it, or refuse to read what I believe ought not be read, I've been reprimanded and warned by the news director to behave myself.

"Cut it out," he scolds, bounding out of his office to a ruckus at the anchor desk, where I'm upbraiding a producer for including mug shots of a black man arrested during a domestic disturbance. A domestic disturbance!

Think of how many domestic disturbances there are every day in greater Chicago, a metropolitan area of more than seven million people. If a domestic disturbance I'm instructed to read isn't news, I don't want to read it. Two minutes to air is a bad time to start a fight, but using a mug shot, especially of an African American in a domestic disturbance, rubs me so wrong I burst.

"C'mon, Jay" (news director Jay Feldman). "Goddamn it. Why do we have to show pictures of some poor guy in a housing project locked up for fighting, allegedly fighting, with his wife? We don't even know that he's done anything wrong, just that she called 911. There are a thousand stories out there that mean things to people. Why do we have to tell this one? Please don't make me read it. Or, at least let's not use the mugs."

Fat chance. Not only do I read the story, with mug shots, but when the broadcast is over, I'm told to leave the newsroom, and to not come back for two days. Suspended. All of which is leaked to the press, so I'm becoming a story about the most difficult anchor in Chicago, the arrogant anchor, a condescending, belligerent, bellicose Peck's Bad Boy. So be it. Whatever the price, I'll just have to pay it.

For a variety of reasons, I'm drawing heat from all corners, most publicly from the newspaper columnist Mike Royko, himself an arrogant, condescending, belligerent, bellicose Peck's Bad Boy. Payback, perhaps, for that day in the Cook County building when I ran off with press releases about a tax increase, scooping him big time. His manner of rant, his way of handing me my lunch, page 3 in the *Daily News*:

> While being interviewed on a TV show recently, Walter Jacobson made a shocking and scurrilous personal attack on me. For days, people have been asking if I am going to respond to Jacobson's allegation. My children have been coming home in tears, their ears ringing with the jeers of their playmates. My employer has called me on the carpet and demanded to know if the charges are true. Like Mayor Daley, I prefer not to respond to reckless mudslinging. But in this case, I have no choice. I did not see the TV show myself, but according to a spokesman, Jacobson flatly stated on the air that he and I are friends. He did not offer any evidence to back up his charge.

Royko's typewriter is prickly as a pin; but is also, when he wants it to be, very funny.

Here he is, not funny:

> Not long ago, Walter wrote a glowing introduction for a recently published book about Chicago politics. It happens that I read the book even before Walter did. I hope he won't be hurt, but the publisher came to me before it was printed and asked me to write the introduction. I told him to bug off because the book was one of the most amazingly idiotic pieces of drivel, junk and pointless blabber that I had ever read. . . . I have not mentioned the title of the book, and I won't. I don't want to encourage anyone to waste $1.95 even out of curiosity. If you feel the need to get rid of $1.95, you might send the money directly to Walter and urge him to use it as tuition for some kind of literature course.

One more Royko column slapping me around, the one under a headline "Wee, Wee Walter." It's about my being five-foot-seven: "Walter's size is the reason he's obsessed by potholes. He's not worried about ruining a tire; he fears that he will tumble into a pothole someday, won't be able to climb out, and a city crew will come along and bury him under a pound of asphalt."

Royko's disdain for not only me, but television news, is boundless. He writes that a TV anchorman is hired for the "lilt in his voice, the tilt of his nose, the gleam in his teeth, the curl of his lip, and the fullness of his hair." He's not entirely wrong about that, but why such venom?

My conjecture is that like his fellows in print, Royko begrudges us our salaries and high profiles, and the fact that more people watch the news on television than read it in the papers. I can't be sure, though, of the source of his loathing because I never talked with him about it. No bellying to a bar for me with Mike Royko. He wouldn't hear of it, and I'd be uneasy. He's a grouchy guy. After a slurp too many, he turns treacherous, egging for a fight, too tough for me. But I've come upon a way if not to punch him out, to at least knock him down—from an anonymous tip about his lifestyle. Mike Royko, the celebrated Everyman who cultivates an image of a blue- collar ethnic, "lives among snoots on North Lake Shore Drive in a luxury condominium overlooking a beach. Check it out, Walter," which I'm delighted to do, discover its accuracy, and am happy to report on the ten o'clock news that Royko is not, as he tells us he is, a Bungalow Baby, a Basement Child, a Flat-above-a-Tavern Youth who never lived any more than staggering distance from Milwaukee Avenue, a Neighborhood Man from shot glass to long underwear, linoleum from Sears.

"None of that stuff," I say. "Truth is that Royko lives a ten-speed-bike distance from Oak Street. He's a high-rise man from his Perrier to his Calvin Klein jeans and a futon mattress." I reveal his lakeshore digs to a million people watching Channel 2, more than twice the number of people reading his columns about me being, as he puts it, "a midget . . . bouncing in his chair at an anchor desk."

I've caught him so for-sure that he's compelled to write, "Because it's already been the subject of an expose by a TV commentator, I might as well make a full confession. Yes, I have moved into a condominium along the city's lakefront. As the commentator indignantly raved, I am no longer a resident of one of the city's inland neighborhoods." Ah, my sweet revenge.

Of course, our war of words is good for both of us, luring his readers to me and my viewers to him, while CBS is luring Bill Kurtis to New York.

15

Council Wars and Newsroom Woes

I t's 1982. Kurtis is leaving Chicago for New York, leaving the station, leaving me, to cash in the chip he was given nine years earlier for coming to WBBM, a chance for a bite of the Big Apple—an anchor chair on *The CBS Morning News*. He'll be teaming up with Diane Sawyer, whose destiny is to go to ABC to become the second woman in television history to solo anchor a network broadcast. (The first will be Katie Couric on *The CBS Evening News*, after coanchoring *The Today Show* on NBC.)

"Musical Chairs" is the name of our game. In Chicago, the list of flagship news anchors who've jumped ship or walked the plank during my years include Fahey Flynn from WBBM to WLS, Carol Marin from WMAQ to CBS to WTTW to WMAQ, Ron Magers from WMAQ to WLS, Robin Robinson from WBBM to WFLD, Don Craig from NBC to WMAQ to WBBM. Mark Suppelsa from WMAQ to WFLD to WGN, Jim Ruddle from WGN to WMAQ, John Drury from WBBM to WGN to WLS to WGN to WLS, Diann Burns from WLS to WBBM (for a reported $2 million a year!), Floyd Kalber from WMAQ to NBC to WLS, Bob Sirott from WMAQ to WFLD to WTTW to WMAQ to WFLD, Kurtis from WBBM to CBS to WBBM to CBS to WBBM, and me from WBBM to WMAQ to WBBM to WFLD to WBBM.

Reasons for change vary, of course, but quite likely the most dramatic one ever in Chicago television news was Carol Marin's. She was anchoring the ten and six o'clock broadcasts with Ron Magers on WMAQ Channel 5 when, in a stunt to gain ratings, management installed Jerry Springer as a news commentator. It was 1997. Springer was at his peak hosting an enormously popular, but awful—he called it "garbage"—daytime tabloid talk show. Either he goes off our broadcasts as a commentator, warned Marin, or I go. He didn't, she did, and Magers soon followed.

Marin landed at CBS News as a network correspondent and WBBM as an investigative reporter. In 2000, WBBM named her solo anchor of a "no-frills," hard-news broadcast at ten P.M. Fewer stories, more in-depth reporting. Result? A dip in the ratings, and Marin is gone. Her talent universally respected, she is, as of this writing, political editor at WMAQ, a regular on WTTW's *Chicago Tonight*, and a columnist at the *Chicago Sun-Times*.

For Bill Kurtis, New York is the mother of all moves, the one he's been aiming at, clearly has earned, and may take him a step closer to being tapped to succeed Dan Rather. It's right for him, wrong, we fear, for WBBM. The "Q" ratings that rank anchor popularity in Chicago have Kurtis in first place, with an unimaginable score of ninety-eight, which means that 98 percent of the news viewers who watch him like him (Fahey Flynn is next, then me).

The press is saying that Kurtis's "Q" may be the highest in the nation, not the kind of anchor a station cares to lose. He's being replaced by Don Craig, a seasoned NBC network correspondent who's been anchoring at Channel 5. The hold that WBBM has on the market has been with Bill-and-Walter. With Don Craig, who can predict?

What worked for Bill and me was the comfort factor, the chemistry. We're good friends who've worked together for a long time. He knows instinctively when I'm about to pop off, and how to handle it. I know he knows, so I don't pause to think about it. Our signals to each other, under the desk off-camera, or up-front, in full view of the camera, delivered by eye or gesture, tell us what to expect, and what to do. He reads a story about Mayor Byrne, I add a comment or a smile or snicker that I know will cause him to react, to which he knows I'll react. If we're spontaneous, and appear to be as unrehearsed as we are, we're doing well; if not, we're not. Mostly we are, so we are happy and sad that after five nights a week for nine years, we're breaking up, and giving runners-up an opening through which to move up in the ratings. For Channels 5 and 7, it could not come at a more opportune time. Big news is breaking.

Harold Washington's era is beginning with Chicago on edge, afraid to imagine what's in store, watching television, and seeing "Beirut on the Lake." The *Wall Street Journal* said it first, now we're all saying it—the generals of government, who are the fifty aldermen we've elected to the city council, are at war.

The fright and newsworthiness of it is that it's all about race, provoked by politicians' self-indulgence, fueled by the utter indecency of a band of white gunmen in the council aiming to deny Mayor Washington the spoils of his victory. They intend to keep from him the patronage he needs to pull the strings to control city government and the politics of Cook County. The mayor's feet on the council floor aren't even wet yet, and already he's up to his knees in trouble.

He needs twenty-six votes to approve his plans for "the renewal of our city" but can count on just twenty-one. The rest belong to the white aldermen commanded by Ed Burke of the southwest side and Ed Vrdolyak of the southeast side, two of Chicago's toughest and most resolute politicians. As divergent as they are, the whites in the council are joined inseparably by suspicion and fear that Mayor Washington will give black people equal access to housing and good schools in white neighborhoods, jobs on LaSalle Street, and a crack at lucrative city contracts—in other words, black power. The fact is that black power means the diminution of white power. The fear is, to what degree?

There is too much real estate and banking, and too many millions of dollars at stake, both on and under the table, for the white guys not to act in self-interest. So they do. In fact they've been acting since the day Harold Washington declared his candidacy in what was to become one of the dirtiest campaigns in the history of American politics—Harold Washington versus a virulently racist attempt to keep him out of city hall.

(Because he's a Democrat, winning the election should have been a breeze. Democrats in Chicago don't lose municipal elections, hadn't lost a mayoral race in fifty-five years, not since 1927, when Al Capone helped his Republican pal, William Hale "Big Bill" Thompson, win one. But Harold Washington is an African American, so his Republican opponent, Bernard Epton, a millionaire insurance lawyer, had a chance. His campaign slogan was "Epton For Mayor before It's Too Late." A not-so-underground song was sung to the tune of the song "Bye, Bye, Blackbird":

> It's not a case of black or white.
>
> We need someone to win the fight.
>
> Your record, Bernie, shows you're tough.
>
> As for us, we've been pushed enough.
>
> Bye, Bye. blackbird.

The captains of both parties distributed lapel pins shaped like a Chicago police badge. "ChiCongo PO-lease" were the words next to a pair of lips and a watermelon. The campaign was disgusting. More than 1,200,000 votes were cast. Harold Washington was elected by just 50,000.)

The white aldermen of the city council are conniving to limit him to one term. What he may accomplish is irrelevant. He's black, so they're committed to running him down, then out. They'll need four years to do it; but by God, they say, they will—by blocking his appointments, and his proposals for transit, infrastructure, and construction projects, and for another World's Fair and expanding O'Hare. Above all, they'll stall his plans for integrating housing, the fire department, and police command.

Whatever the new mayor says the city needs, the gang of whites in the council delay, for no reason other than to eviscerate the politics of Harold Washington. "Council Wars" is a serial story that has seized the city's attention and is a gift to political reporters and commentators on television.

At our morning meetings in the newsroom, we plan the broadcasts coming up—what news to place where and for how much time. Our priority is what's going on in city hall in Chicago, which is much more important to television management than what the ayatollah is pronouncing about his revolution in Iran, or President Reagan about his "Star Wars" initiative. Crime is especially important (or, our sales people say it is), but even the Brinks robbery in London and the seven million dollars stolen from Wells Fargo in Connecticut are paled by splashes of Vrdolyak versus Washington in the Chicago council chamber. We expect their shrieking to be so burlesque that we know how sorry we'll be if we're not there to record it; so we send cameras in anticipation. I stay in the newsroom, ready to go live with city council action, to introduce our coverage.

Announcer (off-camera): "We interrupt this program to bring you the Chicago city council debate on its budget. Here's Walter Jacobson."

Me (on-camera): "Not unexpectedly, but with extraordinary theatrics, the mayor and the aldermen are quarreling over whether to spend a million dollars on street repair and new curbs on the west side."

Alderman Ed Vrdolyak (video of him pacing an aisle, waving his arms, shaking his head, his face red, his voice a howl): "No, Mr. Mayor. No. NO! We can't afford it, don't have the money. This is politics, POLITICS! As always, Mr. Mayor, you're playing politics. How we gonna pay for it? We CAN'T pay for it. So what're you doing? You're playing pol—"

Mayor Washington (hammering his gavel): "Please take your seat, Alderman." Smack-smack goes the gavel, three or four times, harder and faster on the way to five or six. "You haven't been called on. You're out of order, out of order. Sit down, Alderman—"

Vrdolyak chorus (wide shot of the council): "Booooooo."

Washington chorus: "Siddown, siddown."

So it goes, and so we roll for another twenty minutes into CBS's daytime programs, and through three commercials until our sales department implores the news director to please stop. We sign off:

Me (on-camera): "As we've come to expect, the mayor and the alderman are a great show. They ought to take it on the road. As for the budget and street repairs, the council meeting was a waste of time and the taxpayers' money. It'd be interesting, wouldn't it, to know how much—the aldermen's pay by the hour, plus air conditioning, lights, and sound engineers for the microphones. And the cost of using the chamber, the police to protect it, and the maintenance people to set it all up and close it down. I'll try to get the total amount, and have it, and more of the Washington-Vrdolyak show on our news tonight at ten. See you then."

It's the kind of news Kurtis and I love to report together, Bill saying what he's learned about the story, me saying what comes to mind. Me popping-off,

Bill signaling me when I'm over an edge. We add information that we've not yet reported, and sometimes we find something to josh about a bit. Despite grumbles from city hall that we're often "wrong, wrong, wrong, so shut up and read the news," when we're sure of what we're saying, we offer a brief analyses. I have to admit to pleasure in riling the aldermen. They deserve it.

16

Another Mayor Daley and Another TV Station

Bill's been in New York for a year. When we talk on the telephone, occasionally, I hear nostalgia. I wonder if he's thinking he's made a mistake. Anchoring network is much more difficult and more stressful than local. He's in a newsroom smaller, darker, and more crowded than ours in Chicago. He's on a floor below bosses on a floor below bosses watching what he's doing, and scared to death of what he or Diane Sawyer, or anyone at any time, may do "wrong."

At WBBM, we have an executive producer, news director, and general manager over our shoulders; three people, and that's it. When there's a problem, we order-in lunch, and solve it, like working in a parish a thousand miles from the Vatican. At CBS in New York, the pope and his cardinals always are in the room. I suspect Bill is having his fill of the network routine, and would like to come home.

Until he does, if he does, I'm anchoring with Don Craig, and we're flush with news that lights up the switchboard. City hall always is a seductive story, but never before as it is under Harold Washington because never before has a black man been in charge, or white aldermen been so bitter and befuddled. One good thing for the mayor is that by crippling his agenda, the aldermen are crippling themselves. Their hate is so obvious, their business in the city council so despicable, that we're pummeling them in the news—or providing them time on the air to pummel themselves.

When they obstruct a reasonable proposal, one that's objectively reasonable, we go after them with questions: What's wrong with the mayor trying to prevent redlining in housing? What's wrong with his plan for replacing patronage with merit employment? Why are you opposing if?

My cameraman and I follow two aldermen out of the council, skidding down a flight of stairs, which they do to avoid being stuck with us on an elevator. I'm behind them through a revolving door onto LaSalle Street. Turn right, go north, as the pace quickens until one of them turns right, into Randolph, before he gets to it, slamming his nose into the building instead. The chase is over, but I don't want to question him holding his nose. That would be inconsiderate; so I allow him to escape, and I head to the studio to edit the tape for six o'clock, at which time I'll narrate the video, telling our viewers the story.

Only in Chicago, an alderman bumping his nose to avoid a reporter. Mayor Washington may have lost a vote, but he flummoxed two aldermen, a pair of his more zealous saboteurs, who, at the next council meeting, may torment him less.

"Patronage is dead," His Honor declares, a sly arch in his brow. "I'm stomping on its grave, and I assure you it's not alive, and it's never going to be resurrected during the twenty years I'm in office. It's gone." He guarantees it, despite the relentless efforts to embarrass or muddy him into backing off. Hardly a day goes by that I don't answer a call reminding me about the state of Illinois once suspending Harold Washington's law license for charging clients for work not done, or about a federal court sentencing him to forty days in jail for failure to file tax returns (he'd paid the taxes, didn't file the returns).

Whispering voices are reviving old rumors that Harold Washington is gay, and that while he was a member of Congress, he was arrested on charges of child abuse. When I hear that one, I call the police chief in DC, who says other reporters are calling about the mayor, and that the rumors are false. All the dirt being whispered already has been used by the media, printed in gossip columns, and filed under old news that has nothing to do with Council Wars, city services, or the mayor's performance in office. It's trash being belched by the Democratic Party machinery that's warming up to grind Harold Washington out of a race for a second term.

During our staff meetings around the WBBM assignment desk, we talk about what to do with what's being shoveled into our mailboxes and our ears on the telephone. This is what—sift it carefully, extract the pieces of it that may be worth a story, and shelve the rest. With this caveat: Don't lean over backwards for Mayor Washington because he's black or because we like politicians who disrupt the system; don't be politically correct out of fear of agitating the black community. In the 1980s in Chicago, the lines between the races are starkly drawn, the sensitivities acute. Journalists are walking on eggshells.

There are many examples, one of them involving a tip to some information that leads me to a commentary questioning the judgment of Mayor Washington's chief counsel, James Montgomery. Two of his children have summer jobs on the city payroll. Not good, I say, Montgomery using his position to help his family. That's clout. Joe Citizen doesn't have clout to get his children on the public payroll.

"Ridiculous," Montgomery responds. "Walter is ridiculous. My children applied for the job like everybody else." The mayor's chief counsel putting me down like that quickly travels through the media, by phone to my news director. I'm called in to explain:

"I'm not ridiculous. In fact, Montgomery also said, quote, 'If I can't help my children, who can?' He's not supposed to be helping his children to the taxpayers' money."

"I know, I know," says the news director. "But be careful"—that is, lean over a little, be just a little politically correct. "Be careful, okay?"

"I hear you." Nothing more need be said. The lay of the land is perfectly clear—white-reporter–black-mayor. I must be just a little politically correct. That's what reporters in Chicago are thinking, as are reporters around the country—as Kurtis will be thinking when he returns from New York.

"This is not where I want to be," he confides after three years on *The CBS Morning News*, teamed with ever-changing anchors. First Sawyer, then Phyllis George, the former Miss America; then Maria Shriver and Meredith Vieira—a wide variety of "talent," as anchors are called.

"They're not journalists," Bill grumbles. "They're hosts. That's not me. I want to go out on stories. You know, write and produce them myself. Here, all that's done by a staff."

Anchor of *The CBS Morning News* is one of the most prestigious, sought-after, and envied jobs in television. My (educated) guess is that Bill's being paid close to a million dollars a year, which may not be enough to hold him in the job. Sometimes in life, no amount of money is enough to keep a person where he doesn't want to be.

"*Morning News* is competing with *The Evening News* [with Dan Rather] for resources," Bill goes on. "It's an endless battle. We need a crew in London, Dan wants it in Rome, you know where it's going. Same for technical assistance, phone lines, and editors. I understand that. *Evening*'s the flagship . . ."

"There aren't enough resources for *Morning News* and *Evening News*, both?" I interrupt.

"Well, you'd think there are. There ought to be, but it doesn't work that way. *Evening News* has stature. *Morning* is trying to get some. I'm up every day at 2 A.M. and stuck in the studio. Can't get out on a story. I stand in line for my turn on *60 Minutes*, or *CBS Reports*."

Kurtis is offered a job by *Nightline* at ABC to do the kind of journalism he likes to do and to fill in for Ted Koppel when Koppel's off. He's tempted but dissuaded. CBS doesn't want him to go to ABC, or to leave *The Morning News*, but the show is not right for Bill, and he's not right for it. He's a "local guy," not much into being among the East Coast media elite.

He's weary of Manhattan and worn out by his struggle to focus *Morning News* on news, not Hollywood actors, cooks, and self-help authors. He is letting Chicago stations know of his interest in coming back, and because Channels 5 and 7 are interested in him, he's in a strong position to set his price at Channel 2. He yearns for the freedom to write and produce documentaries, and to start up a production company of his own. He's being offered all that, having it written into a contract, and asking for more than $800,000 a year.

That's too much money, say some television executives who note that while Kurtis was gone, Channel 2's ratings didn't falter; in fact, during some months of his absence, the ratings increased. It's demonstrable proof, contend the pin-stripes, of what they've been saying for years—that it's not the personality that makes ratings, it's the content of the broadcast. Offer Kurtis less, they advise, break the myth of personality, put a lid on anchor salaries, and save a whole lot of money.

Maybe that's a good idea, but WBBM isn't about to test it. Kurtis is signed in a hurry, at more than $800,000 a year. I know it's more because I'm being paid $800,000, and when Bill settles in, I'm called upstairs. "We don't want you to feel it's unfair," I'm told. "We're adding $50,000 a year to your contract." Okay. Thank you. And Bill and I are back on the ten o'clock news together.

Our general manager, Gary Cummings, a former television editorial director and newspaper reporter, wants Kurtis on the six o'clock news as well as the ten. Problem is, the six o'clock anchors are Don Craig and Harry Porterfield. To make room for Bill on that broadcast, Craig or Porterfield has to go. Cummings demotes Porterfield to the weekends—Harry Porterfield, the only African American anchor on Channel 2 News, twenty-one years at the station, being pushed out of five nights a week into two on the weekends, out of a first-string position in television news into second-string at a time when Chicago is bristling with tension between the races. Can you believe it?

A more dimwitted move is impossible to imagine. How can Gary Cummings, running a multimillion-dollar CBS business, be so oblivious to the demograph-ics and politics of his market, so utterly unaware of the forces lying in wait for a mistake? It's unfathomable. Bill Kurtis advises him to come up with some combination to keep Harry at an anchor desk during the week.

I try, too. "It's a mistake to move Harry," I plead. "Don't do it. Jesse Jackson will eat you alive. He's being out-sparkled by Mayor Washington and mar-ginalized by the media, less often on the evening news and front pages of the newspapers. He's looking for a cause, Gary. Be careful not to give him one."

"Walter. That's enough. Thank you." I get his drift, assure him I know who's boss, and hush up.

Cummings is replacing a thoroughly competent, well-known, and very popular black anchor with a white one. Just like that, Cummings is snapping Harry Porterfield out of the picture at Channel 2, even though there's not likely a black politician or community leader within a hundred miles who doesn't believe that Chicago television news is insensitive to minority concerns, if not outright racist. There are black reporters, writers, and editors in the network-owned newsrooms, and some black directors in the control booths, but nearly all the anchors, and every one of the political analysts, commentators, news directors, and general managers is white.

Reverend Jackson has been complaining about it, rightly so, for years. Now, he has what he needs to act, and he does. With a boycott. Twice a week he loads up a bus at Operation PUSH on the south side and delivers two dozen picketers to the carpeted, heated, glass-walled entrance to WBBM on McClurg Court. They're carrying placards accusing the station of discrimination, urging passers-by and people who enter or leave the building, or who see the picketers on the news or in the papers, or in *Time* or *Newsweek*, to turn off CBS-WBBM-TV.

How can all this be happening? The lunchroom speculation at WBBM is that Jackson proposed the boycott to Porterfield, who obliged. (If I were Harry Porterfield, I would have obliged; wouldn't you?) There are denials all around, but even if Jesse and Harry did do some plotting, so what? Who's not plotting in our business? Channel 7 is coming after Harry, and Harry's happy to talk (in a whisper). A contract is in the works.

I try Gary Cummings again, to ask if maybe he'll consider a public statement admitting to a mistake and pledging to take steps to correct it. His answer again is "No." But it doesn't matter anymore; it's too late.

Jackson has a platform and is stirring interest nationwide (the newspapers love stories like this). To call off the boycott, he wants Cummings to hire two black anchors, place African Americans in positions to determine what is news and how to cover it, double the number of black and Latino employees from 20 percent of the news department to 40 percent, and to do 35 percent of the station's banking business with black-owned financial institutions. And oh, by the way, he wants $11 million for charities to be selected by Operation PUSH. And, how embarrassing, he pops up at a CBS corporate meeting in Philadelphia to take a few swings at the heavyweights. How painfully uncomfortable for CBS corporate executives.

Harry Porterfield walks into welcoming arms at Channel 7, while Jesse Jackson is standing firm on his demands of Channel 2. His boycott is into its thirty-fifth week. Our numbers are plunging, our leadership is fractured and flawed, and our morale is bottoming out. Gary Cummings has to go. Within a few more weeks he's gone, replaced by Johnathan Rodgers, the first African American to general manage a television station in Chicago, the third largest market in the country. In fact, he's the first black person to manage any CBS-owned station anywhere.

His plate is full. But before he can think about how to clear it, he must muffle the buzz that he's here because of his color, which is not easy to do because the truth is that he is. Short of bowing to all of Jackson's demands, even the $11 million for Operation PUSH charities, there is no way a white general manager can stop the boycott. CBS needs to get the reverend out from in front of WBBM.

Fortunately, the company has Johnathan Rodgers to turn to; and it's a mistake to think he's more symbol than substance. Rodgers is just forty years old but a veteran journalist and television news manager. He is right for the job. His résumé includes Berkeley and Stanford, *Time* magazine, *Sports Illustrated*, *Newsweek*, assistant news director at WBBM-TV in Chicago, station manager at CBS-KNXT in LA, and executive producer of *The CBS Morning News* in New York. He's been a television news writer, producer, reporter, and anchorman. He knows our work and understands our feelings. We need him here.

First things first for Rodgers—get Jesse Jackson off our sidewalk. They know each other, which is a good start. They get together to negotiate an end to the boycott: Rodgers adds twenty new minority employees to the WBBM payroll and commits to hiring more and to raising the stature of those already employed.

He's hired Lester Holt, an African American currently anchoring at WCBS in New York, and is about to hire a woman, Linda MacLennan, currently anchoring in Toronto. No personnel or business quotas, no $11 million for Operation PUSH charities; but an agreement is reached, the boycott is called off, and all involved are saying, as Jackson does, that "great change has come about, and it's going to be for the good of everybody."

Nobody's challenging him, and pictures in the newspapers show Johnathan and Jesse shaking hands in front of the Saturday choir at PUSH. Even Harry Porterfield joins the chorus: "Johnathan deserves an opportunity to succeed, and this gives him that opportunity." So ends a mid-80s public relations nightmare, and so begins better feelings all around. It's the right time, after thirteen years of Bill-and-Walter, to freshen-up Channel 2 News—with Holt and MacLennan, priority to MacLennan. She'll help us off antique row into contemporary Chicago.

We're unanimous about it, that we must have a woman coanchoring our ten o'clock news. Guess who gets to be replaced? Me, because Bill's more of an anchor than I am, and Bill-and-Linda will be a more saleable team than Walter-and-Linda. He has the heft to carry a newcomer into the market.

It's painful after thirteen years, but I have to give way. The only question is how to do it. Channel 2 can't appear to be dumping me just to hire a woman. If Linda's going on the ten because of her gender, I must be coming off because of mine. You can't fight sexism with sexism. The best thing, probably, is for me to talk about it on the news, to explain why we're changing; and, in case there are viewers who may miss me, I'll assure them I'll be here every night with "Perspective." That takes care of that. We hope, but don't have time to pray.

There's a change in Chicago far more important than musical chairs at an anchor desk at Channel 2 News. Mayor Washington is dead, struck down by a heart attack eight months after being reelected for four more years. We knew it would happen. We could see it coming. He weighed 284 pounds of too many cheeseburgers salted with stress.

At eleven in the morning of November 25, 1987, the mayor is at his desk in his office with his press secretary, Alton Miller. In midsentence, he slumps forward in his chair. "I thought he was reaching for something he dropped to the floor," says Miller. "He just didn't straighten up."

Medics in the ambulance and doctors at Northwestern Memorial Hospital a mile away work two and a half hours to bring him back but cannot. Thousands of people in limousines and on buses and trains come to his wake in the lobby of city hall. As most of Chicago mourns, all of Chicago has the jitters.

Again. Black and white partisans tear at each other for votes to succeed him. There will be another temporary mayor and more angry campaigns, until a special election delivers unto us the second Reign of Daley, Richard Michael after Richard Joseph.

At WBBM on McClurg Court, Jesse Jackson's boycott is done, but it still hurts. Our ratings are bad. After owning the market for ten years, Channel 2 is in a slump, the numbers descending precipitously. Our five o'clock news is losing one hundred thousand viewers, the six o'clock two hundred thousand. Channel 7 is clubbing our newscasts in all time periods, at four, five, six, and ten. So is Channel 5. We're drooping from first place to last among the network-owned stations.

Phone lines between Chicago and New York are burning with recriminations. Reasons for the fall? The boycott, for sure, and the same-old-same-old way of the business, up one day, down the next. Or it's another station's turn. Or our CBS lead-ins are weak, and ABC's are strong. Or our viewers are tired of an anchor and want a new on. Or they don't like musical chairs. Or Cubs games on WGN-TV are killing us, or Nielsen must be wrong, or the weather's warm, so our viewers are outside at night instead of inside watching television.

Maybe it's Bill Kurtis's having come back to an audience that considers him disloyal for having left. Maybe it's me picking on Mayor Washington. Or how about the libel suit?

The thinkers in New York are not as interested in what's causing the problem as they are in fixing it. And what often happens in that situation is happening to us. The bad is becoming worse because the medicine is more toxic than the disease. The doctors say the cure for bad ratings in local television news is to dumb-down the product because viewers want more to play with than to think about, more entertainment less information, more Hollywood less city hall, more pictures and music less debate, more gossip less analysis, more crime less government, more weather less news, more sex, less everything.

Some news managers deliver better than others. By 1990, we're about to get a hot one. His name is Bill Applegate. He's en route from New York to Chicago

to boost our numbers with whatever it takes—more murder and rape and titil-
lation. Applegate is (in)famous for adding sparks to a broadcast, and juicing and
jazzing during the "sweeps" rating periods—three months a year during which
the ad agencies focus their visions and scrutinize the numbers.

For me, jazzing up for sweeps means three hours with a makeup artist weath-
ering my eyes, yellowing my teeth, and pasting onto my face a knotted beard. In
filthy baggy pants, a tattered coat, and a cameraman behind, I'm onto the street
into five-below-zero and February's intolerable winds. I'm going "homeless"
for Applegate for forty-eight hours, begging for pennies and morsels, sleeping
in boxes on Lower Wacker Drive, and on a floor with a hundred genuinely
homeless men in a shelter on South State Street.

"I am miserable," I choke and stutter into the camera. "Really, really miserable," which makes for ratings, but provokes the press: "[M]illionaire anchorman could have been wearing designer longjohns to keep his tush warm . . .
self-serving performance art . . . a stunt . . . 48-Hour Man without a Townhouse
. . . something hilarious."

Applegate is erasing from our storyboard news of substance, and chalk-
ing-in trash and thumping sounds, graphics, hollow catchphrases, and whatever else there may be that's over the top. After "homeless," what he wants
from me is a one-on-one interview with John Wayne Gacy, the Chicago sadist
who's been convicted of torture, rape, and murder, and burying the bodies
of more than two dozen young boys and men in a crawl space beneath the
basement of his home on the northwest side. He sinks another one under his
driveway and tosses three more into the Des Plaines River. Gacy's on death
row in the state penitentiary at Menard, downstate Illinois. He has no use for
reporters. All the more reason Team Applegate wants him and is asking me
to get him.

My relationship with Bill Applegate is up-and-down. Right now, it's down,
because he's knocking "Perspective" off the ten o'clock news. He thinks people
are tired of it, that it's not helping the station, is too agitating and negative and
has too much opinion. So, he says, we'll bench it for a stretch.

Yes, I guess we will, which is devastating to me because of how much I don't
want to give it up. He knows precisely how much, so his news director calls me
in to make a deal. If I get Gacy in an interview, I may have my commentary
back at ten o'clock. We shake hands on it (ugh), and I'm off on a mission. I call
Menard once a week for several months.

"Your message has been delivered," I'm advised by the office of the warden.
"That's that's all we can do." So I write it again and send it again many times over
several months. Until I get a letter back from John Wayne Gacy himself. He tells
me about politics (he likes Democrats), and that he likes that I was a Chicago
Cubs batboy. He's been a Cubs fan all his life, he says, and for that reason, he'll

talk to me. The true reason is he wants airtime to profess his innocence, which is fine with me; whatever his reason, it's fine with me.

Prison officials are reluctant to permit me in because interviews, especially on death row, make inmates restive. But the warden also is reluctant to deny an inmate permission to speak. Two weeks after Gacy's letter, in 1992 as the prison bureaucracy churns, I'm hearing good things from Nic Howell, director of prison press relations: "If we okay an interview, when would you want to do it? How many guys in your crew?"

Three weeks after that, two cameramen and I are driving to Menard. We empty our pockets, walk through metal detectors and a steel door, and are led into a twelve-by-twelve-foot windowless room. In the center of it is a fluorescent light over a small metal table, at which I'm instructed to sit. One camera is being readied on a tripod behind my shoulder to get Gacy, the other behind what's to be his chair, to get me.

Then silence, for ten minutes that feel like an hour, until the door is opened from the outside by a guard, who walks in followed by a man shorter and less fearsome than he looks in pictures. He's five-foot-eight or -nine, fifty years old, balding, and sloppy fat in a short-sleeved blue prison shirt. His hands are cuffed in front of him, his feet shackled by a heavy-link chain allowing him no more than a shuffle. I offer him my hand. He brushes it away. The guard unlocks his cuffs, and John Wayne Gacy sits down.

"Whaddaya wanna know?" he mutters.

"Whatever you'll tell me. You okay?"

"Yeah, I'm okay. You people have it all wrong, from day one."

"What do you mean, all wrong?

"You know it. I keep tellin' you, those people are crazy. The Piests and Godziks [families of victims] and all them, they're crazy."

"The families of the boys you killed, and bur—"

"I didn't kill 'em. They say I did, but I didn't kill 'em." (His lawyers argued in court that the deaths were accidental, caused by asphyxia, which is a lack of oxygen in the bloodstream. Eventually, they pled Gacy guilty by reasons of insanity.)

"The only thing I'm guilty of," he now says to me, "was running a cemetery without a license."

The murder spree went on for seven years (1972–78) until he was arrested during his tenure as a precinct captain for the Norwood Park Township Democratic Party. He was director of an annual Polish Constitution Day parade; he wore a Secret Service pin when posing for a picture with First Lady Rosalynn Carter. She autographed it: "To John Gacy. Best wishes."

I ask him about asphyxia and the evidence that he strangled his victims. "You're not a big man," I say. "Most of those boys were teenagers. Weren't some of them hard to handle? How'd you do that?"

"Not hard," he answers, inadvertently admitting to me what he did, and he takes a piece of string from his shirt pocket. "Gimme your pencil." Flabbergasted at what I'm thinking I'm about to get on tape, I push my pencil across the table. "It's easy," he continues. "Like this." He winds the string around the pencil, ties a slipknot, pulls it tight (close-up, close-up, I silently pray to the camera), and hands me the pencil.

"I missed it," I say. "How'd you do that? Can you explain it again?"

He takes the pencil back and winds the string again. I'm thinking if he doesn't do or say anything else, I have all I need. An incredible story. Gacy demonstrating how he murdered his victims.

Suddenly aware that he's contradicted his denials, his self-confidence gone, eyes darting with concern, he stammers: "I'm not talking about those boys. I'm showing you how something like that can be done."

"Whatever you say, Mr. Gacy. I'm here to listen." Which I do into a second hour. I have pure gold, just in time for the February sweeps.

Applegate makes room on the ten o'clock news for five nights of John Wayne Gacy. We edit the interview, dice it for television with pictures of his house, the crawl space, the boys he strangled, and the bodies. The station spends heavily to promote it in prime time and in the newspapers. For a week, Channel 2 nearly doubles its average rating for the ten o'clock news and ends the five nights in first place. As I've been saying, nothing like blood and gore, death and destruction to boost a number.

I have to hand it to Applegate. Despite my distaste for his taste in news, I have to admit he knows how to make a number and is dogged in his pursuit. In the game of guessing what news viewers want to see, he's as good as they get.

When it comes to remembering deals, he forgets. "Perspective" is not coming back at ten, not coming back at all. How naïve of me to think a handshake could make a difference in the business of local television news. For the first time in thirty years, I'm wondering if it's right for me, or me for it. Maybe I made a mistake. Why did I become a reporter in the first place?

Was it my childhood disdain for authority, resenting my mother telling me what to do? Was it my curiosity and nosiness? Liking secrets, and keeping them? Learning to respect the underclass, and how to go after those who abuse it?

Sometimes I think I became a reporter on a day when I was four or five years old on Kenmore Avenue, on my tricycle in front of the Granville Hotel a block from our apartment. The intensity of a gathering crowd straining to see the top of the building. Fire engines and flashing blue lights. And splat! Smack in front of me, a broken and bloody body of a person who had just jumped from a floor high up. I was dumbstruck, couldn't look away. That's how reporters are, aren't they, fascinated by life, and especially death? Reporters like to tell stories.

I remember peddling home faster than my wheels wanted to go, to report to my mother what happened, in the most explicit detail. I love to tell stories.

Now I'm so angry at Channel 2 that I regret delivering Gacy, so angry at Bill Applegate for walking away from our deal that I'm thinking I don't want to be here anymore. But what to do, where to go? Local television news is empty—rat-a-tat, five stories a minute, because wizards in executive suites have decided that attention spans are short, that viewers want a lot, and don't care what it means. Fires, fires, fires, car crashes, crashes, crashes because viewers are gawkers. Animals, animals because people love pets more than they love each other. Three minutes of weather because the reason people turn on the news is to know what it's like outside and what to wear tomorrow.

I don't want to do this anymore. I want out of Channel 2 News!

17

Fox News, Mayor Daley (the second), and Barack Obama

There aren't many jobs in television news in Chicago, not for an anchor with some gray around the edges. Not in 1993, the dawning of the age of unenlightenment, the "Age of Young." Talent scouts for television news are looking for twenty-five-year-old anchorettes, preferably with blonde hair falling over eyes under flashing lashes. Retailers are designing and packaging products for the young, to be pitched to the young on television news. The purveyors of news have divined that the way to entice junior to watch it is to have junior read it. I'm fifty-six, so I'm surprised to get a call from a general manager.

"Let's have lunch," says Stacey Marks-Bronner, the general manager of Fox News Chicago. She's calling from her corner office on North Michigan Avenue, wearing, I suspect, because she always is, a black pinstriped suit. She's about five-four in heels, wears her dark hair at shoulders, and beams bright brown eyes that see everything. She's just been hired by Rupert Murdoch, personally, to run his Fox station in Chicago.

"I want to talk to you, Walter."

"Sure, Stacey, anytime." We've been friends for a year, since she moved to Chicago from Miami in 1991 to be director of marketing at Bill Applegate's Channel 2. He thought up dazzlers, she promoted them. He told her he had the "homeless" and "John Wayne Gacy on Death Row"; she told him how to sell them. And she was so good at it that Murdoch bought her away from Applegate to install her as the first woman to manage a television station in Chicago, first in the nation to manage a station owned by a network.

She's barely thirty years old, from marketing manager to general manager in twenty-four months. Amazing, and she sounds serious on the telephone. What's up? Is she okay?

"I'm fine. I'll tell you when we talk."

What's up is me. She wants to know if I'd be interested in anchoring her Fox nightly news? In this Age of Young? At a time when I'm everything she's not.

Everything she is, I'm not. MTV? I don't know about it. Cyndi Lauper, jelly shoes, grunge. Grunge?

My contract with Channel 2 is about to expire. Applegate's asking me to sign a new one as a reporter, and as host of a weekly news-in-review. At half my salary, $500,000 a year, guaranteed for five years (he's sure to be gone in two, so he doesn't care about the last three—musical chairs executive-style: design a five-year budget that commits less at first, more later on, so when you move out, whoever moves in is stuck with the commitments you leave behind).

Marks-Bronner offers me $750,000 a year for two years, with nothing after that guaranteed. Those numbers are obscene, but what am I to say: No thank you, I don't want the money? My question is, after twenty years at CBS-WBBM, how will I feel at Fox-WFLD? But I realize that's not a deal-breaker. To have "Perspective" back and to anchor again? I'm talking to Stacey, who doesn't play games:

"I want you to anchor with Robin" (Robin Robinson, with whom I once anchored at Channel 2). "You'll be principal anchor" (as Bill Kurtis was to me), "do 'Perspective' every night, and have two legmen to help. Five or six news specials a year, documentaries, and some foreign travel." What's to be included in the broadcast, and what to prioritize, will be decided by the general manager, news director, and anchors together. It's hard for me to imagine that kind of anchor involvement, but it's what she says, and she seems to mean it.

So I ask Applegate to release me from my contract. He agrees, because he can save money and, I suspect, he wants me out of his hair.

I sign on at Fox, and Marks-Bronner meets the press: "Hiring Walter proves our commitment to credible news in Chicago. News is a central part of getting through your life every day. My job is to build an audience where there isn't one, to appeal to a generation of people who can handle a lot at one time"—interpreted by the widely read suburban *Daily Herald* to mean she's hiring "the sort of sassy-yet-respectable personality that may appeal to young viewers who watch Fox's youth-oriented prime-time lineup."

Conventional wisdom is that with a fifty-six-year-old man who's been on Chicago television for thirty years, still using a manual typewriter, she's taking a chance, a big one. To blunt the perceived odds against her, she's promising a broadcast that's "fast-paced, interactive, and in-your-face. I just don't see these hard lines between what's old and what's new. What I see is energy and fire, and I don't think that people on the anchor desk have to be young to attract a young audience."

How refreshing. But to play it safe, she's commanding me to do young things, like wear a turtleneck and sport jacket on the news, or a turtleneck and no jacket.

"Oh, no, I hope you're not serious."

"Of course, I'm serious. Dump the suspenders."

"But I've been wearing them at Channel 2 for twenty years."

"That's the point."

My mission for Stacey, as the newspapers are accurately reporting it, is to help her attract not so much a big audience as a young one, the twenty-year-olds so coveted by advertisers.

"A turtleneck will do that?"

"Try it." Okay, I will. And I'll try to talk a little faster, be more interested in Madonna, and sharpen my edge that's been dulled by two years on the anchor-commentary bench at WBBM.

Stacey is spending half a million dollars to promote her new broadcast, which is fast out of the gate—a 30 percent gain in audience over the same period a year before. Fast, okay, but not up to the competition, not even within sight of the leaders, not 10 percent of the ratings at Channels 5, 7, or 2. We'll see what happens. Meantime, inside Fox News Chicago is a new world for me, run exclusively by women (general manager, sales manager, news director, assistant news director, planning director, and assignment editor)—a sea change from the way things were in 1963 when I began scrambling for news on television.

In the '70s on the news turf in Chicago, women began advancing not only with speed, but with force. Now, in the '90s, women are muscling their way to equality in television studios, editing rooms, control booths, conference rooms, and, most significantly, in the offices of management. Up at the top of the four network-owned stations (WBBM, WMAQ, WABC, and FOX), two general managers are now women, as are all four news directors.

What's that like? At Fox in One Illinois Center on the northeast corner of Michigan Avenue and Lake Street, just south of the Michigan Avenue bridge, I cool my heels outside Marks-Bronner's office, waiting for her to conclude deliberations with her four-year-old Max and one-year-old Jake. When cleared to enter, I step around teddy bears and bubble gum.

Max: "Mom, I want—"

Mom: "Max, you can see I'm talking. Wait 'til I'm finished, then it's your turn."

Max: "Mom—"

Mom: "Max."

That's all it takes to quiet Max, which also, in occasional disputes with Stacey, is all it takes to quiet me, and four score or so other people in the news department. We believe she knows what she's doing. Her station is earning 6 percent of all advertising dollars spent on TV news in the Chicago market. In ten years, the station will be earning 23 percent. And more than half of that will have been earned by the news department, which is spending it as fast as it's coming in— on reporters, editors, cameras, satellite equipment, trucks, and state-of-the-art digital electronics, and on studio designs and promotions, and the overtime and double time that are necessary to keep up with an increasingly rapid pace of Chicago and Illinois politics.

(Women like Stacey surging to prominence in a business presumed to be upscale in ethics, it may be hard to believe what went on in some Chicago television stations just twenty-five years ago: a general manager instructing the distaff ranks of his on-camera roster to come to the studio in gauzy silk blouses, another GM suggesting that women looking for better assignments come to his office, or a news director telling a woman seeking refuge from the nightshift that he might arrange it in exchange for a special favor—tales not of casting couches in Hollywood, but of behind the scenes in newsrooms in Chicago.)

During the second half of the '90s, intrigue behind the scenes in city politics is as compelling as ever. Because Rich Daley the Son, early in his reign, doesn't have the esteem or the fist of the Father, he's more vulnerable to jockeying and conniving in city hall, the internecine warfare among lords of the Democratic Party, and revolutions budding in the neighborhoods. News is busting out all over, and television is eager to get in on it. Station managers are pumping big money into the chase for scoops and exclusives. They're ballooning staff, hiring freelance reporters and photographers, and recruiting more interns to help follow up on tips about politicians on the loose.

Chicago's into a population and housing boom—high-rise apartments and condos in the Loop, gentrification everywhere. Tourists are coming by plane- and train-load, bearing $13 billion a year. It's the bubbling Nineties. Politicians and planners are thinking Millennium Park and a Soldier Field tiara, and more runways at O'Hare. Easy money is being banked, budgets stuffed with civic projects; waves of city jobs are for sale, new varieties of candidates running for office, votes being bought, spoils shared, multimillions in government business dispensed by city hall to pals of the power elite.

There's a surge in corruption, imaginative ways to cover it up, federal sleuths and prosecutors snooping around to uncover it, and reporters keeping score— on average, a Chicago alderman a year is being convicted of bribery or extortion, embezzlement, tax evasion, or conspiracy, or all of them together. On those and so many other subjects Chicago is a landfill of stories.

One of them chilled me to the bone—John Wayne Gacy again. This time, his execution. I'm a witness. He's in baggy blue denim trousers and white cotton shirt, strapped on his back to a gurney in an ugly, antiseptic death chamber inside a small brick building in a courtyard at the Illinois state penitentiary near Joliet, forty-five miles southwest of downtown Chicago. The building is there for no purpose other than the taking an eye for an eye.

Gacy had arrived several hours before, delivered by helicopter from the Menard penitentiary, where he'd been on death row, where I saw him last. He'd been asked his preference for a last meal; and in shackles, seated alone at a table outside his cell, surrounded by prison guards, his family, and his lawyers, he was served his supper as he liked it—a dozen deep-fried shrimp, a bucket of original-recipe Kentucky Fried Chicken, a plate of french fries, another of fresh strawberries, and Diet Coke. He was described to me by his lawyer, Greg Adamski, as "not frightened or nervous. I'd say he was in good spirits, even jovial. He didn't seem to care." After dinner, he was returned to his cell, where he stayed for five hours until being prepped for the execution and visited by a priest.

As the time approached midnight, beyond which neither court nor governor could stay the process, Gacy was placed on the gurney, his left arm invaded by a needle to be attached to a tube that would course the poison through his predrugged and listless body. Before being rolled into the chamber, he had been shot with more than a thousand milligrams—a colossal dose—of Sodium Pentothal that, in less than a minute, reached his brain and put him into a deep sleep to prevent him from feeling anything more.

I was there by chance. As a reporter who'd been covering the story for years—the bodies, the arrest, the trial, the conviction and sentencing—I received a letter from the Illinois Department of Corrections. "Sign here," it said, "if you wish to have your name entered in a drawing to be invited to witness the execution."

Of course I wish to have my name entered. That's what reporters do, isn't it—wish to be entered in and invited to everything? That's what I've been doing since sixth grade, wishing to be invited, and when not invited (especially when not invited) trying to enter anyway. It's not likely I'll slip by security at a state penitentiary and stroll into an execution. So I sign up and, in a week, am called by the DOC, told I've been selected as a media witness, and am advised that I'll be receiving a subsequent call instructing me where to be and at what time, and what to expect.

A surreal experience:

I'm one of about a dozen witnesses (too anxious to count precisely). We're led in the dark on a sidewalk alongside cell blocks that are deathly silent except for a few shouts from somewhere, we can't see where, that jar the air. "So long, John." "See you, John."

A few minutes before death by lethal injection is to begin, a door at our destination is unlocked and opened by a guard who directs us into a waiting area, then through another door into the death chamber, and onto metal folding chairs. The room is small, no more than twenty by thirty feet. In the wall in front of the first row of chairs, hardly an arm's length away, is a large window covered from the inside by blinds that are closed. As if to enhance the drama, the space is lit dimly from the ceiling. It smells of damp concrete, and although the temperature seems like eighty degrees, I am cold and feeling sick, my teeth chattering between waves of nausea. "Eerie" is the best I can do to describe it. "Eerie" or "bizarre."

When we sit down, the blinds are opened, and in the window, under very bright lights like in operating rooms on *ER* or *House*, is John Wayne Gacy, the notorious monster serial killer on his back on the gurney, helpless. His eyes are closed. He appears to be sleeping.

I am too uncomfortable to note whether there is one executioner or two standing next to wall-mounted telephones, in case the governor calls, several switches, and a machine that's to deliver first a chemical to stop Gacy's breathing, which is supposed to take about two minutes, and then a lethal dose of another chemical to stop his heart. We are to witness a doctor with a stethoscope declaring him dead—like clockwork, a fast and flawless procedure that had been rehearsed many times by prison personnel, sometimes with the use of a guard of Gacy's height and weight on the gurney. But that's not what's happening.

Instead, the blinds suddenly are closed, and we're told the execution has been stopped. A malfunction. A liquid in one of the IV tubes has congealed and is stuck. But not to worry. It is being fixed, and, in about ten minutes (I'm stunned and transfixed, can't count the minutes), the tube is removed, replaced by a new one, and the procedure begins again. In about twenty minutes, John Gacy, finally, is gone.

I return to my beat in downtown Chicago. Cross Michigan Avenue, hoof it five blocks to city hall, into the magnificent marbled lobby and up on an elevator to five, to the sanctum of the New Boss. Behind glass doors is a spit-and-polish cop at a desk, and two other cops standing guard. Then another door, two secretaries, and a third door between the press and Mayor Richard M. Daley. A few steps away from his desk is a back door through which he can avoid hangers-on by high-tailing it down the stairs.

He sits where his dad sat for twenty-one years, behind a large wooden desk bathed in sunlight in a warm corner office looking down on the LaSalle Street canyon. I've been there twice, for interviews he is reluctant to grant. Like father like son, he distrusts and disdains the media, with a little extra pique reserved for those of us who, by assignment, have the latitude to stretch beyond the facts to opinion.

One of my surest opinions is that this Mayor Daley in public is not Mayor Daley in private. Face-to-face, one-on-one, he's more contemplative than he is at a podium laden with microphones. With the mayor by myself, I feel his thinking and read his confidence. My questions up close, not shouted from a crowd, don't ring in his ears. He sees me listening, so he senses he's being heard; if he's imprecise or misunderstood, he knows he can clarify what he says, or correct a mistake, or take it back, or decide to say, "It's off the record." He has, after all, granted me the interview and has a right to expect civility, which he cannot expect during the melee of a news conference.

My respect is his due, and my obligation. Neither, however, assures me a story I can claim as a scoop. He's much too savvy to let something loose that may boost me at the expense of other reporters. Unless, of course, he wants to be the lead story on the ten o'clock news, in which case he may give me something new. He understands, better than most politicians, how newsrooms work. If I have a story other reporters do not, I can call it a Fox News Exclusive, and our executive producer will give it premium play, often on all broadcasts. A little story is a big one if it's exclusive.

Mayor Daley knows what kind of information to drop where and when. He rarely sits down with just one reporter. On occasion, though, he will, in response to a query that catches his fancy and may serve him well. When he's looking to be reelected in 1995, I ask his press office if he'd consider riding around town with me in the back seat of his limousine, and a cameraman in front. "Into the neighborhoods," I say in my pitch to his press secretary Jackie Heard that "the mayor can talk about his plans. A picture's worth a thousand words, you know."

"True enough, Walter, but don't count on it."

"I figured. But what's to lose by trying?"

"Okay-okay, Walter, I'll ask."

We drive up Lake Shore Drive and down Western Avenue to Englewood, through Hyde Park and South Shore, up and west to Lawndale, and out to Sauganash. We pass by housing projects, new schools and shopping centers, bus stops, bicycle paths, and the elevated. For two hours, he talks plans, and I try to get him to talk politics.

We come to a draw that is mutually beneficial. I get good pictures of the two of us riding around together, for "A Ride with Mayor Daley. Exclusive Report Tonight at Ten." He gets pictures on television of him loving his city, and a few to show that a reporter respects him, especially one who's always yapping at him. That's why he's doing this. He wants to be on TV. At times when he doesn't, which is most of the time, the wall between us looms as the great one in China. Impenetrable. Access to information in city hall is carefully, very carefully, limited because there are many things the mayor wants us not to see.

Stories he prefers untold:

"I have a good one," discloses Phil Hayes, "Perspective" unit producer who's been poking around an old barn on South Ashland Avenue. And a truck yard on Rockwell at Thirty-First Street. "The city is hiding very expensive flood-control equipment that doesn't work." I ask him how sure he is.

"Sure enough," he says, "because I trust the source. But we can't get inside to check it out." There are ways for us to do what needs to be done to get a story. Not entirely kosher, perhaps, but they do the job. We get into both the barn and the truck yard, take pictures of the evidence, and tell the story.

Another one: We're called by parents of a Little League team that's been waiting two months for the "City That Works" to cut weeds and remove glass and trash from what's called an infield. Two months? That's more than half the season. The parents are getting a runaround, so we design a strategy, also not entirely kosher, to find out who's responsible. That done, I go to the infield, kick up the glass, and tell the story. The response from city hall is to tell Fox management that "Perspective" is "out of line," that it should have alerted the city instead of telling a story.

That's a problem with investigative reporting and commentary—to choose between serving the news department and serving the city. I believe my job is to expose malfunctions of government and malfeasance of politicians who run it, and to look out for the taxpayers' money. If I notify city hall about the trash on the ball field, it'll be cleaned up tomorrow. But then what? Every time I get a call from a neighborhood, I'm to alert the city? No, that's not my job. The city already was alerted by the parents, two months ago. My job is to report it, including the part about the alert. It's the mayor's job to respond to the neighbors.

For any story under any circumstances, my priority must always be to avoid mistakes, to heed that lesson learned long ago at the City News Bureau: If my mother says she loves me, check it out. In other words, be sure-footed, which is what I think I'm being when working with police on a late-night sting next to an empty lot on the west side where gangbangers are selling stolen revolvers. I've been told that one of the cops is in on the deal. He's our story.

We're invited by police internal investigators to position a camera inside their van about thirty yards away. As money and guns are exchanged, three cops dressed like neighbors, weapons drawn, jump from the van, break up the deal, and make arrests. The bad cop, we're told, is wearing a baseball cap. We get it all on tape and move on to the Shakespeare District lockup, where we focus on the baseball cap and the cop under it. Next day, the story's done and on the air.

Before I'm off the air, there's a call to the newsroom. I'm asked to return it when the broadcast is over. I do and am told I made a mistake, a big one. It's the cop under the baseball cap. "Wrong guy, Walter. You blew it. And you're gonna pay for it."

"Wrong guy? What do you mean, wrong guy?"

"You plastered my face all over your fucking tube and said I was in on that deal."

"The Internal Affairs guys identified—"

"I don't give a fuck what they did. That's me wearing the cap. I was in on it, yeah. In on making the arrest. You got the wrong guy, Walter. What the fuck am I supposed to do now? Now that you've told the whole world I'm a crooked cop. This'll cost you, Walter. You can bet your ass on that."

I better not bet my ass on it. I have (accidentally) described a good undercover policeman as a member of a gang of gun dealers. He sues Fox News Chicago, which settles for an undisclosed amount of money (media outlets don't reveal amounts for fear of encouraging lawsuits). What matters to me is that I made a terrible mistake and there's no way to correct it. I apologize on the news, but what's done is done. The station is paying a hefty price, not just in dollars but in credibility.

As the saying goes, "Shit happens." But because I know the consequences of shit happening, I'm careful. It's happened to me maybe half a dozen times in forty years of commentary.

"You have to be more than sure about things, Walter," warns the GM Marks-Bronner. "We have enough trouble. More damage suits against us than any of the other stations." We're first among Murdoch's stations, which means we're costing him more money, embarrassments, and headaches than New York or Los Angeles. "Not good, Walter. No more of those. You know what I mean?"

Yes, I do know what she means and carry it with me in search of errant and arrogant behavior of public officials, the waste of taxpayer dollars, and the secret wheeling and dealing in party headquarters. The range of "Perspective" is wide. We expose city workers who spend more time in the parking lot of a convenience food store than around potholes pouring asphalt. I lambaste a suburb for allowing a noisy factory to locate in a quiet residential area. Typical "Perspective," you say. Likely so, but I'm not always crabby.

When a management engineer in the city water department is discovered dealing drugs, I defend Mayor Daley. "Is it reasonable, do you think," I ask, "to expect the mayor to be watching all the city workers all the time, twenty-four hours a day and night? No, it's not."

I also express sympathy for the latest in a too-long line of Illinois governors and former governors to be indicted for corruption. "There's something about this trial of George Ryan that makes me uncomfortable," I opine. "A feeling that it's not fair, because the US attorney Peter Fitzgerald has an advantage. He can get information from witnesses in ways the defense cannot."

Most of my commentaries are more finger-wagging than the one about George Ryan, and most are about local issues and city, county, and state officials. But I set my sights on national figures, too. On Pete Rose's getting back into baseball: "I see Pete Rose as not only a fake and a liar, but as the ultimate sleaze, . . . conniving and conning his way back into *our* national pastime. He's already mucked it up enough."

About a certain blueblood visiting victims of Hurricane Katrina flooded from their homes and packed into the Houston Astrodome: "It's hard for me to say this in the news business, because I never know what's next. But I believe that now I've heard everything. Barbara Bush, wife of a former president of the

United States, mother of the current president of the United States, after seeing the victims of Katrina stuffed into the Astrodome, comments on National Public Radio that 'so many people in the arenas here, you know, were underprivileged anyway, so this is working very well for them.' The lesson and legacy of Barbara Bush. [Pause.] Barbara Bush. Yuk."

And yuk about her son George, whose second inauguration parties are costing $50 million: "That's $10 million more than the cost of his first inauguration parties, $20 million more than President Clinton spent, $25 million more than his dad spent. It's obscene, . . . American politicians and fat cats in Washington spending $50 million on parties while American troops are dying in Iraq."

It's fun to take shots at Pete Rose, Barbara Bush, and Dubbya, but I feel at my best when standing up for some little guy being rolled over by city hall and the powerfully well-connected.

For instance, this "Perspective": "The Great Chicago Land Grab . . . possibly the Chicago land grab of all time . . . city hall busting into a neighborhood, and taking not only the ground, but the property on it that neighbors say they need for survival . . . a medical center that's providing health care for families that can't get it anywhere else because they can't afford to go anywhere else. The politicians downtown are exercising their power of eminent domain to seize the property for luxury condos. They know the value of condo development, which is why they're aiming to tear the medical center down. Before you do that, would you consider a visit to the neighborhood, to at least meet the people you're about to displace?"

There's enough in my commentaries to rankle Mayor Daley to a point where he's had enough of Fox News Chicago and blows his stack. While watching the Bears on Fox one Sunday, he sees a promotion of a story we've scheduled for our news that night. It's about his capacity and will to intimidate and why people in his government, or who do business with it, refuse to talk about him. The promo sinks in and agitates until the mayor calls the station, demanding that the story be snuffed, which it is. Snuffed dead, taken off our story board.

When His Honor joggles the torpor of a Sunday newsroom, the weekenders in charge are not about to ignore what he has to say. They are unaccustomed to mayoral outbursts, inexperienced in dealing with spits of fire, timid about spitting back, and fearful of some unknown, unpredictable, unimaginable act of retaliation. There is insufficient nerve, or time, or adroit personnel in the newsroom on Sunday to challenge the mayor. A decision is quickly made, therefore, to hold the story for a day when more stubborn minds, and Fox lawyers, are on call.

Indulge me another "Perspective" (I've done more than six thousand of them):

The mayor has just won a third four-year term, scoring 70 percent of the vote, and is prideful and secure enough to swat reporters out of his face as he would mosquitos. Richard M. Daley is at the top of his game in the mid- and late 1990s.

He thinks he's invincible (which he is), so he has no problem raising hell with those of us who rub him the wrong way and takes pleasure in ignoring our questions. That may be difficult for much of the media, but for me it's fine because an unanswered question can be the point of a strong commentary. Best part of a story. Probably I ought not reveal this, but many of my "Perspectives" that are most nettlesome to politicians in city and state government can be blocked before air. All it takes is a return call at the end of a day. For example:

"Sorry, Walter, for getting back to you so late," apologizes (fake apology) a Mayor Daley press person in city hall.

"I understand, but I've been calling for three days. Couldn't get an answer until now. We're going with the story tonight."

"No. You can't do that. The reason for the problem you're asking about [a stop sign missing at a school crossing] is that we're short two crews."

"Why is that?"

"Accumulated time off. We've had it scheduled for tomorrow morning."

"Yes, ma'am." I suspect she's lying about having had it scheduled, but there's no way I can check it out before our news tonight, and I can't run the story until I do. And by tomorrow night the stop sign will be up. An end-of-the-day call is an effective strategy used by city hall to block a commentary it doesn't want on the air.

There's also a strategy for getting a reporter to tell a story city hall *does* want told. The late Mayor Washington was especially adept at that one. In the words of his press secretary Grayson Mitchell: "Jacobson has to come up with a commentary five days a week. A politician who knows that, and understands the pressure, can play Walter. Call him at 3:30 or 4:00 in the afternoon when he's running up the walls looking for a commentary, and give him something we want him to have."

Mayor Daley does not yet maneuver the media as adroitly or with as much finesse as Mayor Washington did, but he's at least as savvy. He knows that news is a business; like all businesses, its priority is to make money. News producers select and position stories depending on what sells. Keeping that in mind, as Daley does, he gets a lot of what he wants on and off the air.

And the mayor knows how to tussle with television. He prepares for news conferences by rehearsing short, declarative statements, and staying on point, always focused on avoiding mistakes. He is smarter and more Machiavellian than he lets on and has a contagious, if often deceptive, sense of humor, and a natural sense of timing. I'm fascinated by Richard M. Daley, his roots, his culture, his neighborhoods, and his brothers practicing politics and law. And I like him (more, I'll bet, than he likes me).

The brother most in sync with Mayor Daley is Bill, a LaSalle Street lawyer and banker. He is six years the mayor's junior but is his brother's guardian and closest and most trusted adviser. Bill also is the most astute and connected political insider in Illinois. The privileges that are his he uses to protect his brother's hold on the mayoralty and all that goes with it. He is very busy with Rich, watching his back, responding to and manipulating the media, and looking for trouble, which he senses long before it's dangerous—as with the ambitions of Barack Obama, an unnoticed member of the Illinois senate.

Bill Daley's instinct tells him Obama better be watched. He's mayor material, so he warrants the planning necessary to get him out of Chicago before it's too late (as their father did with the University of Chicago economist, venerable media-darling, and hugely popular Paul Douglas, whose eye was on that fifth-floor office in city hall; in 1948, Richard J. Daley, then a member of the Cook County Democratic Central Committee, with his own eye on the mayor's office, moved Douglas out of the city council, up to Capitol Hill and the United States Senate).

Brother Bill is President Clinton's secretary of commerce. He will go on to manage Albert Gore's run for the White House, get out of twenty-four-seven politics, and then back in as President Obama's chief of staff. Between the two of them, Bill and Rich together, the second Daley entrenchment is at hand as the twentieth century closes out and the twenty-first begins.

These are delicious times for Mayor Daley. He's rescuing public schools from incompetent management and improving test scores. His economy and public works are booming. His clout in Democratic Party circles, and at national conventions, is beginning to approach his dad's. He's been elected president of the national Conference of Mayors and will be named by *Time* magazine as the best big-city mayor in America.

Good for him, hard on us. The mayor is so pleased with himself and so certain of his authority and popularity that he's rebuffing reporters, dodging scrutiny, muscling publishers. His wins are impeding investigative journalists and mitigating our influence. An imperial mayoralty? That's not a stretch.

But it's not forever. Not now that the ferocious federal prosecutor, Peter Fitzgerald, is riding into town. The corruption-buster—"Eliot Ness with a Harvard law degree" is looking to run loose in city hall, aiming to shoot at elected and appointed public officials as he might shoot at fish in a barrel. Mayor Daley's chiefs of personnel and patronage will be indicted, convicted, and sent to prison.

Tables are turning. We reporters are restless and becoming relentless with questions about evidence of widespread corruption in the Daley domain. It's under his nose. How can he not know of it? He says he can't keep track of thousands of employees, which he cannot, not when they're dealing drugs. But when they're in high positions close to his office, or inside and close to his politics? He says he hopes their behavior is not what it may appear to be. When the columnists and commentators say that it is, the struggle between mayor and reporters escalates, then cools down or heats up depending on the stories of the day and the nature of the comments.

It's all part of a greater struggle between reporters and their news managers over choosing stories to cover. What's news and what's not has a lot, too much, to do with what the ratings are. Our Fox News sales department wants us to back off our insistence on doing stories about corruption in city hall and, especially, the politics in front of and behind it. The ad world is telling us to target twenty- to thirty-five-year-olds who, say the time-buyers, are not interested in politics. I say okay, but let's not dumb-down the news. But we must, say the sales people, because viewers who are tuned to Fox during prime time don't care about Mayor Daley's patronage. They're watching *American Idol* before our ten o'clock news comes on the air, and to keep them tuned-in we must tell *American Idol* kinds of stories—about a contestant's personal life, or about Simon Cowell or Paula Abdul, the show's judges.

In 2004 Stacey Marks-Bronner, the general manager who hired me to help beef-up Fox News, and who's been protecting the news department, is iced in a corporate political scramble by Lachlan Murdoch, Rupert's son in charge of company stations. After twelve years of boosting the quality and ratings of Fox News in Chicago, and ringing the register, Stacey's gone. Suddenly. Just like that. Without warning. When she comes to work one morning, she is handed a pink slip by a corporate executive who flew in the night before. Within two hours, she is out the door onto Michigan Avenue, wondering how to look for a job. Her news director, Debra Juarez, and assistant news director, Terri Cornelius, are next, replaced by sales-types, not news-types. I can see the handwriting on the monitors.

18

Good-bye to Fox

*A*merican Idol* and I don't mesh. I'm not good at dissolving news into entertainment. My heroes in broadcasting are Huntley and Brinkley, and Cronkite, Chancellor, Sevareid, and Edward R. Murrow. I know what Murrow would say about *American Idol* and Rupert Murdoch's Fox News: "Good night, and good-*bye*." He'd have nothing to do with either one of them. Sadly, our news is like Rupert Murdoch himself, dancing with stars. Our broadcasts are star struck. Fox News and I don't get along, not anymore.

My contract will be up soon, and I know that barring a revolution at corporate headquarters in New York, I won't be offered a new one. In fact, an anchor just hired is being described by the media as my replacement-in-waiting. He is Mark Suppelsa from WMAQ-Channel 5, and rumor has it there's a clause in his contract assuring him that by the end of a certain period of time, he'll be lead anchor on our evening broadcast. If not, Fox will pay him a hefty sum. How much, and at what time, I don't know. I'm not privy to the negotiations or the company's plans.

I may get yanked from the anchor desk the way Stacey was yanked from the GM's office, without notice, which is SOP in the TV news business. For now, Suppelsa is a third anchor in the studio with Robin and me, on the set of our late evening news, reading stories for a few minutes every night. This is causing some unease in the shop about how uncomfortable I may be sharing my role.

I'm not happy about it, of course, but can't avoid it, and I must agree that Mark's a good choice to replace me. He's experienced, believable, well-informed (there's always a *New York Times* on his desk in the morning), a seriously committed and competitive journalist of integrity. Unlike so many others on the market for local anchor positions, Mark Suppelsa is not a Ken doll (and Robin Robinson, my coanchor, and his to be, certainly is not a Barbie; on the contrary, she's as no-nonsense a news anchor as there is in the United States, a Chicago fixture as tough as they come).

Mark is patient, respectful, and sensitive to my angst. The newsroom likes him, and the viewers seem to. He's forty years old (I'm sixty-seven), a very nice guy. When I have to raise anchor, if his is the one to be dropped, I'll be okay.

I will not be okay if I have to give up the commentary. There are too many good ones to do. Mayor Daley has now won his fifth term and is being battered by that persistent federal investigation and our exposing shenanigans under his nose. There's a scandal of monstrous proportions looming that involves huge sums of money in the city's trucking business. While under cover of a dark night, the mayor has sparked a fire by cutting up runways at Meigs Field airport to make space for another one of his public parks.

George W. Bush is running for reelection. Barack Obama is running for the US Senate. Former governor George Ryan soon will be in prison, and former governor Rod Blagojevich won't be far behind. With something new to chew on every day, I'm in reporter-anchor-commentator paradise. Unfortunately for my television managers, and for me personally, my paradise sometimes is their paradise lost. Commentary is a threat to the financial well-being of our station. It's inviting our advertisers to attack.

Looking back:

I did a "Perspective" on Fox Chicago one night about a family unable to pay its heating bills. Winter was blowing terrible winds, and the children were cold. No money, no gas. Peoples Gas turned it off. I went after the utility, which accused me of being inaccurate. Desirée Rogers, a Peoples Gas vice president (and future White House social secretary) called Marks-Bronner, my general manager, to demand a retraction, and to threaten to stop spending millions on Fox for advertising time.

Stacey requested my presence in her office. Did I make a mistake? No, I didn't, and I had interviews and paperwork to back up everything I said. But, feeling bad for my GM, and anticipating trouble ahead, I offered to call Peoples Gas to talk about the story. Please do, she said, much relieved.

I made the call. My story was accurate, I told Desirée Rogers, so I won't retract it, but I want to be fair and balanced. I told her if she'd give me an interesting, positive story about her company, I'd be happy to confirm it, then tell it. Call me anytime. Okay, she said. Okay, I said. And she did not stop advertising on Fox.

She was fine, I was fine, my general manager was fine, and that was the end of it. No problem—until the next business executive is peeved by my snooping, and calls to complain, and threatens to strike back—if not Peoples Gas again, then maybe Commonwealth Edison, AT&T, United Airlines, or Bank of America. It's not a picnic managing a television station in Chicago, having to cool a smoldering titan of commerce or industry, and then a TV titan who's the boss smoldering about the smoldering, or about ratings.

At whatever station, owned and operated by whichever network, most general managers in Chicago are so terrified of their bosses in New York that just a sniff of controversy or a dip in a number drives them to the medicine chest in search of a cure. Invariably, they yank the same ol' med that doesn't work—lighten up the broadcast, speed it up, and lead with what bleeds. Expand the weather, add some gossip and a scoop of sex.

And if nothing happens, which is usually what happens, double the dose. And if that doesn't help, double it again, and add more celebrity and sensation. Create a news broadcast featuring Jerry Springer doing political commentary, add more stories about pets. And if still nothing happens, shuffle producers, change anchors, then fire the news director.

So what's the result? Rick Kogan, author and media critic on Chicago radio and in the *Chicago Tribune,* writes about television news: "The [nightly broadcasts] have become inconsequential: filled with video oddities, features, and fluff; and, too often for comfort, a stream of murders, fires, sex, and other notes from the police blotter . . . failing to provide any context, insight, or useful information. They are simply there, as innocuous as the music piped into office-building elevators. This is the age of News-zak."

Amen. During the ratings sweeps in February, May, and November every year, local broadcast time is consumed by "Woman Stalked," "Chicago Centerfolds," "Hotel Bedbugs," and what to eat. Once in a while, a hyped-up News-zak-nothing can kick the numbers for a night or two, but the dip comes back, and the managers go back to figuring out how to kick 'em again.

Opinion polls and surveys? Nope. They're good at discerning what voters will do on election day, choosing between one candidate and another. Polls and surveys are not good at discerning what viewers want to see on the news, choosing between one story and a hundred others.

Rupert Murdoch does not permit his stations to invest in surveys. They're useless, he says, a waste of money. So how does a general manager find out what viewers want? Many of those for whom I've worked, a different one every three or four years, think they can do it by placing a finger on "the pulse of the market." Nice idea, but it doesn't work because in Chicago, there is no pulse of the market. There are pulses of many markets, of extraordinarily wide variety—poor and rich markets; middle-class, black, white, brown, ethnic, religious, and people-who-like-sports, and people-who-don't markets.

It takes time to understand markets. A general manager bolting up the ladder to somewhere else doesn't have the time; when pressed to stop another dip in the ratings, she or he dives into the anchor-résumé drawer to pull out someone from a smaller market who may look and sound good and command less of a salary, but in all likelihood will be at a loss when it comes to reporting with authority what Chicago and suburbs need to know.

Nor does a frantic general manager have time to understand Chicago-style loyalty, or how slowly Chicago responds to change. It's quicker and easier, but dangerous, to do what a predecessor did—change anchors, which often costs a station enough of its viewers to cause a dip in the ratings to become a slide. In Chicago, slides are hard to stop, especially when the content of the broadcasts is frivolous.

Kogan in the *Tribune*: "The aim is to appeal to the most viewers, and with that pressure, news judgment can get cloudy . . . twenty seconds on a forty-foot-wide sinkhole in Ohio! A robber kicking the daylights out of a clerk! A urine-filled toilet. Why am I watching this? So often when it's over, I realize I have not benefited at all. I could have been watching something else, or nothing at all. Stop calling it 'news.'"

Not a bad idea, Rick, to stop calling it news, which is what it isn't. Evening broadcasts, with sports, weather, and commercials, sold and hyped as "news," are making money. Management is not about radical change. How, then, to make the broadcasts what they say they are, and what they're supposed to be? You'd think that having been intimately involved for nearly half a century, I'd be up to answering that question. But I'm not. I don't know.

I do know, though, what I would try. If I were a general manager, I'd call a news conference and fiercely reject the idea that to appeal to television news viewers, we must be News-zak—serving up violence, diets, health, beauty, and freaky pictures from around the world. I'd pledge to inform more than entertain. I'd stop saying that viewers want their news Bud-Lite because it's easy to swallow. I don't think that's true. But even if it is, our mission is to do better than that. I believe we can fulfill it, and make money, too.

The newspapers are being crunched by hard economics; they're shrinking in size and substance, creating a void into which television can charge. If we in TV expand and elevate our coverage and analysis of local events, go deeper into issues that matter instead of insulting our viewers with fluff, we'll hang on to them and attract readers of Chicago and suburban newspapers. Television can tell a story, disseminate information, in immediate, arresting, and dramatic ways that print cannot. A good example is the one about the remarkable career of Barack Obama.

From the beginning:

When he is first elected a state senator in 1997, there's more to be learned by watching him than by reading about him, more clarity to be gained by listening to his words than reading them in a newspaper. It's easier to gauge the honesty of his intentions by looking into his eyes than reading a reporter's description.

At Fox news, I see Obama as the most interesting, under-the-radar elected official in Chicago politics. With a few extra minutes on our nine o'clock news, I can let Obama speak, and I can report what I'm being told by three people

I trust, exceptionally reliable sources—that in the private quarters of Mayor Daley's politics there is concern about Obama emerging as trouble, as African American political dynamite. He's running for reelection to the Illinois senate; there's nobody even bothering to run against him. What if he fancies himself a Harold Washington who can reactivate minority politics, and challenge Daley for mayor in 2007?

The mayor's trusted strategist and publicist, David Axelrod, is encouraging Obama to resist even thinking about city hall, to fancy himself a candidate for the US Senate, and maybe the White House. Axelrod wants that man out of Chicago.

Next thing we know, Axelrod is guiding Obama through a 2004 Democratic primary en route to the US Senate, slicking the way by helping (I believe but can't prove) the *Chicago Tribune* to some whopping election-eve headlines about his opponent's nasty divorce, including allegations of physical abuse. Behind the headlines, there's much to be told, but in newsroom competition for camera crews and air time, hot pants in Hollywood trump analysis in politics.

Axelrod, a former *Tribune* reporter, will lead Obama to the 2004 Democratic National Convention, where an up-and-comer keynote speech will spellbind the nation. Soon Obama will be a US senator, and then president, the trusted Axelrod as his senior adviser. That's Obama.

What about another young, ambitious Chicago politician, Rod Blagojevich of the northwest side of Chicago? His goal is the governor's mansion in Springfield, his senior adviser his father-in-law Dick Mell, an alderman, committeeman, and Democratic Party heavyweight. Dick has been leading Rod along the corridors and alleys of machine politics, landing him two terms in the Illinois General Assembly, three in the US Congress, and he's now aiming at something bigger. Blagojevich is urging me to keep an eye on him. We're poolside at a soiree in Los Angeles tossed by party bigwigs, lobbyists, and fundraisers. "The House of Representatives isn't for me," Blago whispers, scoping the crowd for other Chicago reporters to urge likewise. "Too many people to suck-up to."

"I can imagine," I say. "That's how life is in politics at your age. You're thirty-six, right?"

"Yeah, but I gotta get out of the House . . . out of the audience, onto the stage. I gotta run the show."

"Like what, for instance?"

"Governor."

So that's it. Governor. This guy's planning a run for governor of Illinois. I believe him. Why not? His father-in-law has enough muscle to get him endorsed by the party, and onto a primary ballot.

Blago is charismatic and movie-star handsome, a graduate of Northwestern University in Evanston and Pepperdine's law school in Malibu, child of immigrant parents dreaming of America and crossing the Atlantic with hope in their hearts, zero in their pockets. His dad labored in a steel mill, his mom in a booth taking tickets for the Chicago Transit Authority. He's the grandson of a rural pig farmer in Yugoslavia, a crafted populist, savvy and sophisticated, a Chicago politician who speaks fluent Serbian.

As far as I can tell, all he'll have going against him in a race for governor will be the surfing, pacific-coast cockiness he brought home from law school, and his narcissism. He'll hide them both behind an of-the-people facade, make the necessary connections, swell his coffers, and do what he says he'll do—get out of the audience, and onto the stage, the first Democrat elected governor of Illinois in twenty-seven years. It's a helluva story, Rod Blagojevich and the party machinery. But television news has neither the time nor the inclination to report it.

Television doesn't get it, that in Chicago at family dinner time, the main course is news; at bedtime, the good-night is politics. And that Chicago, more than any other big city in America, will reward with ratings the most inclusive and incisive coverage of politics, the lifeblood of a citizenry deeply affected by the results of elections.

In 1993 I signed up with Fox, contracting to stay for two years. After thirteen, I'm still anchoring and doing commentary. But time and static ratings are coming after me. Mark Suppelsa is ready and waiting, as is our new general manager, Debbie Carpenter, who's come up through the ranks of television sales (every newsy's nightmare because sales people are motivated by numbers, news people by news).

Carpenter's priority is to ease the anchor transition from me to Suppelsa by involving me in the announcement. "Would you mind joining a little party in the newsroom," she asks, "to toast his doing the nine o'clock?" Would I mind? That's irrelevant. Will I do it? Of course.

"I'd like to add my two cents to this celebration," I say, walking up to Mark, and extending my hand, which he takes with a smile, and some relief in his eyes. All people present are relieved, it seems. I continue in words like these: "Change is good. You're the right guy for it, and I believe it's best for Fox News. I'd be dishonest if I said I'm doing cartwheels about it, but now is the right time, and I'll be happy and feel good contributing the commentary. I wish you well, Mark. I wish us all well. And we will be, I know."

The champagne is uncorked, and Debbie Carpenter's platitudes flow. Congratulations and light small talk all around, and that's it. Suppelsa's on the anchor desk, Jacobson's off.

Carpenter's next priority is to transition me off the commentary, off the payroll entirely, and out of the building. There are now six months remaining on my contract, so negotiations are in order. My agent, Steve Mandell, is calling the general manager for an appointment.

"She's not calling me back," he tells me.

"I'm not surprised. She'd rather not. This isn't going to be easy. What do we do?"

"Tell her you want to continue the commentary, three or four nights a week, and that a one-year extension will be enough."

"At half my salary."

"Okay, at half your salary."

Okay for me, but not for Debbie Carpenter. Half my salary is $500,000 a year. Her rulers in New York are pressing her to cut her budget. For close to that money she can hire a couple of young anchors, and probably a reporter, too. Saying good-bye to me is a good way to satisfy the bean counters—and at the same time make her job easier. I'm an irritant, always scratching at management. A grumpy, sixty-eight-year-old broken record: "This isn't news, isn't news, isn't news. It's garbage, garbage, garbage."

For years at the anchor desk, on-camera, live during broadcasts, I've been declaring my objection to stories that don't matter, like man-on-the-street interviews. "The mayor says Chicago needs a third airport," I read on the teleprompter. "Fox News finds out what the people think," and two talking heads appear on the screen, one saying, "It's a good idea," the other saying it's not. They disappear, and I reappear, turning to Robin Robinson, who's coanchoring, then to the camera, and harrumph, "I don't see how two sidewalkers on Michigan Avenue can represent what eight million people in the metropolitan area are thinking about anything." I scrunch my shoulders and furrow my brow, as if to ask, why are we doing this?

Needless to say, that is inappropriate anchor behavior. I know that at times I'm too full of myself, and that news directors, producers, writers, and editors have thought I'm much too full of myself. And I know that general managers are always thinking, enough of Walter already.

I believe that even if I offer Carpenter a few commentaries a week for free, she'll say she's not interested, and she'll add whatever she can to deter me from sounding-off to a Chicago newspaper that's sure to be read in New York. The wrong kind of publicity is as bad for her as a bloated budget. However she puts it to my agent, what she means is there will be no going back to Walter Jacobson as the face of Fox News in Chicago.

Dilemmas abound. Debbie Carpenter's is what to do with me. Mine is what to do with myself. The news department's dilemma is how to dull the edges of unease. It's difficult to dispatch a high-profile anchor without leaving a void. I've been agitating news viewers three or four nights a week for nearly half a century. My "Perspectives" provoke strong feelings, good and bad. They draw attention, loads of it, from politicians, elected officials, activists in the neighborhoods, mayoral pals on LaSalle Street, and columnists in the press. Neither Murdoch in New York, nor Carpenter in Chicago, can wish me off the air, or secret me off. They'll have to take me off in front of everybody. What's the risk, what will people think, and most critically, what will they do with their remote controls?

While Rupert's jaunty claque and Debbie's timid staff ponder, I'll make it as thorny for them as I can. I'll swell my profile with commentaries about arm-twisters in city hall and spillages of taxpayers' dollars. And I'll respond to queries by reporters who keep calendars on anchor contracts. They know mine's coming up, so they'll be calling for information about intrigue and maneuvering inside the station's private meeting places.

Carpenter herself is on the way out but is nonetheless negotiating my contract. She knows in advance how our talks will end but is listening (or is pretending to listen) to my argument to change her mind, that political commentary represents a commitment to high standards of news judgment, and that "Perspective," if nothing else, is a ratings grabber. End of argument. But to lift my heavy heart (and keep me quiet), Carpenter is giving me a news and live-interview show of my own, at the no-viewer hour of eight o'clock on Sunday mornings.

The news director has been told that in conversations with me about my last contract renewal, he's to remind me that when I signed it, I chose to end it in April 2006. When that month rolls around, it will be done. In Fox's scenario of my "retirement," there will be a salute by me in a fond farewell to the station, and a salute by the station to me (to make viewers think it's hard to let me go) in a video celebration of my career, to run three nights on the evening news (in place of stories that matter, no doubt). And a good-bye commentary, a cheek-to-cheek with Robin, and a going-away bash with balloons and a marching band, live on the air! I cringe at the thought of it, and use my last bit of clout to forbid it.

19

The Ups and Downs of Celebrity

Pick a day, any day. I'm at work at my desk when a good friend calls to ask if I'd please make a reservation for him for dinner at RL, on Chicago Avenue off Michigan, currently the most "in" place in town, where Mayor Daley brings a few close friends, and Oprah Winfrey a table-full. It's nearly impossible to get in, especially when calling at four-thirty for a table at six.

I say to my friend, "I don't want to do that. I'll feel like a hypocrite," which is honest. He says to me, "But it's the only way we'll get in," which is true. The choice eateries in Chicago are over-reserved, and full-up for dinner. But they manage to save tables, the good ones, for celebrities who call at the last minute, which most of us do to maintain our status as celebrities. I don't like doing it—and rarely do—because I've made a career out of railing at VIPs flaunting a sense of entitlement, and I don't want to be the subject of a newspaper story about television anchors throwing their weight around in restaurants where people are standing in line for a table.

Also, I can't very well say, "This is Walter Jacobson of Fox News," because I'm not anymore. And I don't want to say, "formerly of Fox News," because who cares? And the worst is how bad I feel when a fresh-out-of-college host answering telephones at RL asks, "Who did you say is calling, Walter who?" That's embarrassing. Celebrity life sometimes is.

Way back when Fahey Flynn was an anchor, I remember one morning standing in line at a ticket counter at an American Airlines departure gate at O'Hare. I watched Fahey, then of Channel 7 News, strut to the front of the line, thrust his ticket onto the counter, and smile. "Oh, Mr. Flynn," fluttered the ticket-taker. "We have space up front and are happy to have you use it."

"Why, thank you," gushed Fahey, off to his seat by a window in row 3. I waited a half hour more for my seat, and a processed ham sandwich in the middle of row 41, between a three-hundred-pound hulk and a mother with a fidgety baby.

Celebrity got Fahey, and gets most media "stars," what we want. Ask any ten anchors in Chicago, including me, how we like being famous, and I bet the answers you get from nine of the ten will include these words: "don't care about being famous." "only want to provide information," "expose corruption," "explain the meaning of things," and "not interested in fame."

Sounds good, but it's not true, because fame is the measure of an anchor's success. If viewers don't know the name of the anchor they're watching, and are not tuning-in to see him or her, then the anchor has no standing in the market and need not be paid a big anchor salary. So we do care about celebrity and ought to be honest about it. The perks come along for the ride.

I began mixing into the celebrity crowd about thirty-five years ago, soon after CBS gambled on Bill Kurtis and me at an anchor desk in a working newsroom. Because that hadn't been tried in Chicago before, it drew us inordinate attention. Day after day, for days on end, there were newspaper columns about things, often nothings, going on at Channel 2 News:

"Sad news to report today, Walter Jacobson's new mustache is going to go," said the *Daily News*.

"Jacobson, as all Chicago knows by now," said the *Tribune*, "got a suspension last week for exchanging hot words with an associate producer."

In his annual Chicago Cubs trivia quiz, Mike Royko asked, "Which TV commentator used to be a Cubs batboy? The answer is the immortal Walter Jacobson. He said he didn't enjoy it because the rowdy players always threw their underwear at him," etcetera, etcetera, etcetera for another five hundred words. "Now I must go and watch the late news show. I don't want to miss Jacobson's commentary. I always throw my underwear at the screen."

Constant attention like that boosted our ratings, which buffeted our celebrity, which drew more attention that buffeted it more, enough to get us into Hollywood movies. Bill's major role was as narrator in Will Ferrell's *Anchorman: The Legend of Ron Burgundy*. Mine was as anchorman in an episode of *The Bob Newhart Show*. Bit parts for sure, but they added to the celebrity.

I was on the screen one minute, Bill a little more than that, and we were described as actors (of limited range), as Walter Cronkite was in his bit part in *Murphy Brown*. But, hey, being in a movie, or on prime-time TV, is fun, and it can't hurt ratings on the news. Anchor Brian Williams hosted *Saturday Night Live*.

And now, all these years later, my Hollywood celebrity is burnished by my son, Peter, who plays Dr. Taub in the hit TV drama *House*. When we're walking a street in Chicago, people push me out of the way to get an autograph from him. Even in the stands in Wrigley Field, my place, where I was the batboy, my son's the one. We were cheering an RBI, and the row in front of us, hearing Peter's voice, jumped around to look through me to see him.

Proud dad, I like it when that happens, mostly because he likes it, but also because I've already had enough of it. My other children are not in the movies, but making me just as proud. Wendy is a consultant on issues involving children and families, Julia an innovator and entrepreneur in the fashion world in New York, and Genevieve, a senior in college, also is in New York.

None of them has ever had the slightest interest in a career in television news. No chips off my ol' block. I believe that growing up, they had enough of TV newsrooms, sitting under anchor desks while Dad was on the air, and in control booths and in editing rooms, and around assignment desks. And they had enough of my job imposing on family time, and too much of my leaving home every night at bedtime. When, on the news, I scolded a parent of one of their friends, my children took the heat.

Interestingly, there are several downsides to celebrity, the big one being loss of privacy. Privacy. Think Tiger Woods. I'll never be in his league, of course, but even down my way in the minor leagues, the public eye can be too searching, as it was for me after I had been drinking champagne at an event for a new publisher of the magazine *Today's Chicago Women*. I was driving home, six blocks, when stopped by police in the alley outside my house, and informed, even before I could think about asking, that I would not get a pass "because you'll put me on TV." I was arrested and ticketed for DUI. And for two days, my mug shot was in the newspapers and on the Internet. Then a Cook County prosecutor was particularly rough on me because, she said, to my lawyer, "Your client is too well-known."

And, of course, I'm not in Robert Redford's league either, but as he once said about being in the movies, "You can't imagine it. You work like hell to get yourself ahead in the business. You could go anywhere before, and suddenly you can't go anywhere. It's like being a cartoon character."

For most men, the celebrity problem is bad behavior. For women, it's gender. Take Amy Jacobson (no relation), for example. For several years she was a high-profile on-air reporter for WMAQ Channel 5. On a day off in 2007, she went swimming with her toddlers and was on the way home when her cell phone chirped. It was a call from a sister of Craig Stebic, who'd been ducking the press since becoming a suspect in the disappearance of his estranged wife.

"Let's talk about the case," Craig's sister said. "C'mon over, right now, we're having a pool party in his backyard." It was the call every reporter in Chicago was hoping for, but Amy Jacobson was the one who got it. Alas, she was in her bikini bathing suit, children in the back seat. What was she to do? Say she's sorry, can't make it, have to change clothes? (I know what I would have done if I had had to: gone naked.) Amy stepped on the gas and drove directly to Craig Stebic's, and to an exclusive interview—and wound up the subject of stories and pictures on television and in newspapers around the country, in a bikini with a towel around her waist.

Knowing of her celebrity, and seeing her in Stebic's backyard, a neighbor had called a competing TV station, which, also knowing of her celebrity, sped to the scene of Amy's "crime"- in-progress, and, over a fence, took pictures of her in her in bikini in a doorway on a telephone.

The photos were then released to all who asked, and Amy instantly became a national celebrity—and was fired. Such is the consequence of America's insatiable appetite for naughty news about celebrities. And such is the price well-known people pay for being well known.

What if John Kass of the *Tribune*, the toughest—and perhaps most celebrated—columnist in town, were in a Speedo bathing suit at a pool party with the mobster Joey "the Clown" Lombardo? Would he be splashed on front pages coast-to-coast, and on Fox News and CNN around the world? No, he would not. John Kass in a Speedo would not be the news that Amy Jacobson in a bikini was. Amy was front-page because she's a woman. Chicago's venerable newspapers, our citadels of gender equality, forever clamoring against the sins of sexism, behave like the bastion of it. They exploited Amy Jacobson's celebrity, and her gender, by making a story out of her being in a bikini that they'd never make out of John Kass in a Speedo. A lesson in all that is that a woman reporter better carry an overcoat, because in pursuit of a scoop she may have to change clothes.

One more thing: Celebrities often are best known as people they are not. I'm not the person in-person that I am on television. Watch me doing a commentary, and you think I'm mean, a bully who pleasures in ridiculing people for minor infractions—a garbage collector who's nipping, or napping for a few minutes on the job, or a seventy-year-old alderman who's clouting a friend, or a policeman who's being rough in a rough neighborhood. "Watch out for Jacobson," people say. "He's out to get you." That's the celebrity me they're talking about. The real me is not a bully. I'm rather timid, actually, very afraid of making a mistake on the air that may hurt someone.

Anyway, back to what I'm doing in television news.

It's spring in 2008. My contract with Fox is up, and I'm gone from the business, no longer fretting about the downsides of celebrity or troubled by enjoying some leftover perks. And since there's nothing I can do about television news, I'm not griping about fluff as passionately as I used to. But news in Chicago has been my life, so I still worry about what it is, and where it's going, which is into the jaws of the Internet. Millions of homes in Chicago and the rest of the country are connected to the Web. And every day, more people are visiting it, loving it, and turning off television news. Advertisers are not spending, revenue's not coming in, and operating costs are over the top.

The stations are desperate. The networks that own them are frantic. One day there's a buzz in the business that CBS is giving up on Channel 2 News, the next day it's that Murdoch of Fox is about to sell all of his owned-and-operated stations. And as always in a crunch in a budget, the first thing carved out is mobility of staff. No more following Mayor Daley around the world or the Cubs and Sox through several weeks of spring training. When the mayor goes to Denmark and is awakened from his dream of hosting the 2016 Summer Olympics, the news team covering him for Fox Chicago consists of a reporter and his computer. No cameraman. The modus in local television news is keeping people home to cut the overtime. Crews en route to news are stopped by the assignment desk, and told to break for lunch. "Get off the clock!"

This is the right time for me to walk away from newsrooms and anchor desks, to travel to purge television's problems from my mind, and to think back to when it all began for me—journalism, and the eternally fascinating combat between politicians and political reporters. For the first time in fifty years I'm on my own, out of work except for an occasional election night on television and a few commentaries on NPR-WBEZ, and to pinch-hit for Roe Conn, the sassy and popular talk show host on WLS Radio, or speculate about Mayor Daley's future, or about the Cubs with Bob Sirott on WGN. Radio is a wonderful medium, more flexible and forgiving than television, less constrained by management's fear of listener/viewer reaction. An "um" or "Let me think about that," or five seconds of dead air are okay on radio. I don't have to wear a suit on radio, or tie a tie, or be made up or make myself up, or sit still, or read a teleprompter. Just listen to what a caller asks or says, and say something back. Have a conversation.

Finally, I'm done with TV—or am I?

20

Yanked from Retirement

"Walter, it's Jeff Kiernan." He's the Channel 2 news director. "I have something I'd like to run by you, you and Bill Kurtis ... to do our ten o'clock broadcast. Rob [Rob Johnson, Channel 2's ten o'clock anchor] will be off on the Friday after next. I'd like you two to sit in for him."

I'm dumbfounded, then flattered, then intrigued. "Interesting idea. It'd be fun to do. But you're in the sweeps. And—"

"So what?"

"You'll get nailed by the press for concocting a stunt for the ratings."

"I don't care about that. It's not a stunt. I want a straightforward broadcast. No nostalgia stuff, or yapping small talk. And I'd like you to do a commentary."

"Are you serious, Jeff? Why?"

"I grew up watching Channel 2 News. You guys are Chicago. I'd like to see you again."

"A regular thirty minutes, including weather and sports?"

"Yes, and the commentary. The ten o'clock news the way you did it when you started."

"That was thirty-six years ago. I haven't read a prompter in three and a half," I say, remembering what it's like when that dreadful thing stops in midsentence, or goes into reverse. Oh, so what? It may even be part of the fun if I blow it. It's just one night. I'm seventy-three, my anchor days are long gone. I'm not looking for an audition. What's to lose? "Okay, Jeff. Why not? What about Bill?"

"He's excited about the idea."

"Great. I'd love to do it."

"Good, Walter. Thanks. We can pay you eight hundred dollars."

"That's fine, Jeff. It's not the money. You said you want a commentary? How long, and on what subject?"

"A minute, minute-fifteen. On whatever you want. Something local, related to the news of the day. However you want to do it. In shirtsleeves and suspenders?"

"You don't think that'll look like an act?"

"No, I don't. But wear what you want. Be comfortable."

"Have you told Rob and the staff?"

"Rob's all for it. We'll tell the staff the day before and then notify the press."

And so he does; and he buys space in the papers for a picture of Bill and me anchoring at Channel 2 thirty-seven years ago. When word gets out, it spreads, and the columnists and talk-show hosts begin talking about it. Bill and I are asked, and happily oblige, to make the rounds like, I hate to say it, celebrities.

I write a commentary about the bumps in Mayor Daley's road:

> You'd think that a polished politician like Daley is too smart to do dumb things, but he's doing them anyway. He is so flummoxed by the recession that he's over the edge on how to handle it . . . choking on a budget that's $500 million in the red . . . planning to run fewer buses and trains . . . telling Chicago police to take four weeks off without pay, even though the force already is two thousand officers short of being able to serve and protect . . . allowing labor unions to charge outrageous fees for setting up conventions at McCormick Place . . . having residents and tourists lug around pockets full of quarters to plug parking meters . . . throwing away money (like Jay Cutler throws away passes) on a lawsuit to prevent us from finding out how a friend got a $100,000 no-bid city contract. So what's going on with His Honor? Is it possible, as some insiders are whispering, that he's had enough, and is seriously considering not running for reelection? Can it be that he's so unhappy about losing the Olympics and being abused by the media, and so worn-out by tales of corruption and pals in prison, that he's thinking of bowing out?

The next day, when asked about my commentary, the mayor brushes it off and adds one of his own. "Listen," he says, "I'm still here and [Walter's] been out of Channel 2 for a long time. Like anything else, he needs publicity and Channel 2 needs help. I don't know if he's helping them."

All-in-all, as Kiernan figures, Kurtis-Jacobson '73 is worth a look. The nostalgia is thick, but not overbearing. We are relaxed, comfortable, and, as we always were, helpful to each other. To us, the fun of thirty minutes thirty-seven years later makes it feel like we never stopped. And I don't once blow the prompter. If there is something missing, it's Bill's not having to dig Walter out of a hole.

Kiernan's one-nighter attracts a bigger audience than he, or his general manager, Bruno Cohen, thought it would. And a big one of the right demographic—the eighteen-to-forty-nine-year-olds coveted by the ad world. For one night, Channel 2 News lurches out of its stagnant last place in the ten o'clock ratings, surges past Channel 5 into a neck-and-neck with Chicago's domineering newscast on Channel 7.

Our postgame speculation is that young people whose parents reminisce about Bill and me tuned in to see what the fuss was all about. And the Boomers, they're looking for some of the past, because they still have an appetite for what Len O'Connor called "sweet Chicago," and for the coverage that holds accountable those who are elected and appointed to lead our way.

I like to think there's a message in the success of that one night, the two of us together back from the past—that despite the subjective, inaccurate, irresponsible, but popular blogging on the Web; the inflamed rhetoric on CNN, MSNBC, and Fox; and the budget calamities shaping local broadcasts into cookie-cutter imitations of each other, there is reason to be positive about television news. Robert Feder says that ever-advancing technology "is making it possible for news and information to be shared and disseminated in ways people could never have dreamed before."

A few weeks after our Bill-and-Walter experiment, Jeff Kiernan, Channel 2 news director, calls to ask if I'd like to try my commentaries again, for a month or so, twice a week on the ten o'clock broadcast. Is he kidding? Does a bear [bleep] in the woods? I take off!

About President Obama: "He and his Chicago mafia are playing games infinitely more complicated than any they've played anywhere anytime before, and dealing with congressional opposition and a press corps infinitely more brutal . . ."

About Vice President Joe Biden: "Oh, no. Not again. What is it about Joe Biden that he can't keep his foot out of his mouth? He knows when cameras are rolling and the microphones are on . . . a Delaware lawyer with seven honorary degrees . . . six times reelected to the United States Senate, chairman of the Foreign Relations Committee. He mixes with leaders of nations, allies and enemies. His big mouth could cause an international crisis. So why doesn't he keep his foot out of it? Maybe he's out of control, in which case he's a hazard. Try to control yourself, Joe. You have to control yourself. Like Carlos Zambrano of the Cubs, Joe, grow up."

About Rod Blagojevich on trial for charges of conspiracy to commit wire fraud, bribery, and extortion. He and his wife, Patti, bring their daughters, fourteen and seven years old, to watch the proceedings: Despicable, I say, "the damage they're doing to their children, dressing them up and shoving them into a horde of reporters and clicking cameras, then into a courtroom of gawkers, to sit still to listen to how evil a person their father is. . . . I don't know about the charges of corruption, but if I were on the jury I'd vote to send Rod and Patti both to prison for child abuse."

And about Mayor Daley directing his inspector general to keep an eye on the city council: "aiming to catch an alderman or two putting pals on the public payroll, or taking money in exchange for favors. An alderman misbehaves and gets caught, the mayor will say that *his* inspector general is the one who caught him or her. Smart move, Mr. Mayor, . . . but you better be careful. While you're siccing the city inspector general on the aldermen, they'll be siccing him onto you."

And Dan Rostenkowski, the legendary Chicago politician, former alderman, member of Congress, chairman of Ways and Means, Mister Democrat, President Lyndon Johnson's BFF on Capitol Hill: "His funeral is sad for me. We grew up together in between politics and the press. I said more bad things about him than good, but we were friends. He liked reporters. I like politicians, especially Rosty, because he talked to me about those games—to the victor go the spoils—which he played like an MVP. When he fouled out was when the games became crimes. On his way into prison he said his conscience is clear, on his way out he said his conscience is clear. Both ways, I believed him."

And the Illinois General Assembly in Springfield: "It's amazing how the leaders of our government don't do what we elect and pay them to do. In the past five months, they've been in session just two weeks, hauling in their $67,000 salaries plus their shares of the $400,000 a year we're spending on their auto mileage, and the $800,000 on their hotels and restaurants. They just walked out on what they promised us they'd be in Springfield to do, in order to schmooze the voters about how much they've done, and about how proud of themselves they are. What they ought to be is ashamed of themselves. "

Even commentaries about the Bears, Lindsay Lohan, and Mel Gibson: "I ran into a man at Starbucks this morning . . . midforties, in pinstripes and white shirt, wearing a wedding ring and carrying a briefcase. A corporate lawyer, he said, on his way to the Daley Center. He asked my opinion of Mel Gibson beating-up on his girlfriend, to which I replied . . . how low rent, about as low as you can get. 'Tsk-tsk,' chortled the lawyer, 'you know how women are. Give the guy a break.' I say break his bank. Planning to go to a movie this weekend? I say boycott Mel Gibson and the movie stars and producers who have anything to do with him."

An ideal retirement—two short commentaries a week on subjects that are comfortable and easy for me, and writing this book. After more than half a life on rigid work schedules, being retired in this way is just right. I'm crazy about the work and like feeling no pressure to get somewhere. And there's joy in the mystery of not knowing what may happen to me next . . .

Epilogue

Which is a stunner. Not in a hundred years, in this profession driven
. . . by Madison Avenue and the dollars of commercial advertising, could
I have guessed I'd get still another call from Channel 2 News. Or that I'd welcome it. I'm a happy member of the American Association of Retired Persons,
remember—on weeknights, in the grandstand at Wrigley, or in Pilsen for tacos,
reading politics in the newspapers instead of on prompter.

It's Jeff Kiernan again, news director calling about anchoring again. He's
thinking about teaming me up with Kurtis again, but this time full time, Monday through Friday on the six o'clock news.

At seventy-two in a world of forty-twos and thirty-twos, I must not be hearing him right. That's fantasy talk, two reporters our age (Bill's now sixty-eight),
wearing hair not salt-and-pepper anymore, but all salt, fitting into television's
youth brigade. There's no way. CBS gambling two-year contracts on an anchor
team of the past, noticeably older than any team in the market? Why is CBS
going old versus the competition going young with anchors of more tender age?
Here's why—Channel 2 News is in the basement of the ratings, being ignored
and suffering an identity crisis. Kiernan and his general manager, Bruno Cohen,
need to attract attention (like the Cubs needing a trusty old-timer to stir the
fans). Bill-and-Walter have done it before, maybe they can do it again, rev things
up just enough to help the station into the game. There's nothing for Kiernan
and Cohen to lose in taking a chance, even a flyer. For Bill and me, like the
one-nighter, why not? In retirement we talk often about how age and experience
ought to be saleable commodities in the business of television news, and we're
being offered a chance to prove it. It's hard to say "No." Of course we'll do it.

On Monday, September 1, 2010, at 6 P.M., after rehearsing for one hour,
we're in the CBS studio, glassed-in on street level on the northeast corner of
Washington and Dearborn, across the street from Pablo Picasso. On my chair

are two pillows like the ones I used for so many years to persuade viewers we're not Mutt and Jeff (Bill's over six feet, I'm under five-seven). On the anchor desk, the scripts; in the air, expectations. After twenty years apart from each other, in different places in our lives, we're still at ease doing a broadcast together. No hidden agendas or subtle rivalry. We admire and trust and genuinely like each other and are having a good time. In an extraordinarily competitive, often self-destructive business that chews up and spits out many more people than it cushions, Bill and I have a fanciful TV news relationship that shows and may work in a market that's a place of neighbors. In Chicago, the familiarity factor counts, as does friendship, as does likeability (Bill) and some irritability (me).

And the timing is good. Incessant change in management and direction, and too many musical chairs on the air, have mired WBBM-TV-CBS in hard times. To try a "Bill-and-Walter" show, it's an appropriate season. The 2012 presidential campaign is underway, the Tea Party is threatening a national debt-ceiling disaster, the state of Illinois is $15 billion in the red, Chicago $635 million in the red. Mayor Rahm Emanuel is on the playing field with his new chiefs of police and the public schools, the crown jewels of local news, Cirque de Soleil of urban politics.

Question is, what happens to Channel 2 going back on its way forward? How many ratings periods will the general manager and news director be granted to convince the supremes in New York to stay out of the way? How long in last place at six o'clock in Chicago before patience in Manhattan wears thin?

A good bet is—not as long as it'll take the Cubs to win a World Series, or even play into one.

Index

Page numbers for images in the photograph gallery, which follows page 100, are indicated by an italicized *G* followed by an italicized page number. The author is referenced in subheadings as "WJ."

Walter Jacobson is a longtime newspaper and television journalist based in Chicago. His "Walter's Perspective" commentaries on three different television stations, CBS-WBBM, NBC-WMAQ, and Fox-WFLD, have won him more than forty Emmys—more than have been won by all the other anchors in the history of Chicago combined.

Mokena Community
Public Library District

3 1985 00246 9703